ASPEN PUBLISHERS

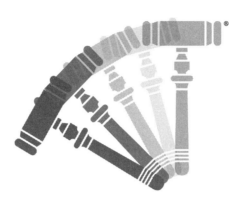

Casenote™ *Legal Briefs*

CONTRACTS

Keyed to Courses Using

Fuller and Eisenberg's
Basic Contract Law

Eighth Edition

Wolters Kluwer
Law & Business

AUSTIN   BOSTON   CHICAGO   NEW YORK   THE NETHERLANDS

This publication is designed to provide accurate and authoritative information in regard to the subject matter covered. It is sold with the understanding that the publisher is not engaged in rendering legal, accounting, or other professional services. If legal advice or other expert assistance is required, the services of a competent professional person should be sought.

— From a Declaration of Principles adopted jointly by a Committee of the American Bar Association and a Committee of Publishers and Associates

To contact Customer Care, e-mail customer.care@aspenpublishers.com, call 1-800-234-1660, fax 1-800-901-9075, or mail correspondence to:

Aspen Publishers
Attn: Order Department
P.O. Box 990
Frederick, MD 21705

Printed in the United States of America.

1 2 3 4 5 6 7 8 9 0

ISBN 978-0-7355-6970-6

About Wolters Kluwer Law & Business

Wolters Kluwer Law & Business is a leading provider of research information and workflow solutions in key specialty areas. The strengths of the individual brands of Aspen Publishers, CCH, Kluwer Law International and Loislaw are aligned within Wolters Kluwer Law & Business to provide comprehensive, in-depth solutions and expert-authored content for the legal, professional and education markets.

CCH was founded in 1913 and has served more than four generations of business professionals and their clients. The CCH products in the Wolters Kluwer Law & Business group are highly regarded electronic and print resources for legal, securities, antitrust and trade regulation, government contracting, banking, pension, payroll, employment and labor, and health-care reimbursement and compliance professionals.

Aspen Publishers is a leading information provider for attorneys, business professionals and law students. Written by preeminent authorities, Aspen products offer analytical and practical information in a range of specialty practice areas from securities law and intellectual property to mergers and acquisitions and pension/benefits. Aspen's trusted legal education resources provide professors and students with high-quality, up-to-date and effective resources for successful instruction and study in all areas of the law.

Kluwer Law International supplies the global business community with comprehensive English-language international legal information. Legal practitioners, corporate counsel and business executives around the world rely on the Kluwer Law International journals, loose-leafs, books and electronic products for authoritative information in many areas of international legal practice.

Loislaw is a premier provider of digitized legal content to small law firm practitioners of various specializations. Loislaw provides attorneys with the ability to quickly and efficiently find the necessary legal information they need, when and where they need it, by facilitating access to primary law as well as state-specific law, records, forms and treatises.

Wolters Kluwer Law & Business, a unit of Wolters Kluwer, is headquartered in New York and Riverwoods, Illinois. Wolters Kluwer is a leading multinational publisher and information services company.

Format for the Casenote Legal Brief

Nature of Case: This section identifies the form of action (e.g., breach of contract, negligence, battery), the type of proceeding (e.g., demurrer, appeal from trial court's jury instructions) or the relief sought (e.g., damages, injunction, criminal sanctions).

Palsgraf v. Long Island R.R. Co.

Injured bystander (P) v. Railroad company (D)

N.Y. Ct. App., 248 N.Y. 339, 162 N.E. 99 (1928).

Party ID: Quick identification of the relationship between the parties.

Fact Summary: This is included to refresh your memory and can be used as a quick reminder of the facts.

NATURE OF CASE: Appeal from judgment affirming verdict for plaintiff seeking damages for personal injury.

FACT SUMMARY: Helen Palsgraf (P) was injured on R.R.'s (D) train platform when R.R.'s (D) guard helped a passenger aboard a moving train, causing his package to fall on the tracks. The package contained fireworks which exploded, creating a shock that tipped a scale onto Palsgraf (P).

though unintended, could have been averted or avoided by observance of such a duty. The scope of the duty is limited by the range of danger that a reasonable person could foresee. In this case, there was nothing to suggest from the appearance of the parcel or otherwise that the parcel contained fireworks. The guard could not reasonably have had any warning of a threat to Palsgraf (P), and R.R. (D) therefore cannot be held liable. Judgment is reversed in favor of R.R. (D).

Rule of Law: Summarizes the general principle of law that the case illustrates. It may be used for instant recall of the court's holding and for classroom discussion or home review.

🏛 RULE OF LAW
The risk reasonably to be perceived defines the duty to be obeyed.

DISSENT: (Andrews, J.) The concept that there is no negligence unless R.R. (D) owes a legal duty to take care as to Palsgraf (P) herself is too narrow. Everyone owes to the world at large the duty of refraining from those acts that may unreasonably threaten the safety of others. If the guard's action was negligent as to those nearby, it was also negligent as to those outside what might be termed the "danger zone." For Palsgraf (P) to recover, R.R.'s (D) negligence must have been the proximate cause of her injury, a question of fact for the jury.

Concurrence/Dissent: All concurrences and dissents are briefed whenever they are included by the casebook editor.

Facts: This section contains all relevant facts of the case, including the contentions of the parties and the lower court holdings. It is written in a logical order to give the student a clear understanding of the case. The plaintiff and defendant are identified by their proper names throughout and are always labeled with a (P) or (D).

FACTS: Helen Palsgraf (P) purchased a ticket to Rockaway Beach from R.R. (D) and was waiting on the train platform. As she waited, two men ran to catch a train that was pulling out from the platform. The first man jumped aboard, but the second man, who appeared as if he might fall, was helped aboard by the guard on the train who had kept the door open so they could jump aboard. A guard on the platform also helped by pushing him onto the train. The man was carrying a package wrapped in newspaper. In the process, the man dropped his package, which fell on the tracks. The package contained fireworks and exploded. The shock of the explosion was apparently of great enough strength to tip over some scales at the other end of the platform, which fell on Palsgraf (P) and injured her. A jury awarded her damages, and R.R. (D) appealed.

ISSUE: Does the risk reasonably to be perceived define the duty to be obeyed?

HOLDING AND DECISION: (Cardozo, C.J.) Yes. The risk reasonably to be perceived defines the duty to be obeyed. If there is no foreseeable hazard to the injured party as the result of a seemingly innocent act, the act does not become a tort because it happened to be a wrong as to another. If the wrong was not willful, the plaintiff must show that the act as to her had such great and apparent possibilities of danger as to entitle her to protection. Negligence in the abstract is not enough upon which to base liability. Negligence is a relative concept, evolving out of the common law doctrine of trespass on the case. To establish liability, the defendant must owe a legal duty of reasonable care to the injured party. A cause of action in tort will lie where harm,

> **ANALYSIS**
>
> The majority defined the limit of the defendant's liability in terms of the danger that a reasonable person in defendant's situation would have perceived. The dissent argued that the limitation should not be placed on liability, but rather on damages. Judge Andrews suggested that only injuries that would not have happened but for R.R.'s (D) negligence should be compensable. Both the majority and dissent recognized the policy-driven need to limit liability for negligent acts, seeking, in the words of Judge Andrews, to define a framework "that will be practical and in keeping with the general understanding of mankind." The Restatement (Second) of Torts has accepted Judge Cardozo's view.

Analysis: This last paragraph gives you a broad understanding of where the case "fits in" with other cases in the section of the book and with the entire course. It is a hornbook-style discussion indicating whether the case is a majority or minority opinion and comparing the principal case with other cases in the casebook. It may also provide analysis from restatements, uniform codes, and law review articles. The analysis will prove to be invaluable to classroom discussion.

Quicknotes

FORESEEABILITY A reasonable expectation that change is the probable result of certain acts or omissions.

NEGLIGENCE Conduct falling below the standard of care that a reasonable person would demonstrate under similar conditions.

PROXIMATE CAUSE The natural sequence of events without which an injury would not have been sustained.

Issue: The issue is a concise question that brings out the essence of the opinion as it relates to the section of the casebook in which the case appears. Both substantive and procedural issues are included if relevant to the decision.

Holding and Decision: This section offers a clear and in-depth discussion of the rule of the case and the court's rationale. It is written in easy-to-understand language and answers the issue presented by applying the law to the facts of the case. When relevant, it includes a thorough discussion of the exceptions to the case as listed by the court, any major cites to the other cases on point, and the names of the judges who wrote the decisions.

Quicknotes: Conveniently defines legal terms found in the case and summarizes the nature of any statutes, codes, or rules referred to in the text.

Rule of Law: Summarizes the general principle of law that the case illustrates.

Note to Students

Aspen Publishers is proud to offer *Casenote Legal Briefs*—continuing thirty years of publishing America's best-selling legal briefs.

Casenote Legal Briefs are designed to help you save time when briefing assigned cases. Organized under convenient headings, they show you how to abstract the basic facts and holdings from the text of the actual opinions handed down by the courts. Used as part of a rigorous study regimen, they can help you spend more time analyzing and critiquing points of law than on copying bits and pieces of judicial opinions into your notebook or outline.

Casenote Legal Briefs should never be used as a substitute for assigned casebook readings. They work best when read as a follow-up to reviewing the underlying opinions themselves. Students who try to avoid reading and digesting the judicial opinions in their casebooks or on-line sources will end up shortchanging themselves in the long run. The ability to absorb, critique, and restate the dynamic and complex elements of case law decisions is crucial to your success in law school and beyond. It cannot be developed vicariously.

Casenote Legal Briefs represents but one of the many offerings in Aspen's Study Aid Timeline, which includes:

- *Casenote Legal Briefs*
- *Emanuel Law Outlines*
- *Examples & Explanations* Series
- *Introduction to Law* Series
- Emanuel *Law in a Flash* Flashcards
- Emanuel *CrunchTime* Series

Each of these series is designed to provide you with easy-to-understand explanations of complex points of law. Each volume offers guidance on the principles of legal analysis and, consulted regularly, will hone your ability to spot relevant issues. We have titles that will help you prepare for class, prepare for your exams, and enhance your general comprehension of the law along the way.

To find out more about Aspen Study Aid publications, visit us on-line at *http://lawschool.aspenpublishers.com* or e-mail us at *legaledu@aspenpubl.com*. We'll be happy to assist you.

How to Brief a Case

A. Decide on a Format and Stick to It

Structure is essential to a good brief. It enables you to arrange systematically the related parts that are scattered throughout most cases, thus making manageable and understandable what might otherwise seem to be an endless and unfathomable sea of information. There are, of course, an unlimited number of formats that can be utilized. However, it is best to find one that suits your needs and stick to it. Consistency breeds both efficiency and the security that when called upon you will know where to look in your brief for the information you are asked to give.

Any format, as long as it presents the essential elements of a case in an organized fashion, can be used. Experience, however, has led *Casenotes* to develop and utilize the following format because of its logical flow and universal applicability.

NATURE OF CASE: This is a brief statement of the legal character and procedural status of the case (e.g., "Appeal of a burglary conviction").

There are many different alternatives open to a litigant dissatisfied with a court ruling. The key to determining which one has been used is to discover *who is asking this court for what.*

This first entry in the brief should be kept as *short as possible.* Use the court's terminology if you understand it. But since jurisdictions vary as to the titles of pleadings, the best entry is the one that addresses who wants what in this proceeding, not the one that sounds most like the court's language.

RULE OF LAW: A statement of the general principle of law that the case illustrates (e.g., "An acceptance that varies any term of the offer is considered a rejection and counteroffer").

Determining the rule of law of a case is a procedure similar to determining the issue of the case. Avoid being fooled by red herrings; there may be a few rules of law mentioned in the case excerpt, but usually only one is *the* rule with which the casebook editor is concerned. The techniques used to locate the issue, described below, may also be utilized to find the rule of law. Generally, your best guide is simply the chapter heading. It is a clue to the point the casebook editor seeks to make and should be kept in mind when reading every case in the respective section.

FACTS: A synopsis of only the essential facts of the case, i.e., those bearing upon or leading up to the issue.

The facts entry should be a short statement of the events and transactions that led one party to initiate legal proceedings against another in the first place. While some cases conveniently state the salient facts at the beginning of the decision, in other instances they will have to be culled from hiding places throughout the text, even from concurring and dissenting opinions. Some of the "facts" will often be in dispute and should be so noted. Conflicting evidence may be briefly pointed up. "Hard" facts must be included. Both must be *relevant* in order to be listed in the facts entry. It is impossible to tell what is relevant until the entire case is read, as the ultimate determination of the rights and liabilities of the parties may turn on something buried deep in the opinion.

Generally, the facts entry should not be longer than three to five *short* sentences.

It is often helpful to identify the role played by a party in a given context. For example, in a construction contract case the identification of a party as the "contractor" or "builder" alleviates the need to tell that that party was the one who was supposed to have built the house.

It is always helpful, and a good general practice, to identify the "plaintiff" and the "defendant." This may seem elementary and uncomplicated, but, especially in view of the creative editing practiced by some casebook editors, it is sometimes a difficult or even impossible task. Bear in mind that the *party presently* seeking something from this court may not be the plaintiff, and that sometimes only the cross-claim of a defendant is treated in the excerpt. Confusing or misaligning the parties can ruin your analysis and understanding of the case.

ISSUE: A statement of the general legal question answered by or illustrated in the case. For clarity, the issue is best put in the form of a question capable of a "yes" or "no" answer. In reality, the issue is simply the Rule of Law put in the form of a question (e.g., "May an offer be accepted by performance?").

The major problem presented in discerning what is *the* issue in the case is that an opinion usually purports to raise and answer several questions. However, except for rare cases, only one such question is really the issue in the case. Collateral issues not necessary to the resolution of the matter in controversy are handled by the court by language known as *"obiter dictum"* or merely *"dictum."* While dicta may be included later in the brief, they have no place under the issue heading.

To find the issue, ask *who wants what* and then go on to ask *why did that party succeed or fail in getting it.* Once this is determined, the "why" should be turned into a question.

The complexity of the issues in the cases will vary, but in all cases a single-sentence question should sum up the issue. *In a few cases,* there will be two, or even more rarely, three issues of equal importance to the resolution of the case. Each should be expressed in a single-sentence question.

Since many issues are resolved by a court in coming to a final disposition of a case, the casebook editor will reproduce the portion of the opinion containing the issue or issues most relevant to the area of law under scrutiny. A noted law professor gave this advice: "Close the book; look at the title on the cover." Chances are, if it is Property, you need not concern yourself with whether, for example, the federal government's treatment of the plaintiff's land really raises a federal question sufficient to support jurisdiction on this ground in federal court.

The same rule applies to chapter headings designating sub-areas within the subjects. They tip you off as to what the text is designed to teach. The cases are arranged in a casebook to show a progression or development of the law, so that the preceding cases may also help.

It is also most important to remember to *read the notes and questions* at the end of a case to determine what the editors wanted you to have gleaned from it.

HOLDING AND DECISION: This section should succinctly explain the rationale of the court in arriving at its decision. In capsulizing the "reasoning" of the court, it should always include an application of the general rule or rules of law to the specific facts of the case. Hidden justifications come to light in this entry; the reasons for the state of the law, the public policies, the biases and prejudices, those considerations that influence the justices' thinking and, ultimately, the outcome of the case. At the end, there should be a short indication of the disposition or procedural resolution of the case (e.g., "Decision of the trial court for Mr. Smith (P) reversed").

The foregoing format is designed to help you "digest" the reams of case material with which you will be faced in your law school career. Once mastered by practice, it will place at your fingertips the information the authors of your casebooks have sought to impart to you in case-by-case illustration and analysis.

B. Be as Economical as Possible in Briefing Cases

Once armed with a format that encourages succinctness, it is as important to be economical with regard to the time spent on the actual reading of the case as it is to be economical in the writing of the brief itself. This does not mean "skimming" a case. Rather, it means reading the case with an "eye" trained to recognize into which "section" of your brief a particular passage or line fits and having a system for quickly and precisely marking the case so that the passages fitting any one particular part of

the brief can be easily identified and brought together in a concise and accurate manner when the brief is actually written.

It is of no use to simply repeat everything in the opinion of the court; record only enough information to trigger your recollection of what the court said. Nevertheless, an accurate statement of the "law of the case," i.e., the legal principle applied to the facts, is absolutely essential to class preparation and to learning the law under the case method.

To that end, it is important to develop a "shorthand" that you can use to make margin notations. These notations will tell you at a glance in which section of the brief you will be placing that particular passage or portion of the opinion.

Some students prefer to underline all the salient portions of the opinion (with a pencil or colored underliner marker), making marginal notations as they go along. Others prefer the color-coded method of underlining, utilizing different colors of markers to underline the salient portions of the case, each separate color being used to represent a different section of the brief. For example, blue underlining could be used for passages relating to the rule of law, yellow for those relating to the issue, and green for those relating to the holding and decision, etc. While it has its advocates, the color-coded method can be confusing and time-consuming (all that time spent on changing colored markers). Furthermore, it can interfere with the continuity and concentration many students deem essential to the reading of a case for maximum comprehension. In the end, however, it is a matter of personal preference and style. Just remember, whatever method you use, underlining must be used sparingly or its value is lost.

If you take the marginal notation route, an efficient and easy method is to go along underlining the key portions of the case and placing in the margin alongside them the following "markers" to indicate where a particular passage or line "belongs" in the brief you will write:

N (NATURE OF CASE)

RL (RULE OF LAW)

I (ISSUE)

HL (HOLDING AND DECISION, relates to the RULE OF LAW behind the decision)

HR (HOLDING AND DECISION, gives the RATIONALE or reasoning behind the decision)

HA (HOLDING AND DECISION, APPLIES the general principle(s) of law to the facts of the case to arrive at the decision)

Remember that a particular passage may well contain information necessary to more than one part of your brief, in which case you simply note that in the margin. If you are using the color-coded underlining method instead of margin notation, simply make asterisks or checks in the margin next to the passage in question in the colors that indicate the additional sections of the brief where it might be utilized.

The economy of utilizing "shorthand" in marking cases for briefing can be maintained in the actual brief writing process itself by utilizing "law student shorthand" within the brief. There are many commonly used words and phrases for which abbreviations can be substituted in your briefs (and in your class notes also). You can develop abbreviations that are personal to you and which will save you a lot of time. A reference list of briefing abbreviations can be found on page xii of this book.

C. Use Both the Briefing Process and the Brief as a Learning Tool

Now that you have a format and the tools for briefing cases efficiently, the most important thing is to make the time spent in briefing profitable to you and to make the most advantageous use of the briefs you create. Of course, the briefs are invaluable for classroom reference when you are called upon to explain or analyze a particular case. However, they are also useful in reviewing for exams. A quick glance at the fact summary should bring the case to mind, and a rereading of the rule of law should enable you to go over the underlying legal concept in your mind, how it was applied in that particular case, and how it might apply in other factual settings.

As to the value to be derived from engaging in the briefing process itself, there is an immediate benefit that arises from being forced to sift through the essential facts and reasoning from the court's opinion and to succinctly express them in your own words in your brief. The process ensures that you understand the case and the point that it illustrates, and that means you will be ready to absorb further analysis and information brought forth in class. It also ensures you will have something to say when called upon in class. The briefing process helps develop a mental agility for getting to the *gist* of a case and for identifying, expounding on, and applying the legal concepts and issues found there. The briefing process is the mental process on which you must rely in taking law school examinations; it is also the mental process upon which a lawyer relies in serving his clients and in making his living.

Abbreviations for Briefs

acceptance	acp	offer	O
affirmed	aff	offeree	OE
answer	ans	offeror	OR
assumption of risk	a/r	ordinance	ord
attorney	atty	pain and suffering	p/s
beyond a reasonable doubt	b/r/d	parol evidence	p/e
bona fide purchaser	BFP	plaintiff	P
breach of contract	br/k	prima facie	p/f
cause of action	c/a	probable cause	p/c
common law	c/l	proximate cause	px/c
Constitution	Con	real property	r/p
constitutional	con	reasonable doubt	r/d
contract	K	reasonable man	r/m
contributory negligence	c/n	rebuttable presumption	rb/p
cross	x	remanded	rem
cross-complaint	x/c	res ipsa loquitur	RIL
cross-examination	x/ex	respondeat superior	r/s
cruel and unusual punishment	c/u/p	Restatement	RS
defendant	D	reversed	rev
dismissed	dis	Rule Against Perpetuities	RAP
double jeopardy	d/j	search and seizure	s/s
due process	d/p	search warrant	s/w
equal protection	e/p	self-defense	s/d
equity	eq	specific performance	s/p
evidence	ev	statute of limitations	S/L
exclude	exc	statute of frauds	S/F
exclusionary rule	exc/r	statute	S
felony	f/n	summary judgment	s/j
freedom of speech	f/s	tenancy in common	t/c
good faith	g/f	tenancy at will	t/w
habeas corpus	h/c	tenant	t
hearsay	hr	third party	TP
husband	H	third party beneficiary	TPB
in loco parentis	ILP	transferred intent	TI
injunction	inj	unconscionable	uncon
inter vivos	I/v	unconstitutional	unconst
joint tenancy	j/t	undue influence	u/e
judgment	judgt	Uniform Commercial Code	UCC
jurisdiction	jur	unilateral	uni
last clear chance	LCC	vendee	VE
long-arm statute	LAS	vendor	VR
majority view	maj	versus	v
meeting of minds	MOM	void for vagueness	VFV
minority view	min	weight of the evidence	w/e
Miranda warnings	Mir/w	weight of authority	w/a
Miranda rule	Mir/r	wife	W
negligence	neg	with	w/
notice	ntc	within	w/i
nuisance	nus	without prejudice	w/o/p
obligation	ob	without	w/o
obscene	obs	wrongful death	wr/d

Table of Cases

CHAPTER 1

Donative Promises, Form, and Reliance

Quick Reference Rules of Law

Dougherty v. Salt

Minor and guardian (P) v. Executor (D)

N.Y. Ct. App., 227 N.Y. 200, 125 N.E. 94 (1919).

NATURE OF CASE: Appeal from dismissal of action for breach of contract.

FACT SUMMARY: The trial court dismissed Dougherty's (P) action to recover on a note finding no consideration supported the note.

🏛 RULE OF LAW
A note which is not supported by consideration is unenforceable.

FACTS: Dougherty (P), a minor, was visited by his aunt who indicated she wished to take care of him. The note was a preprinted form and carried no indication of consideration. Dougherty's (P) guardian was the sole witness who testified the aunt wanted to take care of the child, and thus was motivated to execute the note payable at her death. After her death, suit was brought to enforce the note, which was dismissed, although the jury found the note was supported by consideration. The appellate court reversed, finding sufficient consideration and holding the trial court erred in overruling the jury. Salt (D), the executor, appealed.

ISSUE: Is a note which is not supported by consideration enforceable?

HOLDING AND DECISION: (Cardozo, J.) No. A note which is not supported by consideration is unenforceable. The only evidence available indicated the note was given out of the generosity of the maker. The payee was not a creditor and was not owed support by the maker. Thus, the note was not supported by consideration and was unenforceable. Reversed.

▌ *ANALYSIS*

The note in this case was labeled an executory gift, one which is to be performed or executed in the future. The triggering event here was the death of the aunt. No consideration was found despite the fact the preprinted form stated value had been received. Thus, the court looked to the substance rather than the appearance of the note.

■══■

Quicknotes

CONSIDERATION Value given by one party in exchange for performance, or a promise to perform, by another party.

GIFT A transfer of property to another person that is voluntary and which lacks consideration.

■══■

Schnell v. Nell

Will beneficiary (P) v. Testator's husband (D)

Ind. Sup. Ct., 17 Ind. 29, 79 Am. Dec. 453 (1861).

NATURE OF CASE: Action for breach of contract.

FACT SUMMARY: Out of consideration for his deceased wife, Schnell (D) agreed to pay Nell (P) $200 in return for Nell's (P) payment of one cent and agreement to forbear all claims against the wife's estate.

🏛 RULE OF LAW
A contract will be vitiated for lack of consideration where the consideration given by one party is only nominal and is intended to be so.

FACTS: Theresa Schnell's will left $200 to Nell (P). The will was declared a nullity since Theresa, at the time of her death, held no property in her own name. Nonetheless, Theresa's husband, Zacharias Schnell (D), agreed to give Nell (P) $200 out of the love and respect he had for his wife. In return, Nell (P) agreed to pay Schnell (D) the sum of one cent and also agreed to forbear any claim he might have against Theresa's estate. When Schnell (D) refused to honor his promise, Nell (P) sued for breach.

ISSUE: Will a consideration of one cent, which is intended to be merely nominal, support a contract?

HOLDING AND DECISION: (Perkins, J.) No. The general proposition that inadequacy of consideration will not vitiate a contract does not apply where consideration offered by one party is plainly intended to be nominal. Since Schnell (D) was not bound to honor his promise on a tender of one cent, it is necessary to determine if there was any other sufficient consideration. A moral consideration will not support a promise, nor will forbearance of a legally groundless claim. Honor of a deceased wife for her past services is inadequate since the consideration is past and also because veneration in memory of a deceased person is not a legal consideration for a promise to pay any third money. Schnell's (D) promise is, therefore, unenforceable. Judgment reversed.

▌ ANALYSIS

The holding here represents an exception to the general rule that where an action is at law for breach of contract, a court will not examine the fairness of the bargained-for exchanges. However, where the action is in equity for specific performance of the contract, the general rule is reversed: Before relief will be granted, there must be a showing that the agreed exchanges were substantially equal in value.

Quicknotes

CONSIDERATION Value given by one party in exchange for performance, or a promise to perform, by another party.

MORAL CONSIDERATION An inducement to enter a contract that is not enforceable at law, but is made based on a moral obligation and may be enforceable in order to prevent unjust enrichment on the part of the promisor.

NOMINAL Small; trivial; with reference to name only.

SPECIFIC PERFORMANCE An equitable remedy whereby the court requires the parties to perform their obligations pursuant to a contract.

Kirksey v. Kirksey

Sister (P) v. Brother (D)

Ala. Sup. Ct., 8 Ala. 131 (1845).

NATURE OF CASE: Action to recover damages for breach of a promise.

FACT SUMMARY: Kirksey (D) promised "Sister Antillico" (P) a place to raise her family "if you come down and see me."

🏛 RULE OF LAW
To be legally enforceable, an executory promise must be supported by sufficient, bargained-for consideration.

FACTS: Kirksey (D) wrote to "Sister Antillico" (P) a letter containing the following clause: "If you will come down and see me, I will let you have a place to raise your family." "Sister Antillico" (P) moved sixty miles to Kirksey's (D) residence where she remained for over two years. Kirksey (D) then required her to leave although her family was not yet "raised." "Sister Antillico" (P) contends that the loss which she sustained in moving was sufficient consideration to support Kirksey's (D) promise to furnish her with "a place" until she could raise her family.

ISSUE: Is a promise on the condition, "If you will come down and see me," given as a bargained exchange for the promisee's "coming down and seeing" the promisor?

HOLDING AND DECISION: (Ormond, J.) No. Such a promise is a promise to make a gift. Any expenses incurred by the promisee in "coming down and seeing" are merely conditions necessary to acceptance of the gift. In this case, Kirksey (D) did not appear to be bargaining either for "Sister Antillico's" presence or for her sixty-mile move. Instead, Kirksey (D) merely wished to assist her out of what he perceived as a grievous and difficult situation. Reversed.

▶ ANALYSIS

This well-known case demonstrates the court's insistence on finding a bargained-for exchange before it will enforce an executory promise. A promise to make a gift is generally not legally binding until it is executed. Compare Williston's famous hypothetical in which a benevolent man says to a tramp: "If you go around the corner to the clothing shop there, you may purchase an overcoat on my credit." This hypothetical case highlights the conceptual problem of the present case in that it is unreasonable to construe the walk around the corner as the price of the promise, yet it is a legal detriment to the tramp to make the walk. Perhaps a reasonable (though not conclusive) guideline is the extent to which the happening of the condition will benefit the promisor. The present case might be decided differently today under the doctrine of promissory estoppel which had not yet been developed in 1845.

Quicknotes

BARGAINED-FOR EXCHANGE A requirement for adequate consideration that the promise made by the offeror induce the return promise or performance on the part of the offeree and that the promise or performance on the part of the offeree induce the promise made by the offeror.

EXECUTORY PROMISE A promise to perform an action that has not yet been performed.

GIFT A transfer of property to another person that is voluntary and which lacks consideration.

PROMISSORY ESTOPPEL A promise that is enforceable if the promisor should reasonably expect that it will induce action or forbearance on the part of the promisee, and does in fact cause such action or forbearance, and it is the only means of avoiding injustice.

Feinberg v. Pfeiffer Co.

Retired employee (P) v. Employer (D)

Mo. Ct. App., 322 S.W.2d 163 (1959).

NATURE OF CASE: Appeal from award of damages.

FACT SUMMARY: Feinberg (P), an employee of the Pfeiffer Co. (D), retired after Pfeiffer (D) promised to pay her $200 per month for life upon her retirement, but subsequently the payments were terminated.

🏛 RULE OF LAW
Under the doctrine of promissory estoppel, as stated in § 90 of the Restatement of the Law of Contracts, "a promise which the promisor should reasonably expect to induce action or forbearance of a definite and substantial character on the part of the promisee and which does induce such action or forbearance is binding if injustice can be avoided only by enforcement of the promise," and it is not necessary that such a promise be given for consideration to be enforceable.

FACTS: Feinberg (P) was an employee of the Pfeiffer Co. (D). In 1947, the Board of Directors of the Pfeiffer Co. (D), in recognition of Feinberg's (P) many years of "long and faithful service," adopted a resolution approving payment to Feinberg (P) of $200 per month for life after her retirement. Thereafter, Feinberg (P) retired and received $200 per month for several years. Subsequently, though, Feinberg (P) was notified that she would receive only $100. When she refused to accept this reduced amount, all further payments were terminated. Thereupon, Feinberg (P) brought an action against Pfeiffer Co. (D) for breach of contract. Although the trial court found that there was no consideration for a contract (i.e., past services are not valid consideration for a promise), it did hold that Feinberg (P) was entitled to damages because she justifiably relied on Pfeiffer Co.'s (D) promise. Thereupon, Pfeiffer Co. (D) brought this appeal.

ISSUE: Is a promise per se invalid if it is given without consideration?

HOLDING AND DECISION: (Doerner, Commr.) No. Under the doctrine of promissory estoppel, as stated in § 90 of the Restatement of the Law of Contracts, "a promise which the promisor should reasonably expect to induce action or forbearance of a definite and substantial character on the part of the promisee and which does induce such action or forbearance is binding if injustice can be avoided only by enforcement of the promise;" and such a promise can be enforced even if it was given for no consideration. Of course, even though some cases have considered "promissory estoppel" as a "species of consideration," consideration is not required because an action based upon promissory estoppel is not equivalent to a breach of contract action. Here, Feinberg (P) has no breach of contract action because Pfeiffer's (D) promise was not supported by sufficient consideration (as found by the trial court). Feinberg (P), though, does have an action under the doctrine of promissory estoppel. She justifiably relied on Pfeiffer's (D) promise by retiring from a lucrative position. Furthermore, it is irrelevant that when the payments were terminated Feinberg (P) was unable to work because of illness. Since Feinberg (P) relied, by her retirement, on Pfeiffer's (D) promise, injustice would result by not enforcing this promise regardless of her subsequent illness. Affirmed.

▶ ANALYSIS

This case illustrates the generally recognized doctrine of promissory estoppel. This doctrine is an exception to the general rule that a promise cannot be enforced without valuable consideration. Under promissory estoppel, "substantial detrimental reliance" on a promise takes the place of consideration. Note that the Restatement Second dispenses with the requirement that reliance must be "substantial" and only requires that it be reasonable. Furthermore, the Restatement Second suggests that a court need not enforce the whole promise relied on but may limit the remedy to such relief "as justice requires."

Quicknotes

CONSIDERATION Value given by one party in exchange for performance, or a promise to perform, by another party.

DETRIMENTAL RELIANCE Action by one party, resulting in loss, that is based on the conduct or promises of another.

PROMISSORY ESTOPPEL A promise that is enforceable if the promisor should reasonably expect that it will induce action or forbearance on the part of the promisee, and does in fact cause such action or forbearance, and it is the only means of avoiding injustice.

D & G Stout, Inc. v. Bacardi Imports, Inc.

Liquor distributor (P) v. Liquor company (D)

923 F.2d 566 (7th Cir. 1991).

NATURE OF CASE: Appeal from summary judgment dismissing a complaint for damages based on reliance on a promise.

FACT SUMMARY: When Bacardi (D), after promising to retain General Liquors (P) as its wholesale distributor in northern Indiana, withdrew its product line from General (P), General (P) was forced to sell itself at liquidation prices, after which it sought to recover damages from Bacardi (D).

RULE OF LAW
A promise which the promisor should reasonably expect to induce action or forbearance on the part of the promisee and a third person and which does induce such action or forbearance is binding if injustice can be avoided only by the enforcement of the promise.

FACTS: D & G Stout (P), operating as General Liquors, Inc. (P), was Bacardi's (D) wholesale liquor distributor in northern Indiana. After General (P) survived an industry shake-up and consolidation, it began negotiations with National Wine & Spirits for a possible sale. Bacardi (D), knowing of the negotiations, promised that General (P) would remain its distributor for northern Indiana. Confident that it could continue operating, General (P) then rejected National's offer. But Bacardi (D) reneged on its promise and withdrew its line from General (P). Hiram Walker, General's (P) other major client, also withdrew. Its negotiating leverage destroyed, General (P) was forced to sell to National for $550,000 below the original offer. General (P) sued Bacardi (D) on promissory estoppel grounds for the $550,000 price differential. The district court granted Bacardi's (D) motion for summary judgment. General (P) appealed.

ISSUE: Is a promise which the promisor should reasonably expect to induce action or forbearance on the part of the promisee and a third person and which does induce such action or forbearance binding if injustice can be avoided only by the enforcement of the promise?

HOLDING AND DECISION: (Cudahy, J.) Yes. A promise which the promisor should reasonably expect to induce action or forbearance on the part of the promisee and a third person and which does induce such action or forbearance is binding if injustice can be avoided only by the enforcement of the promise. Through its repudiation, Bacardi (D) destroyed General's (P) negotiating leverage since General (P) no longer had the alternative of continuing as an independent concern. General (P) was left with

one choice: sell at any price. Under these facts, General (P) had a reliance interest in Bacardi's (D) promise, given in full knowledge that General (P) planned to reject National's offer. While General's (P) allegations must still be proven at trial, Bacardi's (D) promise was of a sort on which General (P) might rely, with the possibility of damages for breach. Reversed and remanded.

ANALYSIS

Judge Cudahy emphasized that the lost future income expected from an at-will relationship, whether from wages or from profits, is not recoverable on a theory of promissory estoppel. Although an aspiring employee could not sue for lost wages on an employer's unfulfilled promise of at-will employment, he could sue for moving expenses because moving expenses are reliance costs resulting from a foregone opportunity. In summary, reliance costs are recoverable on a promissory estoppel theory, but expectancy damages are not. As a practical matter, the cost that General (P) incurred when it rejected National's offer was a reliance injury and therefore redressable.

Quicknotes

ANTICIPATORY REPUDIATION Breach of a contract subsequent to formation but prior to the time performance is due.

AT-WILL EMPLOYMENT The rule that an employment relationship is subject to termination at any time, or for any cause, by an employee or an employer in the absence of a specific agreement otherwise.

EXPECTANCY The expectation or contingency of obtaining possession of a right or interest in the future.

PROMISSORY ESTOPPEL A promise that is enforceable if the promisor should reasonably expect that it will induce action or forbearance on the part of the promisee, and does in fact cause such action or forbearance, and it is the only means of avoiding injustice.

The Bargain Principle and Its Limits

Quick Reference Rules of Law

Hamer v. Sidway

Nephew (P) v. Uncle (D)

N.Y. Ct. App., 124 N.Y. 538, 27 N.E. 256 (1891).

NATURE OF CASE: Action on appeal to recover upon a contract which is supported by forbearance of a right as consideration.

FACT SUMMARY: William Story (D) promised to pay $5,000 to William Story 2d (P) if he would forbear in the use of liquor, tobacco, swearing, or playing cards or billiards for money until he became twenty-one years of age.

 RULE OF LAW
Forbearance is valuable consideration.

FACTS: William Story (D) agreed with his nephew William Story 2d (P) that if W. Story 2d (P) would refrain from drinking liquor, using tobacco, swearing, and playing cards or billiards for money until he became twenty-one years of age, W. Story would pay him $5,000. Upon becoming twenty-one years of age, W. Story 2d (P) received a letter from W. Story (D) stating he had earned the $5,000 and it would be kept at interest for him. Twelve years later, W. Story (D) died and this action was brought by the assignees of W. Story 2d (P) against the executor (D) of the estate of W. Story (D). Judgment was entered in favor of W. Story 2d at the trial at Special Term and was reversed at General Term of the Supreme Court. The assignee of W. Story 2d (P) appealed.

ISSUE: Is forbearance on the part of a promisee sufficient consideration to support a contract?

HOLDING AND DECISION: (Parker, J.) Yes. Valuable consideration may consist either of some right, interest, profit, or benefit accruing to the one party, or some forbearance, detriment, loss, or responsibility given, suffered, or undertaken by the other. Order appealed from reversed, and judgment of the special term affirmed.

▌ *ANALYSIS*

The surrendering or forgoing of a legal right constitutes a sufficient consideration for a contract if the minds of the parties meet on the relinquishment of the right as a consideration. Consideration may be forbearance to sue on a claim, extension of time, or any other giving up of a legal right in consideration of a promise.

■■■■

Quicknotes

CONSIDERATION Value given by one party in exchange for performance, or a promise to perform, by another party.

FORBEARANCE Refraining from the assertion of a lawful right or other action.

■■■■

Hancock Bank & Trust Co. v. Shell Oil Co.

Purchaser of leased premises (P) v. Lessor oil company (D)

Mass. Sup. Jud. Ct., 365 Mass. 629, 309 N.E.2d 482 (1974).

NATURE OF CASE: Exceptions to findings and rulings in an action of summary process.

FACT SUMMARY: Hancock (P) asserted that the lease agreement its predecessor entered into with Shell Oil (D) was so lacking in mutuality as to be void as against public policy.

RULE OF LAW
In the absence of statute, the courts traditionally have declined to relieve a party from the terms of a contract supported by consideration merely because it constitutes a bad or uneven bargain on his part.

FACTS: A party had signed an agreement to lease certain property to Shell Oil (D) for a term of 15 years. By the terms of the agreement, Shell (D) had an option to extend the term for an additional 15 years and was entitled to terminate the lease at any time by giving the lessor at least 90 days' notice. Hancock (P) acquired the premises, subject to the lease agreement, at a public auction following foreclosure proceedings against the lessor. When the judge made findings and rulings in an action of summary process which upheld the validity of the lease, Hancock (P) took exception thereto. It argued that a lease which bound the lessor to a 15-year term that could be extended at the lessee's option to 30 years, but which allowed the lessee to terminate the lease upon only 90 days' notice, was "so lacking in mutuality as to be void as against public policy."

ISSUE: Will a party be relieved from the terms of a contract supported by consideration simply because he has made a bad or uneven bargain?

HOLDING AND DECISION: (Quirico, J.) No. Traditionally, in the absence of statute, courts have declined to relieve a party from the terms of a contract supported by consideration merely because he made what he regards as a bad or uneven bargain. On this record, it is not clear that the original lessor made a bad bargain. In any event, there is no basis for treating the lease as void on public policy grounds. There was consideration to support the lessor's obligations under the lease, which is enforceable. Exceptions overruled.

ANALYSIS

Comment E to § 79 of the Restatement, Second, Contract, points out that the requirement of consideration may be met despite a great difference in the values exchanged. It then notes that gross inadequacy of consideration, while it may not render the contract void or voidable, may be a "badge of fraud" justifying a denial of specific performance;

and may help to justify rescission or cancellation on the ground of lack of capacity, fraud, duress, undue influence, or mistake.

Quicknotes

MUTUALITY Reciprocal actions of two parties; in a contract context, refers to mutual promises between two parties to perform an action in exchange for performance on the part of the other party.

RESCISSION The canceling of an agreement and the return of the parties to their positions prior to the formation of the contract.

Batsakis v. Demotsis

Greek resident lender (P) v. Borrower-promisor to repay (D)

Tex. Ct. Civil App., 226 S.W.2d 673 (1949).

NATURE OF CASE: Action to recover on promissory note.

FACT SUMMARY: Batsakis (P) loaned Demotsis (D) 500,000 drachmae (which, at the time, had a total value of $25 in American money) in return for Demotsis's (D) promise to repay $2,000 in American money.

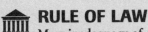 RULE OF LAW
Mere inadequacy of consideration will not void a contract.

FACTS: During World War II, Batsakis (P), a Greek resident, loaned Demotsis (D), also a Greek resident, the sum of 500,000 drachmae which at the time had a distressed value of only $25 in American money. In return, Demotsis (D), eager to return to the United States, signed an instrument in which she promised to repay Batsakis (P) $2,000 in American money. When Demotsis (D) refused to repay, claiming that the instrument was void at the outset for lack of adequate consideration, Batsakis (P) brought an action to collect on the note and recovered a judgment for $750 (which, at the time, after the war, reflected the rising value of drachmae) plus interest. Batsakis (P) appealed on the ground that he was entitled to recover the stated sum of the note—$2,000—plus interest.

ISSUE: Will mere inadequacy of consideration void a contract?

HOLDING AND DECISION: (McGill, J.) No. Only where the consideration for a contract has no value whatsoever will the contract be voided. A plea of want of consideration amounts to a contention that the instrument never became a valid obligation in the first instance. As a result, mere inadequacy of consideration is not enough. Here, the trial court obviously placed a value on the consideration—the drachmae—by deeming them to be worth $750. Thus, the trial court felt that there was consideration of value for the original transaction. Furthermore, the 500,000 drachmae was exactly what Demotsis (D) bargained for. It may not have been a good bargain, but she nonetheless agreed to repay Batsakis (P) $2,000. Accordingly, Batsakis (P) is entitled to recover the $2,000 and not just $750 plus interest. Reformed and affirmed.

▶ ANALYSIS

Official Comment (e) to the Restatement of Contracts, Second, § 81, states, "gross inadequacy of consideration may be relevant in the application of other rules, (such as) lack of capacity, fraud, duress, undue influence or mistake." Section 234 provides for the avoidance of a contract which, at the time it is made, contains an unconscionable term. The Official Comment (c) to this section states that "gross disparity in the values exchanged ... may be sufficient ground, without more, for denying specific performance."

■═■

Quicknotes

ADEQUACY OF CONSIDERATION Value given by one party in exchange for performance, or a promise to perform, by another party that is fair and reasonable in proportion to the value of what is received.

UNCONSCIONABILITY Rule of law whereby a court may excuse performance of a contract, or of a particular contract term, if it determines that such term(s) are unduly oppressive or unfair to one party to the contract.

■═■

William v. Walker-Thomas Furniture Co.

Purchaser (D) v. Retail furniture company (P)

350 F.2d 445 (Fed. Cir. 1965).

NATURE OF CASE: Action in replevin.

FACT SUMMARY: Williams (D) made a series of purchases on credit from Walker-Thomas (P), but defaulted on her payments.

🏛 RULE OF LAW
Where, in light of the general commercial background of a particular case, it appears that gross inequality of bargaining power between the parties has led to the formation of a contract on terms to which one party has had no meaningful choice, a court should refuse to enforce such a contract on the ground that it is unconscionable.

FACTS: Beginning about 1957, Walker-Thomas (P), a retail furniture company, began using a standard form contract for all credit transactions which contained, inter alia, a clause by which the company (P) reserved the right, upon default by a purchaser, to repossess all items contemporaneously being purchased by the buyer at the time of the repossession. This clause was accompanied by one which stated that all credit purchases made from Walker-Thomas (P) were to be handled through one account, with each installment payment spread pro rata over all items purchased (even where purchased separately and at different times), until all items were paid for. Williams (D) began purchasing items from Walker-Thomas (P) in 1957. In 1962, she bought a stereo set there. When she defaulted on a payment soon thereafter, Walker-Thomas (P) filed this action to replevy (i.e., repossess) all items she had purchased (and was still paying for) since 1957. From judgment for Walker-Thomas (P), this appeal followed.

ISSUE: May a court refuse to enforce an unreasonable contract, even though no evidence of fraud can be produced?

HOLDING AND DECISION: (Wright, J.) Yes. Where, in light of the general commercial background of a particular case, it appears that gross inequality of bargaining power between the parties has led to the formation of a contract on terms to which one party has had no meaningful choice, a court should refuse to enforce such a contract on the ground that it is unconscionable. It is true that the common law, operating by the caveat emptor rationale, refused to look into the essential fairness of a contract absent evidence of out and out fraud. The U.C.C., however, notably § 2-302 as adopted in this jurisdiction, has accepted the rule that courts should seek to prevent overreaching in contracts of adhesion such as the one at bar. Williams (D), and others, come from a socioeconomic class in which credit is difficult to obtain. To permit Walker-Thomas (P) to exploit this condition with provisions such as those pointed out above is clearly unconscionable. Remanded to the trial court for further proceedings.

DISSENT: (Danaher, J.) The court ignores many policy considerations in its decision today. For one, the high risk of granting credit to the poor for companies like Walker-Thomas (P) is not even addressed. A more cautious approach is warranted.

▶ ANALYSIS

This case points up the major application which the U.C.C. § 2-302 concept of unconscionability has had to date: adhesion (i.e., form) contracts. Note that the general common-law rule regarding such contracts remains the general rule today. That rule is that a person who signs a contract will be held responsible for any clauses or conditions which a reasonable man making a reasonable inspection would have discovered. The U.C.C. rule merely qualifies this to say that, where one party to a form contract has no real choice over whether to accept the terms because of his relative economic position, then the fact that he knows of the terms will not be enough to constitute a "meeting of the minds" on his part which is necessary to form a valid contract.

Quicknotes

ADHESION CONTRACT A contract, usually in standardized form, that is prepared by one party and offered to another, whose terms are so disproportionately in favor of the drafting party that courts tend to question the equality of bargaining power in reaching the agreement.

INTER ALIA Among other things.

PRO RATA In proportion.

REPLEVIN An action to recover personal property wrongfully taken.

U.C.C. § 2-302 Provides that courts exercise their discretion to limit specific contract provisions that have unconscionable results.

Maxwell v. Fidelity Financial Services, Inc.

Purchaser (P) v. Seller (D)

Ariz. Sup. Ct., 184 Ariz. 82, 907 P.2d 51 (1995) (en banc).

NATURE OF CASE: Review of summary judgment for defendant in an action seeking a declaratory judgment of unconscionability.

FACT SUMMARY: Maxwell (P) sought a declaration that a contract to purchase a solar water heater which was never installed properly and never worked properly was unenforceable on the grounds that it was unconscionable.

> 🏛 **RULE OF LAW**
> A claim of unconscionability can be established with a showing of substantive unconscionability alone.

FACTS: A door-to-door salesman representing a now-defunct solar water heater manufacturer approached Maxwell (P), who agreed to purchase a solar water heater for a total purchase price of $6,512, financed at 19.5 percent interest, making the total cost nearly $15,000. At the time, Maxwell (P) was working part-time as a hotel maid and earning only $400 per month. The purchase was financed by a loan from Fidelity Financial Services (D), which also acquired a lien on Maxwell's (P) house as additional security for payment on the water heater. The market value of her home was approximately $40,000. The water heater was never property installed or worked properly, but Maxwell (P) continued making payments until 1988, when she needed to borrow an additional $800 from Fidelity (D) for purposes unrelated to the original loan. Fidelity (D) created a new contract for the second loan, making the combined amount Maxwell (P) would pay under the two contracts for a non-functioning water heater and the $800 loan approximately $17,000, or nearly one-half the value of her home. Maxwell (P) made payments until 1990, when she brought this declaratory judgment action seeking a declaration that the 1984 contract was unenforceable because it was unconscionable. Fidelity (D) moved for summary judgment, asserting that the statute of limitations had run on Maxwell's (P) claim and, if not, that the 1988 contract worked a novation, thereby barring any action by Maxwell (P) on the 1984 contract. The trial court granted Fidelity's (D) motion on the theory of novation. The court of appeals affirmed. Maxwell (P) appealed.

ISSUE: Can a claim of unconscionability be established with a showing of substantive unconscionability alone?

HOLDING AND DECISION: (Feldman, C.J.) Yes. A claim of unconscionability can be established with a showing of substantive unconscionability alone. This case presents a question of at least substantive unconscionability to be decided by the trial court. The facts present at least a question of grossly excessive price, constituting substantive unconscionability. This contract is made even more harsh by its security terms, which permit Fidelity (D) to foreclose on Maxwell's (P) home in the event of non-payment. The apparent injustice and oppression in these security provisions may also provide evidence of procedural unconscionability. The trial court based its decision entirely on the doctrine of novation without addressing the fundamental question of unconscionability in the manner required by the statute. Reversed and remanded to the trial court.

▶ ANALYSIS

Since the water heater in this case was sold by a door-to-door salesman, the consumer had additional legal protections. The Federal Trade Commission promulgated a regulation permitting buyers to avoid such contracts without a reason within three business days after the seller furnished the buyer with a form explaining this right to cancel. This rule does not, however, cover real estate or insurance sale contracts.

■▬■

Quicknotes

NOVATION The substitution of one party for another in a contract with the approval of the remaining party and discharging the obligations of the released party.

STATUTE OF LIMITATIONS A law prescribing the period in which a legal action may be commenced.

UNCONSCIONABILITY Rule of law whereby a court may excuse performance of a contract, or of a particular contract term, if it determines that such term(s) are unduly oppressive or unfair to one party to the contract.

■▬■

Scott v. Moragues Lumber Co.

Owner of vessel (D) v. Chartering company (P)

Ala. Sup. Ct., 202 Ala. 312, 80 So. 394 (1918).

NATURE OF CASE: Action for breach of an agreement of charter party.

FACT SUMMARY: Although Scott (D) had agreed to charter a vessel to Moragues Lumber (P), subject only to Scott's (D) acquisition of the vessel, he chartered the vessel to a third party after buying it.

🏛 RULE OF LAW
A contract is not void at its inception for lack of mutuality of obligation if one of the parties conditions his performance upon the happening of an event solely within his control.

FACTS: Scott (D) agreed to charter a vessel to Moragues Lumber (P). The offer was subject to Scott's (D) acquisition of the vessel which he did not then own. Although Moragues (P) had accepted the offer before Scott (D) acquired the vessel, upon buying it, Scott (D) chartered the boat to a third party. Moragues (P), thereupon, brought a suit for breach of the agreement.

ISSUE: Is a contract void at its inception for lack of mutuality of obligation if one party conditions his promise upon the occurrence of an event solely within his control?

HOLDING AND DECISION: (Sayre, J.) No. An agreement will not be defeated for lack of mutuality of obligations merely because one party has conditioned fulfillment of the contract on his performing a certain act. While Scott (D) was not bound to purchase the vessel, once he did the offer remained, free of the condition. By accepting Scott's (D) offer, Moragues (P) converted it into a binding contract. The contract was, therefore, to be performed, if at all, within a reasonable time; consideration was provided thereafter by the promises on either side. Scott (D), therefore, is liable for breaching his agreement. Affirmed.

▶ ANALYSIS

Many commentators, in rating the many broad exceptions to the "mutuality of obligation" doctrine have suggested that the term is misleading and should be dispensed with altogether. What is involved in cases which invoke the doctrine, these commentators argue, is not lack of mutual obligation, but, rather, much more basically, the fact that one party has failed to supply sufficient consideration to the other.

Quicknotes

CONDITION Requirement; potential future occurrence upon which the existence of a legal obligation is dependent.

MUTUALITY OF OBLIGATION Requires that both parties to a contract are bound or else neither is bound.

Wickham & Burton Coal Co. v. Farmers' Lumber Co.

Coal supplier (P) v. Coal buyer (D)

Iowa Sup. Ct., 189 Iowa 1183, 179 N.W. 417 (1920).

NATURE OF CASE: Counterclaim by buyer for breach of contract.

FACT SUMMARY: Seller (P) agreed to furnish buyer (D) with as much coal as buyer (D) "would want to purchase" from seller (P).

🏛 RULE OF LAW
A contract to sell personal property is void for want of mutuality if the quantity to be delivered is conditioned entirely on the will, wish, or want of the buyer.

FACTS: Wickham & Burton, a coal supplier, as seller (P), agreed to furnish Farmers' Lumber (D), buyer, as much coal as "(buyer) would want to purchase from (seller) (P)." Delivery was to be in carload lots at a set price per lot. Farmers' Lumber (D), buyer, placed several orders but, after delivering two carloads, Wickham & Burton (P), seller, renounced the contract. Farmers' Lumber (D), which had been forced to secure its coal on the open market for more than the contract price, filed a counterclaim in an action brought by Wickham & Burton (P) (the nature of which is not disclosed) for damages arising from breach of contract.

ISSUE: Where the buyer under a contract for the sale of goods is free to order any quantity he desires, is the contract void?

HOLDING AND DECISION: (Salinger, J.) Yes. If, from lack of mutuality, a promise is not binding, it cannot form a consideration. Thus, a buyer who has the sole discretion to order any quantity of goods cannot enforce the contract. Here, the buyer (D) had no obligation at all under the contract; it did not bind itself to buy all it needed, or to buy all it could sell, or even to buy only from seller (P). To follow a different rule would allow buyer (D) to reject the contract at any time it was able to buy coal for a lesser amount on the market. Since there was never any contract to begin with, seller's (P) part performance does not give rise to any contract. As a result, buyer's (D) counterclaim must fail. Reversed.

▶ ANALYSIS

Since the buyer (D) here can completely escape from meeting any obligation, he has, in fact, promised nothing; his promise is, therefore, termed "illusory." On the other hand, an agreement to purchase "all that I need or require" gives rise to a binding contract. The buyer in this situation has incurred a legal detriment since, if he buys at all, he must secure the named goods from the other party. The only way to evade his obligation legally would be to never place any orders for those goods.

Quicknotes

COVER The purchase of an alternate supply of goods by a buyer, after a seller has breached a contract for sale, for which the buyer may recover the difference between the cost of the substituted goods and the price of the original goods pursuant to the contract, so long as the buyer purchases the alternate goods in good faith and without unreasonable delay.

ILLUSORY PROMISE A promise that is not legally enforceable because performance of the obligation by the promisor is completely within his discretion.

REJECTION The refusal to accept the terms of an offer.

REQUIREMENTS CONTRACT An agreement pursuant to which one party agrees to purchase all his required goods or services from the other party exclusively for a specified time period.

Wood v. Lucy, Lady Duff-Gordon

Licenser of fashion designs (P) v. Fashion designer (D)

N.Y. Ct. App., 222 N.Y. 88, 118 N.E. 214 (1917).

NATURE OF CASE: Action for damages for breach of a contract for an exclusive right.

FACT SUMMARY: Wood (P), in a complicated agreement, received the exclusive right for one year, renewable on a year-to-year basis if not terminated by 90 days' notice, to endorse designs with Lucy's (D) name and to market all her fashion designs for which she would receive one half of the profits derived. Lucy (D) broke the contract by placing her endorsement on designs without Wood's (P) knowledge.

🏛 RULE OF LAW
While an express promise may be lacking, the whole writing may be instinct with an obligation—an implied promise—imperfectly expressed so as to form a valid contract.

FACTS: Lucy (D), a famous-name fashion designer, contracted with Wood (P) that for her granting to him an exclusive right to endorse designs with her name and to market and license all of her designs, they were to split the profits derived by Wood (P) in half. The exclusive right was for a period of one year, renewable on a year-to-year basis, and terminable upon 90 days' notice. Lucy (D) placed her endorsement on fabrics, dresses, and millinery without Wood's (P) knowledge and in violation of the contract. Lucy (D) claims that the agreement lacked the elements of a contract as Wood (P) allegedly is not bound to do anything.

ISSUE: If a promise may be implied from the writing even though it is imperfectly expressed, is there a valid contract?

HOLDING AND DECISION: (Cardozo, J.) Yes. While the contract did not precisely state that Wood (P) had promised to use reasonable efforts to place Lucy's (D) endorsement and market her designs, such a promise can be implied. The implication arises from the circumstances. Lucy (D) gave an exclusive privilege and the acceptance of the exclusive agency was an acceptance of its duties. Lucy's (D) sole compensation was to be one-half the profits resulting from Wood's (P) efforts. Unless he gave his efforts, she could never receive anything. Without an implied promise, the transaction could not have had such business efficacy as they must have intended it to have. Wood's (P) promise to make monthly accountings and to acquire patents and copyrights as necessary showed the intention of the parties that the promise has value by showing that Wood (P) had some duties. The promise to pay Lucy (D) half the profits and make monthly accountings was a promise to use reasonable efforts to bring profits and revenues into existence. Reversed.

▶ ANALYSIS

A bilateral contract can be express, implied in fact, or a little of each. The finding of an implied promise for the purpose of finding sufficient consideration to support an express promise is an important technique of the courts in order to uphold agreements which seem to be illusory and to avoid problems of mutuality of obligation. This case is the leading case on the subject. It is codified in U.C.C. § 2-306 (2) where an agreement for exclusive dealing in goods imposes, unless otherwise agreed, an obligation to use best efforts by both parties.

Quicknotes

BILATERAL CONTRACT An agreement pursuant to which each party promises to undertake an obligation, or to forbear from acting, at some time in the future.

IMPLIED PROMISE A promise inferred by law from a document as a whole and the circumstances surrounding its implementation.

U.C.C. § 2-306 Permits the seller to refuse to deliver unreasonable amounts demanded by a customer under a requirements contract.

Grouse v. Group Health Plan, Inc.

Pharmacist (P) v. Health care company (D)

Minn. Sup. Ct., 306 N.W.2d 114 (1981).

NATURE OF CASE: Appeal of dismissal of action for damages for breach of contract.

FACT SUMMARY: Group Health (D) withdrew an employment offer after Grouse (P) had resigned his previous employment.

🏛 RULE OF LAW
One resigning employment in reliance on a job offer may recover damages if the offer is withdrawn.

FACTS: Grouse (P) was a pharmacist at Richter Drug. Seeking a better position, he interviewed with Group Health Plan, Inc. (D). Elliot, Group Health's (D) chief pharmacist, offered Grouse (P) a position. Grouse (P) gave Richter two weeks' notice. Shoberg, Group Health's (D) general manager, then told Elliot he wanted a reference on Grouse (P). Elliot was unable to obtain one, and the employment offer was withdrawn. It took a period of time for Grouse (P) to find new employment. Grouse (P) sued for lost wages, based on breach of contract. The trial court dismissed, and Grouse (P) appealed.

ISSUE: May one resigning employment in reliance on a job offer recover damages if the offer is withdrawn?

HOLDING AND DECISION: (Otis, J.) Yes. One resigning employment in reliance on a job offer may recover damages if the offer is withdrawn. In a situation such as this, a contract does not exist in a strict legal sense, because due to the bilateral power of termination neither party is committed to performance and therefore no consideration exists. However, when one party reasonably relies to his detriment on the other's promise, under the equitable doctrine of promissory estoppel a contract may be implied in law when none exists in fact. Here, Grouse (P) in good faith quit his job on the basis of what he reasonably believed to be a firm employment offer, and in so doing detrimentally relied on Group Health's (D) offer. This was sufficient to invoke promissory estoppel to supply needed consideration. Reversed and remanded.

▌ ANALYSIS

Promissory estoppel, like most equitable doctrines, is a flexible tool courts may use to fill in gaps where strict adherence to the rules of actions at law would lead to seemingly unjust results. As the court here says, it is a substitute for consideration. One changing his position in reliance on another's promise will constitute the consideration to make a nonbinding unilateral offer into a binding bilateral contract.

Quicknotes

BILATERAL CONTRACT An agreement pursuant to which each party promises to undertake an obligation, or to forbear from acting, at some time in the future.

DETRIMENTAL RELIANCE Action by one party, resulting in loss, that is based on the conduct or promises of another.

PROMISSORY ESTOPPEL A promise that is enforceable if the promisor should reasonably expect that it will induce action or forbearance on the part of the promisee, and does in fact cause such action or forbearance, and it is the only means of avoiding injustice.

Slattery v. Wells Fargo Armored Service Corp.

Independent contractor (P) v. Employer (D)

Fla. Dist. Ct. App., 366 So. 2d 157 (1979).

NATURE OF THE CASE: Appeal from entry of summary judgment against plaintiff in claim for collection of posted reward.

FACT SUMMARY: Slattery (P) attempted to collect reward offered by Wells Fargo (D) for acts he was obligated to perform.

🏛 RULE OF LAW
Performance of a pre-existing duty does not create consideration sufficient to support a contract.

FACTS: Wells Fargo (D) offered a reward for information leading to the arrest and conviction of persons involved in the shooting of a Wells Fargo agent. While employed by government agencies as an independent contractor to administer polygraph tests, Slattery (P) conducted a polygraph interrogation of the perpetrator on an unrelated matter. In the course of that interrogation, the individual stated that he had shot and killed the guard and was subsequently convicted and sentenced for the crime. Slattery (P) contends that he was entitled to the reward posted by Wells Fargo (D). The trial court entered summary judgment against Slattery (P), who appealed.

ISSUE: Can one collect a reward for performing tasks that one was previously under contractual obligation to perform?

HOLDING AND DECISION: (Per curiam) No. One cannot collect a reward for performing tasks that one was previously under contractual obligation to perform. Performance of a pre-existing duty does not create consideration sufficient to support a contract. Slattery (P) was under a pre-existing duty to give his employers all useful information obtained in the course of his employment as an independent contractor performing polygraph interrogations for law enforcement. Accordingly, by giving the information about the shooting to the authorities, Slattery (P) did not perform an act that would amount to sufficient consideration to support the contract offered by Wells Fargo (D). In effect, Slattery (P) did nothing to accept Wells Fargo's (D) offer. In addition, public policy dictates that the integrity of law enforcement would be undermined if Slattery (P) were allowed to collect a reward for furnishing information he was under an obligation to furnish. Affirmed.

▶ ANALYSIS

The court adopted a straightforward analysis: Since Slattery (P) was already obligated to tell his employers everything he learned from the interrogation regarding the shooting of the guard, he was incapable of performing the consideration necessary to accept the offer of a contract created by Wells Fargo's (D) offer of reward. The court cited no provision of Slattery's (P) employment contract with the government agencies that would establish the scope of his duties, but simply asserted that he was bound to reveal all that he knew.

■━■

Quicknotes

INDEPENDENT CONTRACTOR A party undertaking a particular assignment for another who retains control over the manner in which it is executed.

SUMMARY JUDGMENT Judgment rendered by a court in response to a motion made by one of the parties, claiming that the lack of a question of material fact in respect to an issue warrants disposition of the issue without consideration by the jury.

■━■

Lingenfelder v. Wainwright Brewery Co.

Executor for architect (P) v. Brewery (D)

Mo. Sup. Ct., 103 Mo. 578, 15 S.W. 844 (1891).

NATURE OF CASE: Action to enforce a contract.

FACT SUMMARY: Jungenfeld, an architect, discontinued the building of a brewery when a refrigeration contract was awarded to a competitor. He was induced to return to work by the promise of a bonus.

🏛 RULE OF LAW
A new employment contract made to keep an employee from quitting in the middle of a job he has contracted to complete is not supported by consideration.

FACTS: Jungenfeld, an architect, was hired by Wainwright Brewery (D) to build a new brewery. He was also the president of a refrigeration company, and he expected his company to be awarded the contract to construct a refrigeration plant for Wainwright Brewery (D). It, however, awarded the contract to another firm. This so angered Jungenfeld that he quit. In order to avoid the delay of hiring a new architect, Wainwright (D) agreed to pay Jungenfeld a five percent bonus if he would return to work. Jungenfeld did return to work and completed the brewery. Shortly thereafter, he died. The Brewery (D) then refused to pay the bonus. Lingenfelder (P), executor of Jungenfeld's estate, then sued to collect the bonus. The trial court held for Lingenfelder (P), and Wainwright (D) appealed, contending that there was no consideration for the new contract. Lingenfelder (P) argued that the old contract had been canceled and that a new one, binding on the Brewery (D), had been formed.

ISSUE: Is a new contract to complete the same job for more money binding on the promisor where it was entered into in order to keep the promisee from defaulting?

HOLDING AND DECISION: (Gantt, J.) No. There is no consideration to support such a contract. Jungenfeld merely did the same work he was already obligated to perform under the old contract. To allow one to take advantage of an emergency or of an inconvenience of the employer by requiring him to pay more for the same job is contrary to public policy, and an agreement to that effect is not supported by adequate consideration. The fact that Wainwright (D) agreed to pay the additional sum does not estop it from showing that there was no consideration for its promise. Finally, there is no merit in Lingenfelder's (P) contention that the bonus was for the compromise of a doubtful claim which Jungenfeld had against the brewery for not awarding the refrigeration contract to his company. There is no evidence whatsoever that Wainwright (D) had agreed to do so or had, in any other way, breached its contract with Jungenfeld. Reversed.

▶ ANALYSIS

In *Schwartzreich v. Bauman-Basch, Inc.*, 231 N.Y. 196 (1921), the court held that an employment contract for a specified period of time could be mutually rescinded and a new contract entered into to perform the same duties at a higher wage. The new agreement would be valid even though the employee was merely performing the same duties he had previously promised to perform at the lower wage. To enforce such an agreement, it is necessary that at the time of executing the new contract there had been a mutual agreement to void the old contract.

◼══◼

Quicknotes

MUTUAL RESCISSION An agreement by both parties to a contract to nullify the contract as if it had never existed.

PRE-EXISTING DUTY A common law doctrine that renders unenforceable a promise to perform a duty, which the promisor is already legally obligated to perform, for lack of consideration.

◼══◼

Foakes v. Beer

Debtor (D) v. Creditor (P)

House of Lords, 9 App. Cas. 605 (1884).

NATURE OF CASE: Suit for interest on debt.

FACT SUMMARY: Beer (P) agreed to forgo interest on a debt if Foakes (D) would pay her part of the debt immediately and the remainder in installments.

🏛 RULE OF LAW
The court cannot pass on the adequacy of the consideration, and if any consideration is present, it is sufficient to support the contract.

FACTS: Foakes (D) owed Beer (P) money. Beer (P) agreed to forgo all interest on the debt if Foakes (D) would pay her part then and the rest in set installment payments. Foakes (D) complied with Beer's (P) terms and paid off the debt. Beer (P) then brought suit for the interest on the debt. She claimed there was no consideration for the contract since Foakes (D) did no more than he was already obligated to do. The trial court and court of appeals both found for Beer (P) on the basis of *Cumber v. Wane.*

ISSUE: Is there any consideration present where a debtor makes a new agreement to perform that which he is already obligated to do?

HOLDING AND DECISION: (Selborne, L.C.) No. What the law imposes as duty is no consideration. Already being obligated to repay the debt, there is no consideration present where the debtor makes a new agreement to do that which he is already obligated to do. No payments were received ahead of time, and the creditor, Beer (P), obtained no advantage whatsoever by the terms of her agreement with Foakes (D). The mere fact that she would not have to pursue legal remedies to collect the obligation is not consideration. While we agree with Foakes's (D) counsel's argument that the court cannot pass on the adequacy of consideration where the parties have freely bargained for it, in the present case there is no consideration whatsoever. Therefore, judgment for Beer (P) is affirmed.

CONCURRENCE: (Lord Blackburn) Businessmen understand that prompt partial payment may be more beneficial than insisting on their rights and enforcing payment in full, particularly with a solvent debtor. With a debtor of doubtful credit, this is more so the case.

CONCURRENCE: (Lord Fitzgerald) Because the resolution in *Pinnel's Case* (the doctrine that payment of a lesser sum cannot be a satisfaction of a greater sum) has been the law for 280 years it should not be overturned, but it would be better and wiser if it were not the law.

▶ ANALYSIS

This is the same situation as *Cumber v. Wane,* 1 Str. 425 (1717). The payment of less than one's full legal obligation will not support a settlement agreement. There is no consideration to support the promise. Two exceptions to this are where the promisee agrees to perform a duty not called for under the contract (e.g., pay early), which will be of some benefit to the promisor, or when the amount of the debt is in dispute. Where there is interest on the loan, a creditor will always be bound by an agreement to extend the time of performance. The consideration is the extra interest earned by the creditor.

■=■

Quicknotes

PRE-EXISTING DUTY A common law doctrine that renders unenforceable a promise to perform a duty, which the promisor is already legally obligated to perform, for lack of consideration.

■=■

Austin Instrument, Inc. v. Loral Corp.

Seller (P) v. Buyer (D)

N.Y. App. Div., 35 A.D.2d 387, 316 N.Y.S.2d 528 (1970).

NATURE OF CASE: Appeal from judgment for plaintiff in contract dispute, and dismissal of defendant's claim of economic duress.

FACT SUMMARY: Loral (D) claimed that Austin (P) had extorted higher price increases for gear parts and assemblies covered by a first subcontract and sought damages for economic duress.

🏛 RULE OF LAW
To establish economic duress, a party must show he has been the victim of a wrongful or unlawful act or threat which deprived him of his unfettered free will and judgment in the transaction.

FACTS: Loral (D) had agreed to furnish radar dopplers for Navy use and negotiated subcontracts with Austin Instrument (P) for the manufacture and delivery of precision gear parts and assemblies. When Loral (D) was awarded an additional government contract for radar equipment, it began negotiations with Austin (P). About the same time, Austin (P) claimed it was losing money on the existing job that it could not afford and demanded retroactive price increases. Loral (D) claimed that Austin (P) stopped all work on the first subcontract and refused to proceed unless its demands were met. Loral (D) then wrote a letter saying it feared the drastic consequences if it defaulted under the Navy contract, and that it had no choice but to accept Austin's (P) terms. When Austin (P) sued for the balance owing on the subcontracts, Loral (D) sought to recover damages for economic duress in Austin's (P) alleged extorting of higher price increases under the first subcontract. The Referee found that Loral (D) had failed to establish its cause of action and dismissed Loral's (D) complaint. Loral (D) appealed.

ISSUE: To establish economic duress, must a party show he has been the victim of a wrongful or unlawful act or threat which deprived him of his unfettered free will and judgment in the transaction?

HOLDING AND DECISION: (Eager, J.) Yes. To establish economic duress, a party must show he has been the victim of a wrongful or unlawful act or threat which deprived him of his unfettered free will and judgment in the transaction. Here, it is clear Loral (D) weighed all the considerations and determined as a matter of business judgment to continue with Austin (P) and acted voluntarily. Loral's (D) efforts to obtain the items elsewhere were neither reasonable nor commensurate with the alleged urgency and gravity of the situation. Without a finding that the items were not obtainable elsewhere, there was no basis for a finding of duress. Loral (D) was at no time under any immediate urgency or government pressure for deliveries under the Navy contract. The self-serving letters it wrote were deliberately and voluntarily planned to set the stage for an alleged cause of action for economic duress. A threat to break a contract does not in itself constitute duress. Affirmed.

▶ ANALYSIS

The court here accused Loral (D) of deliberately staging economic duress by writing self-serving letters exaggerating the gravity of the situation. In fact, the court found, there was no interruption in delivery of machine parts covered by the first subcontract, as Loral (D) had claimed. The court's factual findings were at odds with Loral's (D) allegations.

■=■

Quicknotes

BREACH OF CONTRACT Unlawful failure by a party to perform its obligations pursuant to contract.

ECONOMIC DURESS A defense to an action that a party was unlawfully coerced into the performance of an action by another due to fear of imminent economic loss and was not acting in accordance with his own free volition in performing the action.

FINDING OF FACT A conclusion reached by a court or agency based on evidence presented.

SUBCONTRACTOR A contractor who enters into an agreement with a principal contractor, or other subcontractor, to perform all or a part of a contract.

■=■

Austin Instrument, Inc. v. Loral Corp.

Subcontractor (P) v. Radar set producer (D)

N.Y. Ct. App., 29 N.Y.2d 124, 272 N.E.2d 533 (1971).

NATURE OF CASE: Action to recover damages for breach of contract.

FACT SUMMARY: Austin (P) threatened to withhold delivery of precision parts unless Loral (D) would raise the contract price.

🏛 RULE OF LAW
A contract modification is voidable on the ground of duress when the party claiming duress establishes that its agreement to the modification was obtained by means of a wrongful threat from the other party which precluded the first party's exercise of free will.

FACTS: Loral (D) was under contract to produce radar sets for the government. The contract contained a liquidated damage clause for late delivery and a cancellation clause in case of default by Loral (D). Loral (D), who did a substantial portion of its business with the government, awarded Austin (P) a subcontract to supply some of the precision parts. Subsequently, Austin (P) threatened to cease delivery of the parts unless Loral (D) consented to substantial increases in the subcontract price. After contacting 10 manufacturers of precision gears and finding none who could produce the parts in time to meet its commitment to the government, Loral (D) acceded to Austin's (P) demand.

ISSUE: Is a contract modification acceded to by one party under circumstances amounting to economic duress enforceable against that party?

HOLDING AND DECISION: (Fuld, C.J.) No. A contract modification "is voidable on the ground of duress when it is established that the party making the claim was forced to agree to it by means of a wrongful threat precluding the exercise of his free will." Loral (D) has made out a classic case of economic duress in that: (1) Austin (P) threatened to withhold delivery of "needful goods" unless Loral (D) agreed, (2) Loral (D) could not obtain the goods from another source of supply, and (3) the ordinary remedy of an action for breach of the original subcontract would not be adequate [since so much was riding on Loral's (D) own general contract with the government]. Thus it is "manifest" that Austin's (P) threat deprived Loral (D) of his free will. "Loral (D) actually had no choice." Reversed in part and affirmed in part.

▶ ANALYSIS

Although it has generally been held that a threat to breach a contract does not constitute economic duress, courts have recently begun to hold that various kinds of unethical business compulsion do constitute duress. The present case is an example of this trend. Note that even under the U.C.C. (which recognizes modification without consideration—§ 2-209) the requirement of good faith is ever present.

■■■

Quicknotes

ECONOMIC DURESS A defense to an action that a party was unlawfully coerced into the performance of an action by another due to fear of imminent economic loss and was not acting in accordance with his own free volition in performing the action.

U.C.C. § 2-209 Provides that a contract for the sale of goods needs no additional consideration to be modified.

■■■

McMahon Food Corp. v. Burger Dairy Co.

Dairy product vendor (P) v. Dairy product supplier (D)

103 F.3d 1307 (7th Cir. 1996).

NATURE OF THE CASE: Appeal from award of relief to defendant in plaintiff's action for declaratory judgment.

FACT SUMMARY: McMahon Food Corp. (MFC) (P) tendered checks to Burger Dairy Co. (Burger) (D) containing or accompanied by notations asserting that disputed accounts were thereby paid in full. Burger (D) negotiated the checks but denied that they effected an accord and satisfaction of the accounts in arrears.

RULE OF LAW
(1) To effect an accord and satisfaction, the instrument must be tendered in good faith as full satisfaction of the claim and the amount of the claim must be unliquidated or subject to a bona fide dispute.
(2) A check will not create an accord and satisfaction where: (a) the specific debt in question is unclear, (b) the person processing the check is unaware of the accord and satisfaction, and (c) there is no just basis for the dispute.

FACTS: MFC (P) purchased dairy products delivered by the truckload in plastic open-topped milk cases from Burger (D). Burger (D) charged a deposit for milk cases delivered and paid a credit for milk cases returned. Burger (D) also purchased used milk cases from MFC (P). Over time, accounting disputes arose and Burger claimed that MFC was $58,518.41 in arrears ("the February debt"). McMahon, MFC's (P) vice president, met with Bylsma, Burger's (D) general manager, to resolve the February debt issue, but without success. MFC (P) continued to purchase dairy products from Burger (D) after this meeting and paid the new invoices with checks and vouchers that included typed notations stating, "paid in full through 8/8/92" and "paid in full through 8/15/92" (the August checks). Burger (D) deposited the August checks without comment. McMahon then met with Carter (who had replaced Bylsma as general manager) to review the account and advised that he had settled the February debt with Bylsma. After reviewing post-February debt invoices with Carter, McMahon tendered a check for $51,812.98 containing restrictive endorsements indicating that MFC (P) was current with Burger (D). Burger (D) later struck the restrictive language from the check, cashed it, and informed MFC (P) that (1) it had done so and (2) MFC still owed Burger (D) over $64,000. MFC (P) filed suit seeking declaratory judgment that it had reached an accord and satisfaction of any debt to Burger (D). Burger (D) countersued, seeking the money it claimed was still owed.

The trial court found MFC (P) to be $58,518.41 in arrears and awarded that amount plus interest and costs to Burger (D). This appealed followed.

ISSUE:
(1) Will the successful negotiation of a check for a disputed claim effect an accord and satisfaction of a debt where: (a) the check is clearly intended to discharge the claim, (b) the recipient understood the purpose of the check and intentionally scratched out and/or altered the restrictive endorsement, but (c) the check was tendered in bad faith?
(2) Will accord and satisfaction occur where a voucher accompanying a check contains potentially unclear language indicating that it is intended to satisfy outstanding debts to date, and the check is processed by an employee who has no responsibility for an accord and satisfaction?

HOLDING AND DECISION: (Coffey, J.)
(1) No. The successful negotiation of a check for a disputed claim will not effect an accord and satisfaction of a debt where: (a) the check is clearly intended to discharge the claim, (b) the recipient understood the purpose of the check and intentionally scratched out and/or altered the restrictive endorsement, but (c) the check was tendered in bad faith. For accord and satisfaction, payment must be tendered "in good faith." There was no honest dispute between the parties at the time the payment was tendered because McMahon was found by the trial court to have dishonestly taken advantage of Carter by claiming to have settled the February debt with Bylsma. Even though Burger's (D) attempt to negate the restrictive endorsements by removing and/or altering them had no effect (because words of protest cannot change the legal effect of accord and satisfaction), McMahon's bad faith precludes accord and satisfaction as a threshold matter.
(2) No. Accord and satisfaction will not occur where a voucher accompanying a check contains potentially unclear language indicating that it is intended to satisfy outstanding debts to date and the check is processed by an employee, who has no responsibility for an accord and satisfaction. First, vouchers with notations purporting to be "payment in full" which can reasonably be understood to refer to more than one disputed debt are ambiguous and cannot serve as full satisfaction of a claim. Second, the assistant controller who processed the checks for Burger (D) had no knowledge of the dispute with MFC (P) and no responsibility for accord

Continued on next page.

and satisfaction. Accordingly, whether she saw or understood the "paid in full" language is irrelevant because her knowledge is not imputed to Burger (D). Burger's (D) failure to instruct her to look for accord and satisfaction statements does not constitute a lack of due diligence. Third, even though McMahon had refused to pay the February debt by the time MFC (P) tendered the August checks, the trial court found that MFC (P) had no credible reason for believing the February debt had been discharged. Accordingly, MFC (P) was still in bad faith when it tendered the August checks, thus failing to meet the "good faith dispute" element of accord and satisfaction. Affirmed.

▶ *ANALYSIS*

The appellate court considered the trial court's finding that McMahon intentionally misrepresented the circumstances and results of his negotiations with Bylsma to be dispositive: once bad faith enters the analysis, there can be no accord and satisfaction. Not only must the tender of satisfaction be made in good faith, but the dispute must itself have valid grounds. Even though there was testimony that McMahon believed that Burger's (D) accounts were in error, a debtor cannot unilaterally create an accord and satisfaction. Accordingly, the tender of satisfaction must be conspicuously made to one who knows of and understands the dispute and the specific debt at issue must be unambiguously identified. In short, one cannot create an accord and satisfaction of a debt by trickery or technicality.

■══■

Quicknotes

ACCORD AND SATISFACTION The performance of an agreement between two parties, one of whom has a valid claim against the other, to settle the controversy.

DECLARATORY JUDGMENT A judgment of the court establishing the rights of the parties.

UNLIQUIDATED CLAIM Disputed claim; one not finally determined as to damages or liability.

■══■

Angel v. Murray

Taxpayers (P) v. Disposal contractor (D)

R.I. Sup. Ct., 113 R.I. 482, 322 A.2d 630 (1974).

NATURE OF CASE: Action for breach of contract.

FACT SUMMARY: Maher (D) asked for $10,000 more per year to collect refuse even though his contract with the city to provide this service had not yet expired.

🏛 RULE OF LAW
Where unanticipated circumstances or conditions have occurred, the parties to a contract may voluntarily increase the amount of compensation due even if no additional consideration is given.

FACTS: Maher (D) entered into a 5-year contract with the city to provide it refuse collection services. A totally unanticipated growth in construction increased the number of units from which Maher (D) had to collect refuse by 20–25%. Maher (D) requested an additional $10,000 per year for the remainder of the contract because of this unexpected increase. The Council discussed the matter at a public meeting and agreed to give Maher (D) $10,000 for that year, and an additional $10,000 was given him the following year. Apparently, Angel (P), a taxpayer, and others (P) brought a civil action against Maher (D) and Murray (D), the City Treasurer, to compel Maher (D) to repay the $20,000 in additional compensation received by him. Angel (P) alleged that there was no new consideration to support the modification since Maher (D) was already under a duty to collect the refuse.

ISSUE: May a contract be voluntarily modified by the parties without new consideration where unexpected situations or conditions have arisen?

HOLDING AND DECISION: (Roberts, C.J.) Yes. The preexisting duty rule has, in the past, been used to hold such contracts invalid for lack of consideration. A modification of a contract is itself a contract which must be supported by consideration. We find that where the parties voluntarily agree to modify an existing contract, without coercion or duress, because of unanticipated conditions or circumstances, the modification is valid. There is no reason to prevent the parties from modifying their contractual agreements. The new contract is valid. Reversed and remanded.

▶ ANALYSIS

Some courts have gone through elaborate attempts to avoid the preexisting duty rule by first finding a rescission and then a new contract. *Linz v. Schuck*, 106 Md. 220 (1907). Many jurisdictions no longer temper application of the pre-existing duty rule along the lines mentioned in *Angel*. Modifications made before the contract is fully executed on either side will be upheld if they are equitable and free from coercion. Restatement (Second) Contracts § 89D(a).

■══■

Quicknotes

CONTRACT MODIFICATION A change to the terms of a contract without altering its general purpose.

PRE-EXISTING DUTY A common law doctrine that renders unenforceable a promise to perform a duty, which the promisor is already legally obligated to perform, for lack of consideration.

■══■

Clark v. West

Writer of treatise (P) v. Publisher (D)

N.Y. Ct. App., 193 N.Y. 349, 86 N.E. 1 (1908).

NATURE OF CASE: Action for breach of contract and an accounting.

FACT SUMMARY: West (D) paid Clark (P) only $2 per page for writing a legal treatise and Clark (P) demanded the $6 per page he had been promised if he quit drinking, alleging that West (D) had not objected when he continued to drink.

🏛 RULE OF LAW
A condition in a contract may be waived, but no waiver is implied by mere acceptance of the proffered performance.

FACTS: West (D) entered into a contract with Clark (P) whereby Clark (P) was to write a multi-volume treatise on corporations for West (D). The contract price was $6 per page if Clark (P) totally abstained from liquor during the contract or $2 per page if he drank. West (D) became aware that Clark (P) was drinking moderately during the term of the contract but made no objection. West (D) accepted Clark's (P) work and paid him $2 per page. Clark (P) sued for the difference, claiming that he was owed $6 per page. West (D) demurred, and both the trial court and the court of appeals sustained the demurrer. Clark (P) appealed, claiming that West (D) had waived the abstinence requirement and that the waiver was effective since abstinence was a mere condition precedent to West's (D) obligation to pay $6 per page.

ISSUE: May a condition precedent to performance be waived?

HOLDING AND DECISION: (Werner, J.) Yes. A condition to a contract may be waived, but mere acceptance of performance does not constitute a waiver. While it is West's (D) contention that Clark's (P) abstinence was the consideration for the payment of $6 rather than $2, a careful analysis of the contract shows that it was the writing of the treatise, rather than abstinence, which was the bargained-for consideration. Since abstinence was not the consideration for the contract, it was a condition which could be waived without a new agreement based upon a good consideration. No formal agreement or additional consideration is required to waive a condition precedent to performance. West (D) received and accepted the bargained-for consideration, i.e., the treatise. If the condition was waived, then West (D) is liable for the $6 contract price, but mere silence and acceptance of performance will not be deemed a waiver of the condition. However, since Clark (P) alleges an express waiver of the condition, he should be allowed to prove this at trial. The demurrer is, therefore, overruled and the case remanded for trial.

▶ ANALYSIS

Frequently, as in *Clark*, it is difficult to determine whether one is dealing with a promise or a condition. Modification of a promise typically requires a new consideration, while the waiver of a condition does not. A condition may be described as qualifying a contractual duty by providing either that performance is not called for unless a stated event occurs or fails to occur, or that performance may be suspended or terminated if a stated event occurs or fails to occur. Stated more simply, the condition is outside of and modifies the promised performance called for under the contract.

Quicknotes

CONDITION PRECEDENT The happening of an uncertain occurrence, which is necessary before a particular right or interest may be obtained or an action performed.

DEMURRER The assertion that the opposing party's pleadings are insufficient and that the demurring party should not be made to answer.

Past Consideration

Quick Reference Rules of Law

Mills v. Wyman

Caretaker (P) v. Father (D)

Mass. Sup. Jud. Ct., 20 Mass. (3 Pick.) 207 (1825).

NATURE OF CASE: Action on appeal to recover upon alleged promise.

FACT SUMMARY: Mills (P) took care of Wyman's (D) son without being requested to do so, and for so doing was promised compensation for expenses arising out of the rendered care by Wyman (D). Wyman (D) later refused to compensate Mills (P).

> ## 🏛 RULE OF LAW
> A moral obligation is insufficient as consideration for a promise.

FACTS: Mills (P) nursed and cared for Levi Wyman, the son of Wyman (D). Upon learning of Mills's (P) acts of kindness toward his son, Wyman (D) promised to repay Mills (P) his expenses incurred in caring for Levi Wyman. Later, Wyman (D) refused to compensate Mills (P) for his expenses. Mills (P) filed an action in the Court of Common Pleas where Wyman (D) was successful in obtaining a non-suit against Mills (P). Mills (P) appealed.

ISSUE: Is a moral obligation sufficient consideration for a promise?

HOLDING AND DECISION: (Parker, C.J.) No. It is said that a moral obligation is a sufficient consideration to support an express promise. However, the universality of the rule cannot be supported. Therefore, there must be some other pre-existing obligation which will suffice as consideration. Affirmed.

▶ ANALYSIS

In cases such as this one, the nearly universal holding is that the existing moral obligation is not a sufficient basis for the enforcement of an express promise to render the performance that it requires. The general statement is that it is not sufficient consideration for the express promise. The difficulties and differences of opinion involved in the determination of what is a moral obligation are probably much greater than those involved in determining the existence of a legal obligation. This tends to explain the attitude of the majority of courts on the subject and justifies the generally stated rule.

■━■

Quicknotes

MORAL OBLIGATION A duty that is not enforceable at law, but is consistent with ethical notions of justice.

■━■

Webb v. McGowin

Lumber employee (P) v. Executors of passerby's estate (D)

Ala. Ct. App., 27 Ala. App. 82, 168 So. 196 (1935).

NATURE OF CASE: Action on appeal to collect on a promise.

FACT SUMMARY: Webb (P) saved the now deceased J. McGowin from grave bodily injury or death by placing himself in grave danger and subsequently suffering grave bodily harm. J. McGowin, in return, promised Webb (P) compensation. McGowin's executors (D) now refuse to pay the promised compensation.

🏛 RULE OF LAW
A moral obligation is a sufficient consideration to support a subsequent promise to pay where the promisor has received a material benefit.

FACTS: Webb (P), while in the scope of his duties for the W.T. Smith Lumber Co., was clearing the floor, which required him to drop a 75-lb. pine block from the upper floor of the mill to the ground. Just as Webb (P) was releasing the block, he noticed J. McGowin below and directly under where the block would have fallen. In order to divert the fall of the block, Webb (P) fell with it, breaking an arm and leg and ripping his heel off. The fall left Webb (P) a cripple and incapable of either mental or physical labor. In return for Webb's (P) act, J. McGowin promised to pay Webb (P) $15 every two weeks for the rest of Webb's (P) life. J. McGowin paid the promised payments until his death eight years later. Shortly after J. McGowin's death, the payments were stopped and Webb (P) brought an action against N. McGowin (D) and J.F. McGowin (D) as executors of J. McGowin's estate for payments due him. The executors (D) of the estate were successful in obtaining a nonsuit against Webb (P) in the lower court. Webb (P) appealed.

ISSUE: Was the moral obligation to compensate as promised sufficient consideration?

HOLDING AND DECISION: (Bricken, J.) Yes. It is well settled that a moral obligation is a sufficient consideration to support a subsequent promise to pay where the promisor has received a material benefit, although there was no original duty or liability resting on the promisor. Reversed and remanded.

▶ ANALYSIS

In most cases where the moral obligation is asserted, the court feels that the promise ought not be enforced; instead of going into the uncertain field of morality, the court chooses to rely upon the rule that moral obligation is not a sufficient consideration. On the other hand, in cases where the promise is one which would have been kept by most citizens, and the court feels that enforcement is just, a few courts will enforce the promise using the *Webb v. McGowin* rule. In general, the *Webb v. McGowin* rule is the minority rule and the *Mills v. Wyman* rule is the majority rule.

■■■

Quicknotes

MATERIAL BENEFIT An advantage gained by entering into a contract that is essential to the performance of the agreement and without which the contract would not have been entered into.

MORAL OBLIGATION A duty that is not enforceable at law, but is consistent with ethical notions of justice.

■■■

Webb v. McGowin

Lumber employee (P) v. Executors of passerby's estate (D)

Ala. Sup. Ct., 168 So. 199 (1936).

NATURE OF CASE: Appeal of judgment by the executors of an estate.

FACT SUMMARY: N. Floyd and Joseph N. McGowin (D), executors of Greeley McGowin's estate, appealed a judgment based upon the distinction between the moral obligation of a promisor and the obligation in which material benefits were received by the promisor.

🏛 RULE OF LAW
A promisor's duty based upon received material benefits is different from the duty under a moral obligation.

FACTS: Floyd and Joseph McGowin (D), executors of J. Greeley McGowin's estate, appealed a judgment based upon the distinction between the moral obligation of a promisor and the obligation in which material benefits were received by the promisor.

ISSUE: Is a promisor's duty based upon received material benefits different from the duty under a moral obligation?

HOLDING AND DECISION: (Foster, J.) Yes. A promisor's duty based upon received material benefits is different from the duty under a moral obligation. If a promisor, rather than his estate, receives a material benefit, then the promisor has the privilege of recognizing and compensating the provider of the benefits. The obligation is also present where the promisee suffers injuries to property or person by reason of the services rendered. This is a different type of obligation than that owed by a promisor out of a moral obligation. Writ denied.

▶ ANALYSIS

The Supreme Court's decision in this case has been edited down to a mere recitation of the rule. Thus, it is unclear what promises were made by J. Greeley McGowin and what alleged benefits were received by him before his death. Generally, promises require consideration in order to be enforceable.

■═■

Quicknotes

MATERIAL BENEFIT An advantage gained by entering into a contract that is essential to the performance of the agreement and without which the contract would not have been entered into.

MORAL OBLIGATION A duty that is not enforceable at law, but is consistent with ethical notions of justice.

■═■

CHAPTER 4

The Limits of Contract

Quick Reference Rules of Law

In re the Marriage of Witten

Sperm donor (D) v. Egg donor (P)

Iowa Sup. Ct., 672 N.W.2d 768 (2003).

NATURE OF CASE: Appeal from decree in dissolution of marriage action.

FACT SUMMARY: Trip Witten (Trip) (D) and Tamara Witten (Tamara) (P) divorced and now dispute control and disposition of their 17 embryos held in frozen storage.

RULE OF LAW

An agreement governing the release of frozen embryos is not enforceable once one party changes his or her mind as to the disposition of the embryos.

FACTS: During their marriage, Trip (D) and Tamara (P) underwent an in vitro fertilization process which resulted in 17 embryos being held in frozen storage pursuant to an "Embryo Storage Agreement" with the storage facility. The agreement was silent regarding the effect of dissolution of their marriage but provided that the embryos will be stored until: (1) both parties authorize release or destruction, (2) the death of one or both donors, (3) failure to pay the storage fee, or (4) ten years from the date of agreement. Trip (D) later sought dissolution of the marriage and Tamara (P) sought "custody" of the embryos which Trip (D) opposed. The trial court enforced the storage agreement and enjoined either party from using or destroying the embryos without consent of the other. Tamara (P) appealed.

ISSUE: Is an agreement governing the release of frozen embryos enforceable once one party changes his or her mind as to the disposition of the embryos?

HOLDING AND DECISION: (Ternus, J.) No. Agreements governing the release of frozen embryos are not enforceable once one party changes their mind as to the disposition of the embryos. Simply enforcing contract terms entered into at the time the eggs were fertilized fails to protect adequately the individual and societal interests unique to the issue of becoming a parent and is contrary to the public policy of Iowa. Nor should the court substitute its judgment for that of the parties as would occur under any analysis that attempts to balance the competing interests and public policy concerns. Instead, the ability of the donors to make family and reproductive decisions based on their current views and values must be protected. Accordingly, the contract is enforceable, but subject to the right of a donor to change his or her mind up to the point of use or destruction of the embryo. Because Trip (D) no longer agrees to the earlier planned disposition of the embryos and since Trip (D) and Tamara (P) have been unable to date to reach a new agreement regarding the future disposition of the embryos, neither can use or destroy them until there is a mutual contemporaneous agreement. Until then, whoever opposes destruction of the embryos is responsible for the storage fees. Affirmed.

ANALYSIS

Although the court in effect upheld the enforceability of the storage agreement by affirming the trial court's decree, it did so only because the agreement happened to be consistent with the contemporaneous mutual consent model. The court considered approaches advocated by commentators and other jurisdictions, but rejected the contractual model (New York) and the balancing test (New Jersey), opting instead for the contemporaneous mutual consent model, which recognizes that an agreement does not necessarily violate public policy as long as neither party has a change of heart. The court did not explain how to apply the contemporaneous mutual consent model to the question of what will happen when the storage contract expires in ten years. At that time, assuming the parties still feel the same, the court's reliance on the contemporaneous mutual consent model will no longer resolve the issue. If the parties do not agree at the point when the storage agreement expires, there is no status quo to maintain and doing nothing would result in the destruction of the embryos and effectively enforce the contract as written against the wishes of the parties.

Quicknotes

DISSOLUTION DECREE A decree terminating a marriage.

IN VITRO FERTILIZATION The fertilization of a human egg using donor sperm in a controlled environment outside the womb.

PUBLIC POLICY Policy administered by the state with respect to the health, safety and morals of its people in accordance with common notions of fairness and decency.

T.F. v. B.L.

Child's biological mother (P) v. Mother's former partner (D)

Mass. Sup. Jud. Ct., 442 Mass. 522, 813 N.E. 1244 (2004).

NATURE OF CASE: Action for order of child support.

FACT SUMMARY: T.F. (P) sought child support from B.L. (D) who had agreed to co-parent a child conceived by T.F. (P) by artificial insemination while the two were a couple.

> ## 🏛 RULE OF LAW
> An implied agreement to co-parent a child is unenforceable as against public policy because parenthood by contract is not the law of Massachusetts.

FACTS: While living together as a same sex couple, T.F. (P) and B.L. (D) agreed that B.L. (D) would take on the responsibilities of a parent and T.F. (P) would conceive by artificial insemination and deliver a child. After T.F. (P) became pregnant, the couple separated. T.F. (P) delivered the child and B.L. (D) refused to provide support. T.F. (P) sought an order requiring child support and the trial court posed the question of whether parenthood by contract was the law of Massachusetts to the court of appeals.

ISSUE: Is an implied agreement to co-parent a child unenforceable as against public policy because parenthood by contract is not the law of Massachusetts?

HOLDING AND DECISION: (Cowin J.) Yes. An implied agreement to co-parent a child is unenforceable as against public policy because parenthood by contract is not the law in Massachusetts. There was sufficient evidence for the trial court to find that B.L. (D) agreed to take on parental responsibilities in that she expressed a desire to adopt the child, referred to herself as a separated parent, visited the mother and child in the hospital, promised to support the child and promised to change her work hours to help raise the child. In order to protect freedom of personal choice, however, agreements to enter into parenthood should not be enforced against persons who subsequently reconsider. Remanded to lower court for further proceedings consistent with this opinion.

CONCURRENCE AND DISSENT: (Greaney, J.) Parenthood by contract is not the law of Massachusetts, but the equitable authority of the Probate and Family court extends to protect the best interest of the child such that the agreement should be enforced. The fact that B.L. (D) is not a parent and there is no statutory remedy should not preclude an order requiring child support. The American Law Institute's analysis recommends that B.L's (D) prior conduct equitably estops her from denying a support obligation to the child.

▶ ANALYSIS

By phrasing the issue in terms of whether one can become a parent by operation of contract rather than as a function of conduct, the court here took the opposite approach from that taken in *Elisa B. v. Superior Court*, 37 Cal. 4th 108, 117 P.3d 660, 33 Cal. Rptr. 3d 46 (2005). In *Elisa B.*, the court reasoned from the premise that a de facto parenthood relationship existed and can exist between a person and the child of their same sex partner.

Quicknotes

BEST INTERESTS OF CHILD Standard used by courts when rendering decisions which involve a child or children.

CHILD SUPPORT Payments made by one parent to another in satisfaction of the non-custodial parent's legal obligation to provide for the sustenance of the child.

ESTOPPEL An equitable doctrine precluding a party from asserting a right to the detriment of another who justifiably relied on the conduct.

PUBLIC POLICY Policy administered by the state with respect to the health, safety and morals of its people in accordance with common notions of fairness and decency.

CHAPTER 5

An Introduction to Contract Damages

Quick Reference Rules of Law

Hawkins v. McGee

Patient (P) v. Surgeon (D)

N.H. Sup. Ct., 84 N.H. 114, 146 A. 641 (1929).

NATURE OF CASE: Action in assumpsit for breach of an alleged warranty.

FACT SUMMARY: McGee (D), a surgeon, performed an unsuccessful operation on Hawkins's (P) hand after having guaranteed to make the hand 100% perfect. Hawkins (P) was awarded damages for pain and suffering and for "what injury he has sustained over and above the injury he had before."

🏛 RULE OF LAW
The purpose of awarding damages for breach of contract is to put the plaintiff in as good a position as he would have been had the defendant kept his contract.

FACTS: McGee (D), a surgeon, performed an operation on Hawkins's (P) hand. Before the operation, McGee (D) had repeatedly solicited an opportunity to perform the operation and had guaranteed to make the hand 100% perfect. The operation was not successful, and Hawkins (P) seeks to recover on the basis of McGee's (D) warranty. The trial court instructed the jury that Hawkins (P) would be entitled to recover for his pain and suffering and for "what injury he has sustained over and above the injury he had before."

ISSUE: Is the measure of damages for breach of a contract what the defendant contracted to give the plaintiff?

HOLDING AND DECISION: (Branch, J.) Yes. McGee's (D) words, if taken at face value, indicate the giving of a warranty. Coupled with the evidence that McGee (D) repeatedly solicited the opportunity to perform the operation, there is a reasonable basis for a jury to conclude that McGee (D) spoke the words with the intention that they be taken at face value as an inducement for Hawkins's (P) submission to the operation. The jury instruction on damages was erroneous. The purpose of awarding damages is to put a plaintiff in as good a position as he would have been in had the defendant kept his contract. The measure of recovery is what the defendant should have given the plaintiff, not what the plaintiff has given the defendant or has otherwise expended. Hence, the measure of Hawkins's (P) damages is the difference between the value of a perfect hand, as promised by McGee (D), and the value of his hand in its present condition. Hawkins's (P) pain is not relevant to this determination. Also, damages might be assessed for McGee's (D) failure to improve the hand, even if there was no evidence that the operation had made it worse. New trial ordered.

▶ ANALYSIS

The measure of damages is the actual loss sustained by reason of the breach, which is the loss of what the promisee would have made if the contract had been performed, less the proper deductions. The plaintiff may recover damages not only for the net gains which were prevented by the breach, but also for expenses incurred in reliance on the defendant's performance of his contract promise. In a proper case, prospective profits which were lost because of the breach are also recoverable.

■═■

Quicknotes

ACTION IN ASSUMPSIT Action to recover damages for breach of an oral or written promise to perform or pay pursuant to a contract.

■═■

United States Naval Institute v. Charter Communications, Inc.

Copyright assignee (P) v. Media group (D)

936 F.2d 692 (2d Cir. 1991).

NATURE OF CASE: Appeal and cross-appeal from a judgment on remand awarding damages and profits in an action for breach of contract.

FACT SUMMARY: When Charter Communications (D), the exclusive licensee for a paperback edition of a book, for which Naval (P) was the author's assignee, shipped the paperback edition to retail stores prior to the date set in the contract, Naval (P) filed suit for damages and Charter's (D) profits on the hardback edition of the book.

> 🏛 **RULE OF LAW**
> Damages for breach of contract are generally measured by a plaintiff's actual loss.

FACTS: Naval Institute (P), as the assignee of the author's copyright in The Hunt for Red October, granted Charter Communications (D) and Berkley Publishing Group (collectively Berkley) (D) an exclusive license to publish a paperback edition of the book "not sooner than October 1985." However, Berkeley shipped the paperbacks to retailers earlier than October, so that the paperback went on sale September 15, 1985. Naval (P) sued for breach of the licensing agreement. The court awarded damages to Naval (P), calculating actual damages as the profits Naval (P) would have earned from hardcover sales in September if the competing paperback edition had not been released. The court also awarded Berkeley's (D) profit on the displacing copies to Naval (P). Naval (P) appealed as to the profits award, and Berkeley (D) cross-appealed.

ISSUE: Are damages for breach of contract generally measured by a plaintiff's actual loss?

HOLDING AND DECISION: (Kearse, J.) Yes. Damages for breach of contract are generally measured by a plaintiff's actual loss. While on occasion a defendant's profits are used as the measure of damages, this generally occurs when those profits tend to define the plaintiff's loss. Here, Berkley's (D) alleged profits did not define Naval's (P) loss because those who bought the paperback would most likely not have bought the hardcover version in any event. However, the court correctly calculated Naval's (P) actual damages by relying on August sales rather than the lower September sales of the hardcover version. Nothing in the record foreclosed the possibility that, absent Berkley's (D) breach, sales of hardcover copies in the latter part of September would have outpaced sales of those copies in the early part of the month. Thus, it was within the prerogative of the court as finder of fact to look to Naval's (P) August sales to quantify Naval's (P) loss. Reversed as to the award of profits but affirmed in all other respects. Reversed in part and affirmed in part.

▶ ANALYSIS

In its analysis, the court of appeals looked to §§ 347 and 356 of the Restatement (Second) of Contracts. An award of a defendant's profits where they greatly exceed the plaintiff's loss and where there has been no tortious conduct on the part of the defendant would tend to be punitive, and punitive awards are not part of the law of contract damages. However, it is proper to lay the normal uncertainty in hypothesizing possible sales at the door of the wrongdoer who altered the proper course of events.

■═■

Quicknotes

ACTUAL DAMAGES Measure of damages necessary to compensate victim for actual injuries suffered.

PUNITIVE DAMAGES Damages exceeding the actual injury suffered for the purposes of punishment, deterrence and comfort to plaintiff.

■═■

Coppola Enterprises, Inc. v. Alfone

Seller of residential property (D) v. Buyer of residential property (P)

Fla. Sup. Ct., 531 So. 2d 334 (1988).

NATURE OF CASE: Action for recovery of benefit of bargain.

FACT SUMMARY: Seller of residential property Coppola (D) refused to give buyer Alfone (P) reasonable time to obtain financing after Coppola's (D) delays postponed an original closing date.

🏛 RULE OF LAW
A seller's initial postponement of the closing date waives "time is of the essence" provisions in a contract for sale of residential property such that the seller must give the buyer reasonable time to fulfill the buyer's obligations under the contract.

FACTS: Alfone (P) contracted with Coppola (D) to purchase a residential lot and house to be constructed on the property for $105,690.00. The contract provided that the closing would occur ten days from written notice from Coppola (D). The original closing date was postponed because of construction delays. When Alfone (P) was unable to obtain financing within the ten days before the rescheduled closing, Coppola (D) claimed that time was of the essence and sold the property to another purchaser for $170,000. At trial, Alfone (P) successfully sought damages of benefit of the bargain plus interest. The trial court's judgment was affirmed on appeal to the District Court of Appeal.

ISSUE: Did Coppola's (D) postponement of the original closing date due to construction waive the requirement that Alfone (P) obtain financing for the closing within ten days of written notice of the rescheduled closing such that Alfone (P) must be given reasonable time to obtain financing?

HOLDING: (Kogan, J.) Yes. Coppola's (D) postponement of the original closing date due to construction delays waived the provisions of the contract making time of the essence and Alfone (P) was entitled to a reasonable time to obtain financing. By selling the property to the third party, Coppola (D) breached the contract to sell to Alfone (P). A seller is not permitted to profit from his own breach of a contract, even if made in good faith. Accordingly, Alfone (P) was entitled to damages equal to Coppola's (D) profits from the sale. Affirmed.

▶ ANALYSIS

The case turns on who first breached the contract. When Coppola (D) was unable to deliver the property due to its construction delays, it lost the ability to assert that time was of the essence.

Quicknotes

BENEFIT OF THE BARGAIN Calculation of assessing damages in actions for breach of contract measured as the difference between the actual value and the purported value of the goods being bought.

The Expectation Measure

Quick Reference Rules of Law

Louise Caroline Nursing Home, Inc. v. Dix Construction Co.

Nursing home (P) v. Construction company (D)

Mass. Sup. Jud. Ct., 362 Mass. 306, 285 N.E.2d 904 (1972).

NATURE OF CASE: Motion to recommit an auditor's report.

FACT SUMMARY: Louise Caroline (P) contended it was entitled to recover the value of the construction had Dix (D) not breached its contract.

🏛 **RULE OF LAW**
The proper measure of damages for breach of a construction contract is the amount of the reasonable cost of completing the contract and repairing the defective performance less the unpaid contract price.

FACTS: Louise Caroline Nursing Home (P) contracted with Dix (D) for the construction of a nursing home. Dix (D) began the work and then subsequently abandoned the project. Louise (P) contracted elsewhere, and the project was completed at a cost within the contract price with Dix (D). Louise (P) sued, and the case was referred to an auditor who found Dix (D) had breached, yet no compensable damages were incurred. Louise (P) appealed.

ISSUE: Can a party recover damages for the breach of a construction contract beyond that which it must pay in excess of the contract price?

HOLDING AND DECISION: (Quirico, J.) No. The proper measure of damages for the breach of a construction contract is the amount of the reasonable cost of completing the contract and repairing the defective performance less the unpaid contract price. In this case no additional expense was incurred due to Dix's (D) breach, and, therefore, no damages were recoverable. Exceptions overruled.

▌ *ANALYSIS*

Louise (P) may have recovered some damages had they presented their case properly. They alleged damages caused by the delay in construction yet presented no evidence to establish such damages. They also contended they were forced to pay additional interest on the construction loan, yet again failed to present any supporting evidence.

■▬■

Quicknotes

BREACH OF CONTRACT Unlawful failure by a party to perform its obligations pursuant to contract.

MEASURE OF DAMAGES Monetary compensation that may be awarded by the court to a party who has sustained injury or loss to his or her person, property or rights due to another party's unlawful act, omission or negligence.

■▬■

Peevyhouse v. Garland Coal & Mining Co.

Farm owner (P) v. Coal mining company (D)

Okla. Sup. Ct., 382 P.2d 109 (1962), *cert. denied*, 375 U.S. 906 (1963).

NATURE OF CASE: Appeal from award of damages for breach of contract.

FACT SUMMARY: Peevyhouse (P) leased his farm for five years to the Garland Coal & Mining Co. (D) for strip-mining subject to the condition that the Mining Co. (D) perform restorative work at the end of the five years, but such work was never done.

RULE OF LAW
The measure of damages for breach of a contract obligation to perform construction or excavation work is usually the reasonable "cost of performance" of such work; but where the economic benefit which would result by full performance is "grossly disproportionate" to (i.e., much less than) the cost of performance, damages are limited to the "diminution in value" to the premises because of nonperformance.

FACTS: Peevyhouse (P), in 1954, leased his farm containing coal deposits to the Garland Coal & Mining Co. (D) for five years. Under this lease agreement, the Coal Co. (D) was permitted to conduct strip-mining operations subject to the condition that it perform certain restorative and remedial work at the end of the lease period. At the end of the lease period, though, when all other covenants in the lease contract had been carried out, the Coal Co. (D) refused to do the restorative work. Thereupon, Peevyhouse (P) brought an action against the Coal Co. (D) to recover $25,000 in damages (i.e., the approximate cost of doing the restorative work). In response, the Coal Co. (D) argued that such damages were excessive because the value of the farm would only be improved by $300 if the restorative work was done. After a jury awarded Peevyhouse (P) $5,000 in damages, both Peevyhouse (P) and the Coal Co. (D) brought this appeal on the issue of damages.

ISSUE: Are damages for breach of a contract obligation to perform construction or excavation work automatically measured by the "cost of performance" of such work?

HOLDING AND DECISION: (Jackson, J.) No. The measure of damages for breach of a contract obligation to perform construction or excavation work is usually the reasonable "cost of performance" of such work; but where the economic benefit which would result by full performance is "grossly disproportionate" to (i.e., much less than) the cost of performance, damages are limited to the "diminution in value" to the premises because of nonperformance. Of course, damages must be limited when the benefit from full performance is much less than the cost of performance in order to promote "substantial justice"

(i.e., avoid "unconscionable and oppressive damages") and to prevent "economic waste." Here, the remedial excavation work is only incidental to the main purpose of the contract (i.e., to lease the farm), and performance of this work would involve considerable waste. It would cost approximately $29,000 to complete the work, while the value of the farm would only increase by $300. As such, damages must be limited to $300 (i.e., the "diminution in value" from nonperformance). Affirmed as modified.

DISSENT: (Irwin, J.) It is well settled that "the law will not make a better contract for parties than they themselves have seen fit to enter into, or alter it for the benefit of one party and to the detriment of others." Yet the majority has altered the contract here for the benefit of the Coal Co. (D) and to the detriment of Peevyhouse (P). The record fully indicates that Peevyhouse (P) would not have entered into the lease agreement unless the Coal Co. (D) agreed to fully restore his land. Furthermore, at the time of the execution of the contract, the Coal Co. (D) knew that the cost of the restorative work might be disproportionate to the value received by Peevyhouse (P) but still thought that it would be to its economic advantage to enter into the contract. As such, the Coal Co. (D) should not be released from its obligation under the contract to perform the restorative work or to fully pay for the cost of doing it.

ANALYSIS

This case illustrates the general rule regarding the measure of recovery of damages by an owner of real property when a construction contract is defectively performed. Note, though, that if the structure contracted for is unusable or unsafe in its defective condition, there is never any "economic waste" by allowing the owner damages measured by the cost of remedying the defect regardless of such cost. Note, further, that if a builder abandons construction prior to completion, normal damages are the reasonable cost of completion, plus any damages suffered by delay in completion. The damages for such delay are measured by the rental or use value that the premises would have had during the delay period.

Quicknotes

COVENANT A written promise to do, or to refrain from doing, a particular activity.

PERMISSIVE WASTE The mistreatment of another's property by someone in lawful possession by the failure to make ordinary repairs or maintenance.

Aiello Construction, Inc. v. Nationwide Tractor Trailer Training and Placement Corp.

Construction company (P) v. Property owner (D)

R.I. Sup. Ct., 122 R.I. 861, 413 A.2d 85 (1980).

NATURE OF CASE: Appeal from award of damages in breach of contract action.

FACT SUMMARY: Shortly after Aiello (P) began performance of its construction contract, Nationwide (D) stopped payments due Aiello (P) under the terms of the contract.

🏛 RULE OF LAW
A builder in a construction contract may recover damages for breach measured by the builder's expenditures to the date of breach, less the value of materials on hand, plus the profit that the builder proves with reasonable certainty that he would have realized from full performance.

FACTS: Aiello (P) and Nationwide (D) entered into a contract in which Aiello (P) was to perform grading and removal work on Nationwide's (D) property. Shortly after Aiello (P) began performance, Nationwide (D) stopped making the monthly payments due under the contract. Aiello (P) sued for breach of contract. The court awarded Aiello (P) damages for Nationwide's (D) breach of contract. The damages were calculated by calculating the costs incurred by Aiello (P) in its performance prior to the date of breach, plus the amount Aiello (P) would have realized in profit had the contract been fully performed, less payments previously made by Nationwide (D). Nationwide (D) appealed on the ground that the court incorrectly assessed damages.

ISSUE: May a builder in a construction contract recover damages for breach measured by the builder's expenditures to the date of breach, less the value of materials on hand, plus the profit that the builder proves with reasonable certainty he would have realized from full performance?

HOLDING AND DECISION: (Weisberger, J.) Yes. A builder in a construction contract may recover damages for breach measured by the builder's expenditures to the date of breach, less the value of materials on hand, plus the profit that the builder proves with reasonable certainty he would have realized from full performance. Here, the trial court scrupulously followed this method of assessment of damages, and the judge's findings of fact were supported by ample evidence, and the judge did not overlook or misconceive evidence in arriving at his conclusion. Affirmed.

▶ ANALYSIS

The formula used to measure Aiello's (P) damages in the principal case is the same formula that is contained in Comment h of the Restatement of Contracts, § 346. Another formula contained in § 346 is contract price, less the cost of completion that the builder saved by not completing the work, and the amount paid by the owner prior to breach. The two methods of computation of damages will normally result in equivalent amounts of recovery.

Quicknotes

BREACH OF CONTRACT Unlawful failure by a party to perform its obligations pursuant to contract.

MEASURE OF DAMAGES Monetary compensation that may be awarded by the court to a party who has sustained injury or loss to his or her person, property or rights due to another party's unlawful act, omission or negligence.

Egerer v. CSR West, LLC

Land developer (P) v. Fill supplier (D)

Wash. Ct. App., 116 Wash. App. 645, 67 P. 3d 1128 (2003).

NATURE OF CASE: Appeal from award of damages in breach of contract case.

FACT SUMMARY: After CSR (D) failed to deliver "shoulder excavation" fill as agreed by contract with Egerer (P), Egerer (P) brought suit seeking "hypothetical cover" damages.

🏛 RULE OF LAW
Where an equivalent cover material is unavailable, the measure of damages under "hypothetical cover" is the most reasonable cover available, even if it is of higher quality than the material specified in the contract.

FACTS: Egerer (P) contracted with Wilder to provide "shoulder excavation" fill at $1.10/cu. yd. Egerer (P) also contracted with CSR (D) to provide all "shoulder excavation" fill from a highway construction project at $.50/cu.yd. CSR (D) brought some of the shoulder excavation fill to Egerer's (P) construction site in July 1997, but soon determined that it could use the material elsewhere and delivered no more material to Egerer (P). Egerer (P) was unable to find other "shoulder excavation" fill. Higher quality "pit run" fill at a time the weather permitted its use on Egerer's (P) construction site was quoted at between $8.25 and $9.00/cu. yd., which Egerer determined was too expensive for his project. In 1999, Egerer (P) was able to purchase "slide material" at $6.39/cu.yd. Egerer (P) filed suit alleging that CSR breached its contract and the trial court awarded Egerer (P) damages equal to the difference between the market price of $8.25/cu.yd. and the contract price of $.50/cu.yd. CSR appealed, acknowledging the breach, but arguing that the trial court improperly calculated damages.

ISSUE: Where an equivalent cover material is unavailable, is the measure of "hypothetical cover" damages the best reasonable alternative?

HOLDING AND DECISION: (Becker, C.J.) Yes. Where an equivalent cover material is unavailable, the measure of "hypothetical cover" damages is the best reasonable alternative. U.C.C. § 2-712 provides that the buyer may recover as damages the difference between the market price at the time when the buyer learned of the breach and the contract price. Because other "shoulder excavation" fill was unavailable at the time and because a court has reasonable leeway in measuring market price, the trial court's calculation using the pit run quotes at the time of the breach was reasonable and customary. Affirmed.

▌ANALYSIS

This case illustrates the difficulty in balancing damage calculations under U.C.C. §§ 2-713 and 2-712. Depending on the urgency of the buyer's need to find replacement goods and the vagaries of the market, the aggrieved buyer can potentially maximize the benefit realized by the breach. For example, where the buyer is in no hurry, the buyer can sue for hypothetical cover damages at the time of the breach but wait until the market drops before actually finding a replacement. This scenario provides the impetus for recent amendments to U.C.C. § 2-713.

Quicknotes

BREACH OF CONTRACT Unlawful failure by a party to perform its obligations pursuant to contract.

DAMAGES Monetary compensation that may be awarded by the court to a party who has sustained injury or loss to his person, property or rights due to another party's unlawful act, omission or negligence.

COVER The purchase of an alternate supply of goods by a buyer, after a seller has breached a contract for sale, for which the buyer may recover the difference between the cost of the substituted goods and the price of the original goods pursuant to the contract, so long as the buyer purchases the alternate goods in good faith and without unreasonable delay.

Delchi Carrier SpA v. Rotorex Corp.

Buyer (P) v. Seller (D)

71 F.3d 1024 (2d Cir. 1995).

NATURE OF CASE: Appeal from judgment for plaintiff for contract damages.

FACT SUMMARY: Delchi (P) was awarded damages for lost profits and other consequential damages when Rotorex (D) shipped nonconforming compressors for air conditioners.

🏛 **RULE OF LAW**
A contract plaintiff may collect damages to compensate for the full loss, which includes, but is not limited to, foreseeable lost profits.

FACTS: Rotorex (D), a New York corporation, contracted to sell compressors to Delchi (P), an Italian manufacturer of air conditioners. Prior to executing the contract, Rotorex (D) sent a sample compressor and written performance specifications. When the compressors arrived in Italy, they were rejected in quality control checks because they had lower cooling capacity and consumed more power than the sample model and specifications. Rotorex (D) refused to supply new, conforming compressors, claiming the performance specifications were inadvertently communicated to Delchi (P). Delchi (P) then cancelled the contract and suffered a loss in its sales volume because it could not obtain substitute compressors in time. Delchi (P) filed suit under the United Nations Convention on Contracts for the International Sale of Goods (CISG) for breach of contract and failure to deliver conforming goods. The court granted Delchi's (P) motion for summary judgment and awarded damages that included lost profits. Delchi (P) appealed, claiming the judge erroneously denied damages for various consequential and incidental damages because they would allegedly constitute a double recovery.

ISSUE: May a contract plaintiff collect damages to compensate for the full loss, which includes, but is not limited to, foreseeable lost profits?

HOLDING AND DECISION: (Winter, J.) Yes. A contract plaintiff may collect damages to compensate for the full loss, which includes, but is not limited to, foreseeable lost profits. The award for lost profits did not compensate Delchi (P) for costs actually incurred that led to no sales. Awarding damages for costs actually incurred in no way creates a double recovery. Affirmed in part, reversed in part and remanded.

▶ **ANALYSIS**

The CISG did not expressly provide for calculating lost profits. The district court applied the standard formula most American courts use and deducted only variable costs from sales revenue. On appeal, the district court's decision in that regard was upheld as correct.

∎≡∎

Quicknotes

BREACH OF CONTRACT Unlawful failure by a party to perform its obligations pursuant to contract.

CONSEQUENTIAL DAMAGES Monetary compensation that may be recovered in order to compensate for injuries or losses sustained as a result of damages that are not the direct or foreseeable result of the act of a party, but that nevertheless are the consequence of such act and which must be specifically pled and demonstrated.

LOST PROFITS The potential value of income earned or goods which are the subject of the contract; may be used in calculating damages where the contract has been breached.

∎≡∎

KGM Harvesting Co. v. Fresh Network

Seller (D) v. Buyer (P)

Cal. Ct. App., 36 Cal. App. 4th 376, 42 Cal. Rptr. 2d 286 (1995).

NATURE OF CASE: Appeal from damages awarded for breach of contract.

FACT SUMMARY: Fresh Network (P) was awarded damages for the cost of buying substitute lettuce when KGM (D) refused to deliver the quantity of lettuce required under a contract.

RULE OF LAW
Where a buyer covers by making in good faith and without unreasonable delay any reasonable purchase of goods in substitution for those due from the seller, the buyer may recover the difference between the cost of cover and the contract price.

FACTS: KGM (D) had contracted to deliver 14 loads of lettuce each week to Ohio lettuce broker Fresh Network (P). When the price of lettuce rose dramatically in May and June 1991, KGM (D) refused to deliver the required amount of lettuce, and Fresh Network (FN) (P) had to purchase lettuce on the open market to fulfill contractual obligations to third parties. A jury awarded FN (P) damages in an amount equal to the difference between the contract price and the cover price. KGM (D) appealed, alleging that, because of FN's (P) "cost plus" contract with a lettuce broker who sold the lettuce to the fast food industry, FN (P) was able to pass on the extra expenses occasioned by its breach, and that the damages awarded amounted to a windfall.

ISSUE: Where a buyer covers by making in good faith and without unreasonable delay any reasonable purchase of goods in substitution for those due from the seller, may the buyer recover the difference between the cost of cover and the contract price?

HOLDING AND DECISION: (Cottle, J.) Yes. Where a buyer covers by making in good faith and without unreasonable delay any reasonable purchase of goods in substitution for those due from the seller, the buyer may recover the difference between the cost of cover and the contract price. This gives the buyer the benefit of its bargain. FN (P) should have received prejudgment interest from the time the original complaint was filed, not from thirty days before trial. Affirmed in part, reversed in part and remanded.

ANALYSIS

The court distinguished damages awarded under U.C.C. § 2712 for cover from those under § 2713. In some cases, damages may be limited to actual losses under § 2713. Usually this occurs when there is a showing of bad faith.

Quicknotes

BAD FAITH Conduct that is intentionally misleading or deceptive.

BREACH OF CONTRACT Unlawful failure by a party to perform its obligations pursuant to contract.

Neri v. Retail Marine Corp.

Boat purchaser (P) v. Boat retailer (D)

N.Y. Ct. App., 30 N.Y.2d 393, 285 N.E.2d 311 (1972).

NATURE OF CASE: Action for breach of a sales contract.

FACT SUMMARY: Neri (P) contracted to purchase a boat from Retail Marine (D). Later Neri (P) wrongfully rescinded the contract and then brought suit for recovery of his deposit. Marine (D) counterclaimed seeking damages for its lost sale.

RULE OF LAW
A seller may recover his lost profit from a sales contract when the buyer defaults on the purchase if the contract market differential measure of damages is inadequate to put the seller in as good a position as performance would have done.

FACTS: Neri (P) contracted to purchase a boat from Retail Marine (D). Neri (P) gave a deposit of $4,250, and Marine (D) ordered the boat from the factory. A week later Neri (P) rescinded the contract stating that because he was about to undergo an operation he would be unable to make the payments on the boat. In his rescission Neri (P) requested a refund on his deposit which Marine (D) refused, whereupon Neri (P) brought suit for restitution. Marine (D) counterclaimed alleging that they were entitled to a setoff $2,580 which was their lost profit. The trial court held that Marine (D) was only entitled to a setoff of its incidental damages—the costs of holding the boat for one month at which time Marine (D) was able to resell the boat to another purchaser for the same price. On the issue of damages Marine (D) appealed. Affirmed as modified.

ISSUE: May a seller recover his lost profit when a buyer defaults on a purchase contract if the contract market differential measure of damages is inadequate to put the seller in as good a position as performance would have done?

HOLDING AND DECISION: (Gibson, J.) Yes. A seller may recover his lost profit when a buyer defaults on a sales contract if the contract market differential measure of damages is inadequate to put the seller in as good a position as performance would have done. U.C.C. § 2708(1) provides that the measure of damages for nonacceptance or repudiation by the buyer is the difference between the market price at the time and place of tender and the unpaid contract price. U.C.C. § 2708(2) provides that if U.C.C. § 2708(1) is inadequate to make the seller whole (to put him in the same position as if the contract had been performed) then the measure is the lost profit on the contract. In this case, Marine (D) resold the boat within a month for the same price. Thus, U.C.C. § 2708(1) is inade-

quate to make the seller whole and U.C.C. § 2708(2) would apply as Marine's (D) real damage was its lost profit on the contract. We conclude that Marine (D) is entitled to an offset of $2,580 (lost profit) against Neri's (P) claim for restitution.

ANALYSIS

The principal case is an example of the U.C.C. provisions to protect sellers of goods from defaulting purchasers. Here the code gives a specific remedy which does justice for the seller by allowing the seller to recover his lost profit. The principal case is also noteworthy as an illustration of the code's position on restitution for defaulting purchasers. U.C.C. § 2718 allows a defaulting purchaser to acquire restitution for money advanced by allowing the defaulting purchaser to recover that money in excess of the seller's damages. Prior to the code, a defaulting purchaser was usually remediless.

Quicknotes

LOST PROFITS The potential value of income earned or goods which are the subject of the contract; may be used in calculating damages where the contract has been breached.

MEASURE OF DAMAGES Monetary compensation that may be awarded by the court to a party who has sustained injury or loss to his or her person, property or rights due to another party's unlawful act, omission or negligence.

REPUDIATION The actions or statements of a party to a contract that evidence his intent not to perform, or to continue performance, of his duties or obligations thereunder.

RESCISSION The canceling of an agreement and the return of the parties to their positions prior to the formation of the contract.

RESTITUTION The return or restoration of what the defendant has gained in a transaction to prevent the unjust enrichment of the defendant.

Rockingham County v. Luten Bridge Co.

Locality (D) v. Bridge building company (P)

35 F.2d 301 (4th Cir. 1929).

NATURE OF CASE: Action in damages for breach of contract.

FACT SUMMARY: Luten Bridge Co. (P), after receiving notice that the contract was being canceled, went ahead and constructed the bridge and brought suit for the full contract price.

🏛 RULE OF LAW
When notice of cancellation is received while a contract is still executory, the party cannot complete it and claim the contract price.

FACTS: Rockingham County (D) contracted with Luten Bridge Co. (P) to build a bridge. Shortly after the contract had been signed and before construction was begun, Rockingham (D) notified Luten (P) that the contract was deemed canceled and that it would not pay for any construction work. Luten (P) went ahead and built the bridge anyway and sued for the entire contract price which the court awarded it.

ISSUE: After notice of cancellation while a contract is still executory, may a party complete performance and sue for the entire contract price?

HOLDING AND DECISION: (Parker, J.) No. The County's (D) rescission was wrongful. However, Luten (P) had no right to increase the damages resulting from the breach. Luten's (P) sole remedy is to treat the contract as broken and to bring suit for damages, including any lost profits. There is a positive duty to mitigate the defendant's damages. Since Luten's (P) only real loss is lost profits, there was no benefit to anyone in constructing the bridge. Reversed and remanded.

▶ ANALYSIS

Mitigation means avoidance of unnecessary damages. While the common law is similar to the U.C.C. in this area, it must be remembered that it is inapplicable to construction contracts. Only reasonable efforts to mitigate are required. No penalty is assessed for failure to mitigate successfully. Any benefit conferred on the defendant must be paid for regardless of the plaintiff's failure to mitigate. Failure to mitigate merely bars the recovery of damages which could have been prevented by mitigation.

Quicknotes

EXECUTORY CONTRACT A contract in which performance of an obligation has yet to be rendered.

MITIGATION OF DAMAGES A plaintiff's implied obligation to reduce the damages incurred by taking reasonable steps to prevent additional injury.

Shirley MacLaine Parker v. Twentieth Century-Fox Film Corp.

Actress (P) v. Film company (D)

Cal. Sup. Ct., 3 Cal. 3d 176, 474 P.2d 689 (1970).

NATURE OF CASE: Action for damages for breach of a contract for employment.

FACT SUMMARY: Parker (P), an actress, was to have the lead role in the motion picture "Bloomer Girl," to be produced by Fox (D), and she was to receive $750,000 in salary. Fox (D) decided not to make the movie and offered the leading role in a film, "Big Country, Big Man," instead, which Parker (P) refused.

RULE OF LAW

The general measure of recovery by a wrongfully discharged employee is the amount of salary agreed upon for the period of service less the amount which the employer affirmatively proves the employee has earned or, with reasonable effort, might have earned from other comparable or substantially similar employment.

FACTS: Parker (P), an actress whose professional name is Shirley MacLaine, was hired for the lead role in the film "Bloomer Girl," to be produced by Fox (D). She was to receive a salary of $750,000 for 14 weeks. Under the contract, Parker (P) was to have approval over the director or any substitute, the dance director, and the screenplay. Fox (D) decided not to make the film and offered Parker (P) the lead in "Big Country, Big Man," which, unlike the other film, was not a musical, but a western. Also, Fox (D) did not offer Parker (P) approval of the director or screenplay (and there was no need for a dance director). "Bloomer Girl" was to have been filmed in Los Angeles; "Big Country, Big Man" was to be made in Australia. Parker (P) rejected the second film offer and sued for her salary and resulting damages.

ISSUE: Is the general measure of recovery by a wrongfully discharged employee the amount of salary agreed upon for the period of service less the amount which the employer affirmatively proves the employee has earned or, with reasonable effort, might have earned from other comparable or substantially similar employment?

HOLDING AND DECISION: (Burke, J.) Yes. Fox (D), in claiming that Parker (P) unreasonably refused the second film offer, must show that the other employment was comparable to the first or, at least, substantially similar to that of which their employee had been deprived. The employee's rejection of, or failure to seek, other available employment of a different or inferior kind may not be used to mitigate damages. If the western film offer were found different or inferior to the musical film offer, it makes no difference whether Parker (P) reasonably or unreasonably refused the second offer. The western was a different and inferior film where Parker (P) could not use her singing and dancing talents as in the musical. The western required travel to Australia for extensive outdoor filming rather than the use of sound stages in Los Angeles. The "Big Country" offer impaired or eliminated several rights of approval. Accordingly, as the second offer was different and inferior to the first, Parker (P) was awarded $750,000. Affirmed.

ANALYSIS

The court points out that if the other offer of employment is of a different or inferior kind, it does not matter whether the employee acts reasonably or unreasonably in rejecting the offer. The person with the duty to mitigate need not expose himself to undue risk, expense, or humiliation. It may be possible, considering the kinds of movies Parker (P) had made in the past, which included no westerns, that such a film may have been considered a career risk or even a humiliation. Also, many cases have held that the employee is not required to accept employment unreasonably distant from the original location. The court apparently thought that Australia was unreasonably distant when Parker (P) was regularly working in Los Angeles and had intended to work on "Bloomer Girl" there. Note that in mitigating, the employee does not have to accept a position of lesser rank or at a lower salary. Also, Parker (P) asked for damages in addition to her salary, but such special damages are rarely awarded in cases of wrongful discharge. Damages for injury to the reputation of the employee are considered to be too remote and not within the contemplation of the parties. There is authority for damages when the denied employment would have enhanced the employee's reputation, e.g., with a motion picture credit, but this has only been applied once in the United States, although it is common in England. The dissent would apparently foist an unacceptable film role upon an actress. Due to the nature of the industry and its regularly accepted business practices, the majority probably kept in mind the actor's need "to feel right" about a role and script before accepting it.

■==■

Quicknotes

MITIGATION OF DAMAGES A plaintiff's implied obligation to reduce the damages incurred by taking reasonable steps to prevent additional injury.

■==■

Hadley v. Baxendale

Mill operator (P) v. Carrier company (D)

Ct. of Exchequer, 9 Exch. 341 (1854).

NATURE OF CASE: Action for damages for breach of a carrier contract.

FACT SUMMARY: Hadley (P), a mill operator in Gloucester, arranged to have Baxendale's (D) company, a carrier, ship his broken mill shaft to the engineer in Greenwich for a copy to be made. Hadley (P) suffered a £300 loss when Baxendale (D) unreasonably delayed shipping the mill shaft, causing the mill to be shut down longer than anticipated.

🏛 **RULE OF LAW**
The injured party may recover those damages as may reasonably be considered arising naturally from the breach itself and, second, may recover those damages as may reasonably be supposed to have been in contemplation of the parties, at the time they made the contract, as the probable result of a breach of it.

FACTS: Hadley (P), a mill operator in Gloucester, arranged to have Baxendale's (D) shipping company return his broken mill shaft to the engineer in Greenwich who was to make a duplicate. Hadley (P) delivered the broken shaft to Baxendale (D) who, in consideration for his fee, promised to deliver the shaft to Greenwich in a reasonable time. Reopening of the mill was delayed five days, costing Hadley (P) lost profits and paid-out wages of £300. Hadley (P) had paid Baxendale (D) £2 4s. to ship the mill shaft. Baxendale (D) paid into court £25 in satisfaction of Hadley's (P) claim. The jury awarded an additional £25 for a total £50 award. [Note: The headnote taken from the English reporter and reprinted in the casebook is in error when it states that Hadley's (P) servant told Baxendale (D) the mill was stopped and the shaft must be sent immediately.]

ISSUE: May the injured party recover those damages as may reasonably be considered arising naturally from the breach itself, and may recover those damages as may reasonably be supposed to have been in contemplation of the parties, at the time they made the contract, as the probable result of a breach of it, be recovered?

HOLDING AND DECISION: (Alderson, B.) Yes. The jury requires a rule for its guidance in awarding damages justly. When a party breaches his contract, the damages he pays ought to be those arising naturally from the breach itself and, in addition, those as may reasonably be supposed to have been in contemplation of the parties, at the time they made the contract, as the probable result of the breach of it. Therefore, if the special circumstances

under which the contract was made were known to both parties, the resulting damages upon breach would be those reasonably contemplated as arising under those communicated and known circumstances. However, if the special circumstances were unknown, then damages can only be those expected to arise generally from the breach. Hadley's (P) telling Baxendale (D) that he ran a mill and that his mill shaft which he wanted shipped was broken did not notify Baxendale (D) that the mill was shut down. Baxendale (D) could have believed reasonably that Hadley (P) had a spare shaft or that the shaft to be shipped was not the only defective machinery at the mill. Here, it does not follow that a loss of profits could fairly or reasonably have been contemplated by both parties in case of breach. Such a loss would not have flowed naturally from the breach without the special circumstances having been communicated to Baxendale (D). New trial ordered.

▶ *ANALYSIS*

This case lays down two rules guiding damages. First, only those damages as may fairly and reasonably be considered to be arising from the breach itself may be awarded. Second, those damages which may reasonably be supposed to have been in contemplation of the parties at the time they made the contract as the probable result of a breach of it may be awarded. The second is distinguished from the first because with the latter, both parties are aware of the special circumstances under which the contract is made. Usually, those special circumstances are communicated by the plaintiff to the defendant before the making of the contract. But that is not an absolute condition. If the consequences of the breach are foreseeable, the party which breaches will be liable for the lost profits or expectation damages. Foreseeability and assumption of the risk are ways of describing the bargain. If there is an assumption of the risk, the seller or carrier must necessarily be aware of the consequences. A later English case held that there would be a lesser foreseeability for a common carrier than for a seller, as a seller would tend to know the purpose and use of the item sold while the common carrier probably would not know the use of all items it carried. If all loss went on to the seller, this would obviously be an incentive not to enter into contracts. Courts balance what has become a "seller beware" attitude by placing limitations on full recovery. The loss must be foreseeable when the contract is entered into. It cannot be overly speculative. The seller's breach must be judged by willingness, negligence, bad faith, and

Continued on next page.

availability of replacement items. Restatement 1st, § 331 (2), would allow recovery in the situation in this case under an alternative theory. If the breach were one preventing the use and operation of property from which profits would have been made, damages can be measured by the rental value of the property or by interest on the value of the property. U.C.C. § 2-715 (2) allows the buyer consequential damages for any loss which results from general or particular needs of which the seller had reason to know.

■══■

Quicknotes

CONSEQUENTIAL DAMAGES Monetary compensation that may be recovered in order to compensate for injuries or losses sustained as a result of damages that are not the direct or foreseeable result of the act of a party, but that nevertheless are the consequence of such act and which must be specifically pled and demonstrated.

EXPECTATION DAMAGES The measure of damages necessary to place the nonbreaching party in the same position as he would have enjoyed had the contract been fully performed.

U.C.C. § 2-715 (2) Provides that any damages which seller is aware of and cannot cover against are includable as consequential damages.

■══■

Kenford Co. v. Erie County

Dome construction company (P) v. Locality (D)

N.Y. Ct. App., 67 N.Y.2d 257, 493 N.E.2d 234 (1986).

NATURE OF CASE: Appeal in action for damages for breach of contract.

FACT SUMMARY: Kenford (P) filed suit for loss of profits when County of Erie (D) failed to construct a domed stadium that Kenford (P) was going to operate.

🏛 RULE OF LAW
To establish loss of future profits as damages for breach of contract, a party must demonstrate with certainty that such damages have been caused by the breach, and the alleged loss must be capable of proof with reasonable certainty.

FACTS: In 1969, pursuant to a resolution adopted by its legislature, the County of Erie (D) entered into a contract with Kenford (P) and Dome Stadium, Inc. (DSI) (P) for the construction and operation of a domed stadium facility near Buffalo. The contract provided that construction of the facility would begin within twelve months of the contract date, and that a mutually acceptable forty-year lease between Erie (D) and DSI (P) for the operation of the facility would be negotiated within three months of the receipt by Erie (D) of preliminary plans, drawings, and cost estimates. Although extensive negotiations followed, the terms of the lease were never agreed upon and the construction of a domed facility never occurred. In June 1971, Kenford (P) and DSI (P) commenced an action for breach of contract. The trial court awarded a multimillion dollar judgment for Kenford (P) and DSI (P), but the appellate division modified the judgment and remanded on the issue of loss of profits during the twenty-year period of proposed management contract. The appellate court concluded that the use of expert opinion to present statistical projections of future business operations involved the use of too many variables to provide a rational basis on which lost profits could be calculated, and it was therefore insufficient as a matter of law to support an award of lost profits.

ISSUE: To establish loss of future profits as damages for breach of contract, must a party demonstrate with certainty that such damages have been caused by the breach and that the alleged loss is capable of proof with reasonable certainty?

HOLDING AND DECISION: (Per curiam) Yes. To establish loss of future profits as damages for breach of contract, a party must demonstrate with certainty that such damages have been caused by the breach, and the alleged loss must be capable of proof with reasonable certainty. Damages may not be merely speculative, possible, remote, or caused by intervening events. The procedure for com-

puting damages selected by DSI (P) was in accord with contemporary economic theory and was presented through the testimony of recognized experts. Nonetheless, the proof is insufficient to meet the required standard. The provisions in the contract addressing remedy for a default do not suggest or provide for such a heavy responsibility on the part of Erie (D). Furthermore, the multitude of assumptions required to establish projections over the twenty-year life of the contract do not add up to reasonable certainty no matter how sophisticated the calculations. Although the appellate court's verdict was correct, their application of a "rational basis" test was not. Affirmed.

▶ ANALYSIS

The expectation measure seeks to compensate an aggrieved party even when they have not changed their position in reliance on the breaching party. The goal of this measure is to put the party in the same position they would have been in had the contract been performed. The court's analysis follows the traditional definition of the expectation measure; however, it places a very high burden of proof on the party seeking damages.

■■■

Quicknotes

LIQUIDATED DAMAGES An amount of money specified in a contract representing the damages owed in the event of breach.

LOST PROFITS The potential value of income earned or goods which are the subject of the contract; may be used in calculating damages where the contract has been breached.

■■■

Valentine v. General American Credit, Inc.

Employee (P) v. Employer (D)

Mich. Sup. Ct., 420 Mich. 256, 362 N.W.2d 628 (1984).

NATURE OF CASE: Appeal of dismissal of an action for damages for breach of contract.

FACTS: Valentine (P) sued for mental distress resulting from a breach of an employment contract.

RULE OF LAW
Mental distress damages are not recoverable in an action for breach of an employment contract.

FACTS: Valentine (P) was terminated by General American Credit, Inc. (D). She sued for mental distress allegedly arising out of the termination. She alleged that she had a right to job security that had been violated. The trial court dismissed the suit, and Valentine (P) appealed.

ISSUE: Are mental distress damages recoverable in an action for breach of an employment contract?

HOLDING AND DECISION: (Levin, J.) No. Mental distress damages are not recoverable in an action for breach of an employment contract. Generally speaking, damages for mental anguish are not recoverable in a breach of contract action. Since the obligation to provide job security was contractual, mental anguish damages are not recoverable. The only exception to this rule occurs when the contract is inherently personal, such as breach of a promise to marry. Employment does have a personal element, but the main purpose is economic, not personal. Affirmed.

ANALYSIS

The rule stated here was once universally recognized. However, the trend has been to recognize breach of an express or implied employment contract as a tort as well as breach of contract. The tort has been characterized as intentional infliction of emotional distress, and also as wrongful termination.

Quicknotes

QUASI-CONTRACT An implied contract created by law to prevent unjust enrichment.

EMOTIONAL DISTRESS Extreme personal suffering which results in another's conduct and in which damages may be sought.

Wasserman's, Inc. v. Middletown

Commercial property lessor (P) v. Municipality (D)

N.J. Sup. Ct., 137 N.J. 238, 645 A.2d 100 (1994).

NATURE OF CASE: Appeal from judgment awarding stipulated damages in breach of contract action.

FACT SUMMARY: A lease between Wasserman's, Inc. (P) and the Township of Middletown (D) contained a stipulated damages provision based on Wasserman's (P) gross receipts.

🏛 RULE OF LAW
Provisions for liquidated damages are enforceable only if they are a reasonable forecast of just compensation for the harm caused by the breach.

FACTS: The Township of Middletown, N.J. (D) leased a commercial property to Wasserman's, Inc. (P). The lease contained a provision fixing damages in the event of a breach by the Township (D) as follows: a pro rata reimbursement of any improvement costs, plus 25% of Wasserman's (P) gross receipts for one year. Wasserman's (P) subsequently sublet the premises to Jo-Ro, Inc. (P). Years later, the Township (D) canceled the lease and sold the property. Wasserman's (P) and Jo-Ro (P) sued to enforce the stipulated damages provision. The trial court upheld the clause and, applying it, awarded $346,058.45. The appellate division affirmed, and the state supreme court granted review.

ISSUE: Are provisions for liquidated damages enforceable if they are a reasonable forecast of just compensation for the breach?

HOLDING AND DECISION: (Pollock, J.) Yes. Provisions for liquidated damages are enforceable if they are a reasonable forecast of just compensation for the breach. At common law, courts generally looked with suspicion on such clauses. This was because such provisions often constituted a penalty and were more or less forced upon the party having lesser bargaining power. Also, they often did not reflect actual loss, as contractual remedies are designed to do. Finally, courts felt that allowing parties to set their own measure of damages usurped a judicial function. Today, this early unfavorable attitude has relaxed somewhat. Stipulated damage provisions that constitute a legitimate attempt to predict actual damages are valid liquidated damage provisions; those that do not are considered penalty provisions which do not advance the aims of contract law and thus are not enforceable. In general, gross receipts do not reflect actual losses incurred when a lease is canceled. It is not possible to determine from the record here whether the stipulated damages are arbitrary or would be likely to flow from the breach. The court should consider the parties' reasoning behind the damages calculation, the duty to mitigate and the market value of replacement space. Therefore, this matter must be remanded to the trial court for a determination of whether the stipulated damages clause based on gross receipts is a valid liquidated damages clause. Affirmed in part, reversed in part, and remanded.

▶ ANALYSIS

A subissue that can arise when the reasonableness of a damages provision is challenged is that of timing. Some courts set the time for considering damages as of the time the contract is executed. Others look to the time of the breach. The modern trend is to assess reasonableness at either time. The U.C.C. reflects this trend in § 2-718 with a reference to "anticipated or actual harm."

⬛▬■

Quicknotes

LIQUIDATED DAMAGES An amount of money specified in a contract representing the damages owed in the event of breach.

MITIGATION Reduction in penalty.

U.C.C. § 2-718 Provides that a liquidated damages provision is valid if reasonably related to either the harm anticipated at the time of contracting, or the actual damages suffered.

⬛▬■

CHAPTER 7

Specific Performance

Quick Reference Rules of Law

London Bucket Co. v. Stewart

Heating system installer (D) v. Purchaser (P)

Ky. Ct. App., 314 Ky. 832, 237 S.W.2d 509 (1951).

NATURE OF CASE: Appeal from a decree of specific performance.

FACT SUMMARY: Stewart (P) sought specific performance of a contract with London Bucket Co. (D) by which the latter agreed to properly furnish and install a heating system.

🏛 RULE OF LAW
Specific performance of a contract will not be decreed unless the ordinary common-law remedy of damages for breach would afford inadequate and incomplete relief.

FACTS: Stewart (P) sought specific performance of his contract with London Bucket Co. (D) whereby it was to properly furnish and install a heating system. Stewart (P) alleged that London (D) installed the system in an incomplete, unskilled, and unworkmanlike manner. The trial court issued a decree for specific performance.

ISSUE: Are there circumstances in which a court cannot decree specific performance of a contract?

HOLDING AND DECISION: (Stanley, Commr.) Yes. Specific performance of a contract will not be decreed unless the ordinary common-law remedy of damages for breach would afford inadequate and incomplete relief. It is the general rule that contracts for building construction will not be specifically enforced because damages are ordinarily an adequate remedy and because the court is incapable of supervising performance. This case falls within the general rule that there may be, as Stewart (P) suggests, some difficulty in proving the damages. This fact is insufficient to justify the application of an exception to the general rule. The judgment decreeing specific performance is, therefore, reversed.

▌ ANALYSIS

For centuries, the English system of justice had two types of courts administering two different systems of law. The "regular" or common-law courts had jurisdiction over actions at law, while the courts of equity or chancery had jurisdiction over suits in equity. Their function was to act in those cases where "the legal remedy was inadequate." Most American states no longer have separate courts of law and equity. However, this does not mean that the two systems do not, to a considerable extent, remain distinct. In cases involving a demand for specific performance, the court will apply the rules of equity. Generally, contracts for land and those for the sale of unique goods are the only ones for which specific performance will be decreed.

The basis for allowing specific performance in those cases is that since each item involved is unique, the buyer cannot, with an award of money damages, go out in the market and buy an exact replacement. In addition, legal contracts not to compete will be specifically enforced since money damages are difficult to measure and are considered inadequate.

■=■

Quicknotes

MONEY DAMAGES Monetary compensation sought by, or awarded to, a party who incurred loss as a result of a breach of contract or tortious conduct on behalf of another party.

SPECIFIC PERFORMANCE An equitable remedy whereby the court requires the parties to perform their obligations pursuant to a contract.

■=■

Walgreen Co. v. Sara Creek Property Co.

Retail pharmacy store (P) v. Landlord (D)

966 F.2d 273 (7th Cir. 1992).

NATURE OF CASE: Appeal from a grant of permanent injunctive relief in suit for breach of contract.

FACT SUMMARY: Walgreen (P) filed suit to enforce a clause contained in its lease agreement that provided that no space in the mall would be rented to a competing pharmacy.

🏛 RULE OF LAW
Where the costs of injunctive relief are less than the costs of a damages remedy, injunctive relief is an appropriate remedy, even when the damage remedy is not shown to be inadequate.

FACTS: Walgreen (P) operated a pharmacy in a mall under a lease that provided that the landlord, Sara Creek (D), would not lease space to anyone else who wanted to operate a pharmacy or store containing a pharmacy in the mall. After losing its primary tenant, Sara Creek (D) informed Walgreen (P) that it intended to lease space to Phar-Mor, a "deep discount" chain. The Phar-Mor store would include a pharmacy. Walgreen (P) filed a diversity suit for breach of contract and asked for injunctive relief mandating compliance with the nonrental clause. Evidence was offered by Sara Creek (D) that Walgreen's (P) damages were readily ascertainable. The injunction was granted and Sara Creek (D) appealed.

ISSUE: Where the costs of injunctive relief are less than the costs of a damages remedy, is injunctive relief an appropriate remedy even when the damage remedy is not shown to be inadequate?

HOLDING AND DECISION: (Posner, J.) Yes. Where the costs of injunctive relief are less than the costs of a damages remedy, injunctive relief is an appropriate remedy, even when the damage remedy is not shown to be inadequate. Generally, the plaintiff seeking an injunction has the burden of persuasion. In the case of a permanent injunction, it must be shown that damages are inadequate. If it is likely that the costs of the damages remedy would exceed the costs of the injunction, then for the sake of efficiency, the injunction is the proper remedy. In this case, despite testimony by Sara Creek (D) to the contrary, the damage remedy would have been difficult to compute. It would have required calculation of lost profits for at least ten years into the future. An injunction, on the other hand, removes the evidentiary issue from the court. And since supervision of the injunction would rest with Walgreen (P), the future cost to the court is likewise minimal. By imposing the injunction on Sara Creek (D), the issue becomes one of private bargaining. The parties are free to negotiate a fee for the removal of the injunction. The trial court properly weighed the costs and benefits of injunctive relief. Affirmed.

▶ ANALYSIS

Certain categories of contracts will regularly win equitable remedies. Where subject matter is unique, such as with real estate, specific performance will usually be granted. The rationale is that money damages cannot adequately compensate for the loss of a unique item. This is, however, something of a fallacy since most individuals would be willing to bargain away rights to a specific item for some price. The problem, however, rests with the trier of fact, as it is next to impossible to determine the appropriate premium to pay for the loss of a unique item.

■==■

Quicknotes

INJUNCTIVE RELIEF A court order issued as a remedy, requiring a person to do, or prohibiting that person from doing, a specific act.

■==■

Laclede Gas Co. v. Amoco Oil Co.

Gas distributor (P) v. Propane gas company (D)

522 F.2d 33 (8th Cir. 1975).

NATURE OF CASE: Action to enjoin a breach of contract.

FACT SUMMARY: Amoco (D) argued that its contract to supply propane gas to Laclede (P) was not specifically enforceable because, among other things, a damage remedy at law was adequate.

🏛 RULE OF LAW
While specific performance will not be ordered when the party claiming breach of contract has an adequate remedy at law, a remedy at law adequate to defeat the grant of specific performance must be as certain, prompt, complete, and efficient to attain the ends of justice as a decree of specific performance.

FACTS: A written agreement called for Amoco (D) to pipe propane gas directly into Laclede's (P) lines to be distributed within subdivisions that would eventually be converted to natural gas (a process often taking years). Only Laclede (P) had a right to cancel, but Amoco (D) gave notice of its intention to terminate the agreement. Laclede (P) sued for injunctive relief or, in the alternative, damages for breach of contract. The court of appeals, in the first part of its opinion, reversed the trial court's decision holding the contract invalid for lack of mutuality. It then addressed the issue of whether specific performance should be ordered. Amoco (D) argued against it, contending that, among other things, a damages remedy at law was available and adequate.

ISSUE: In order to defeat a grant of specific performance, must a remedy at law be as certain, prompt, complete, and efficient to attain the ends of justice as a decree of specific performance?

HOLDING AND DECISION: (Ross, J.) Yes. As long as the party claiming breach of contract has an adequate remedy at law, specific performance will not be ordered. However, to be adequate to defeat the grant of specific performance, a remedy at law must be as certain, prompt, complete, and efficient to obtain the ends of justice as a decree of specific performance. Here, it is doubtful that Laclede (P) could obtain a contract for the long-term supply of propane from another source, given the uncertain future of worldwide energy supplies. Even if it were possible, there would still be considerable expense and trouble which cannot be estimated in advance in making arrangements for its distribution to the residential subdivisions. Thus, the remedy at law is not "adequate" to defeat the grant of specific performance in this case. The decision of the district court is reversed and the cause remanded for issuance of a decree of specific performance.

▶ ANALYSIS

Section 370 of the Restatement, Contracts (1932), provides: "Specific enforcement will not be decreed unless the terms of the contract are so expressed that the court can determine with reasonable certainty what is the duty of each party and the conditions under which performance is due."

Quicknotes

INJUNCTIVE RELIEF A court order issued as a remedy, requiring a person to do, or prohibiting that person from doing, a specific act.

MUTUALITY OF PERFORMANCE The requirement for a valid contract that the parties are required to perform.

SPECIFIC PERFORMANCE An equitable remedy whereby the court requires the parties to perform their obligations pursuant to a contract.

The Reliance and Restitution Measures

Quick Reference Rules of Law

Security Stove & Mfg. Co. v. American Rys. Express Co.

Exhibit owner (P) v. Shipper (D)

Mo. Ct. App., 227 Mo. App. 175, 51 S.W.2d 572 (1932).

NATURE OF CASE: Action for damages.

FACT SUMMARY: American Railway Express Co. (D) was late in delivering an exhibit shipped by Security Stove (P). Security (P) was awarded its expenses as damages.

🏛 RULE OF LAW
Where a carrier has notice that a delay will cause a shipper an unusual loss, and where the notice was such that the carrier will be presumed to have contracted with reference thereto, he is responsible for the actual damages occasioned by his delay.

FACTS: Security Stove (P) contracted with American Railway Express Co. (D) to have the latter ship an exhibit to Atlantic City for a convention. Security (P) emphasized that the exhibit had to be there by October 8th. American (D) assured Security (P) that it could deliver it by that date. However, a package containing part of the shipment did not arrive until after the convention had closed. The trial court allowed as damages the express charges, transportation expenses, and hotel costs incurred by the employees whom Security (P) had sent to the convention, as well as the cost of the booth rental at the convention.

ISSUE: Can a carrier be held liable for actual damages sustained as a result of its delay in delivery of a shipment?

HOLDING AND DECISION: (Bland, J.) Yes. Ordinarily, the measure of damages for a carrier's failure to deliver a shipment within a reasonable time is the difference between the market value of the goods at the time of delivery and their value at the time they should have been delivered. However, where the carrier has notice that a delay will cause the shipper an unusual loss, and where the notice was such that the carrier can be presumed to have contracted with reference thereto, he is responsible for the actual damages occasioned by the delay in delivery. Here, the suit was not to recover loss of profits or goods. Hence, unless Security (P) is allowed to recover its actual expenses, it will be deprived of any substantial compensation for its loss. In cases like the one at bar, the method of estimating damages should be the one which is the most definite and best serves the purpose of compensation. Thus, although Security (P) would have incurred its expenses whether or not the contract had been breached, it should be allowed to recover them. Affirmed.

▶ ANALYSIS

The principle that damages, to be recoverable, must have been in the contemplation of the parties at the time the contract was entered into does not require that the defaulting party could have foreseen the specific details of the injury or damages which did occur. For example, it has been held sufficient that the defaulting party could have foreseen that its failure to make delivery would cause the other party's factory to shut down, since details of the losses that resulted may be determined at trial. This same principle is applied in other types of cases provided, of course, that the losses are proved with reasonable certainty.

■■■■

Quicknotes

ACTUAL DAMAGES Measure of damages necessary to compensate victim for actual injuries suffered.

COMPENSATORY DAMAGES Measure of damages necessary to compensate victim for actual injuries suffered.

■■■■

Osteen v. Johnson

Parent of singer (P) v. Promoter (D)

Colo. Ct. App., 473 P.2d 184 (1970).

NATURE OF CASE: Action for breach of an oral contract.

FACT SUMMARY: The trial court held that Johnson (D) had specifically substantially performed the agreement with Osteen (P) and so awarded just $1 in damages for his "minor" breaches thereof.

🏛 RULE OF LAW
Restitution is available as a remedy where there has been a contract breach of vital importance, variously defined as a substantial breach or a breach which goes to the essence of the contract.

FACTS: In return for a payment of $2,500, Johnson (D) agreed to promote Osteen's (P) daughter, Linda, as a singer and composer of country-western music. Specifically, he agreed to advertise her for one year in various mailings; implement her recording of several songs; prepare two records; press and mail out copies of one of the records to disc jockeys throughout the country; and press and mail out copies of the second record if the first record met with any success. Osteen (P) brought an action for breach of contract, claiming among other things that Johnson (D) had failed to press and mail out a second record despite success of the first and had wrongfully caused another party's name to appear on the label of the first record as coauthor of a song that had been composed solely by Linda. The trial court found that Johnson (D) had substantially performed the agreement but entered a judgment of damages for $1 and costs for what it considered Johnson's (D) "minor" breaches of the agreement.

ISSUE: Is restitution available as a remedy where there has been a contract breach of vital importance?

HOLDING AND DECISION: (Dufford, J.) Yes. It is the court's opinion that the remedy which Osteen (P) proved and upon which he can rely is that of restitution, which is available where there has been a contract breach of vital importance (variously defined as a substantial breach of a breach which goes to the essence of the contract). Since no evidence was presented which would justify an award of other than nominal damages, the essential question here becomes whether any breach by Johnson (D) was substantial enough to justify the remedy of rescission. The failure to press and mail out a second record after success of the first constituted a substantial breach and, therefore, justifies the remedy of rescission. However, restitution cannot be required unless Osteen (P) returns in some way what he received as a result of Johnson's (D) part performance. So, the amount restored to Osteen (P) will be the $2,500 he paid minus the reasonable value of the services rendered by Johnson (D). Reversed and remanded.

▶ ANALYSIS

According to Restatement, Second, Contracts § 371, the sum of money awarded to protect a party's restitution interest may, as justice requires, be measured either by the reasonable value to the other party of what he received or the extent to which the other party's property has been increased in value or his other interests advanced.

■=■

Quicknotes

NOMINAL DAMAGES A small sum awarded to a plaintiff in order to recognize that he sustained an injury that is either slight or incapable of being established.

RESCISSION The canceling of an agreement and the return of the parties to their positions prior to the formation of the contract.

RESTITUTION The return or restoration of what the defendant has gained in a transaction to prevent the unjust enrichment of the defendant.

■=■

United States v. Algernon Blair, Inc.

Federal government (P) v. General contractor (D)

479 F.2d 638 (4th Cir. 1973).

NATURE OF CASE: Action to recover for labor and equipment furnished.

FACT SUMMARY: Blair (D), as general contractor, was sued by its subcontractor in the name of the United States (P) to recover for the labor and equipment that had been supplied before the subcontractor ceased work on the project due to a breach of contract by Blair (D).

🏛 RULE OF LAW
A subcontractor who justifiably ceases work under a contract because of the prime contractor's breach may recover in quantum meruit the value of labor and equipment already furnished pursuant to the contract irrespective of whether he would have been entitled to recover in a suit on the contract.

FACTS: Blair (D) was acting as general contractor in constructing a naval base and had subcontracted certain work to Coastal. Coastal stopped performance when 28% of its work was done because of a material breach of the subcontract by Blair (D). Another subcontractor was hired to complete the job. Coastal then brought an action, in the name of the United States (P), to recover for labor and equipment furnished. The district court found $37,000 was still due Coastal under the contract but held that it would have lost more than that if it had to complete the contract. Therefore, there could be no recovery on the contract.

ISSUE: When a subcontractor justifiably ceases work because of the general contractor's breach, can he recover in quantum meruit the value of labor and equipment already supplied?

HOLDING AND DECISION: (Craven, J.) Yes. Whether or not he would be entitled to recover in a suit on the contract, a subcontractor who justifiably ceases work under a contract because of the prime contractor's breach, as in this case, may recover in quantum meruit the value of the labor and equipment already supplied. The impact of quantum meruit is to allow a promisee, such as Coastal, to recover the value of services he gave to the defendant irrespective of whether he would have lost money on the contract and been unable to recover in a suit on the contract. The standard for measuring the reasonable value of services rendered is the amount for which such services could have been purchased from one in the plaintiff's position at the time and place the services were rendered. The case must be remanded for findings as to the reasonable value of the labor and equipment Coastal furnished. Reversed and remanded.

▶ ANALYSIS

According to Palmer, the courts regularly deny restitution of the value of the plaintiff's performance where he has fully performed and the defendant's obligation is to pay money. He notes this is incongruous, since restitution of an amount in excess of the contract price for full performance has been permitted in many decisions where the plaintiff has only partially performed. 1 G. Palmer, The Law of Restitution 378–79 (1978).

Quicknotes

QUANTUM MERUIT Equitable doctrine allowing recovery for labor and materials provided by one party, even though no contract was entered into, in order to avoid unjust enrichment by the benefited party.

RESTITUTION The return or restoration of what the defendant has gained in a transaction to prevent the unjust enrichment of the defendant.

Kutzin v. Pirnie

Seller of real estate (P) v. Buyer of real estate (D)

N.J. Sup. Ct., 124 N.J. 500, 591 A.2d 932 (1991).

NATURE OF CASE: Appeal of award for damages in action on contract for sale of residential property.

FACT SUMMARY: The Pirnies (D) signed a contract to purchase the Kutzins' (P) house and later changed their mind, refusing to go through with the purchase. The Kutzins (P) retained a deposit that was in excess of actual damages pursuant to the contract that contained neither forfeiture nor a liquidated damages clause.

> ## 🏛 RULE OF LAW
> A seller is not entitled to retain the entire deposit in excess of actual damages when a buyer breaches a contract that does not contain a liquidated damages or forfeiture clause.

FACTS: The Pirnies (D) signed a contract to purchase real property from the Kutzins (P). The contract did not contain a liquidated damages or forfeiture clause and was not specific about what would happen to the escrowed deposit if the sale did not go through. The contract provided time and opportunity for the attorneys for the parties to negotiate. Pursuant to the contract, the Pirnies (D) made a $36,000 deposit on the property. Thereafter, the Pirnies (D) decided not to purchase the property and sought the return of their deposit. The Kutzins refused to return the deposit and, after selling the property to another, sued for damages. The trial court ordered the Kutzins to return $18,675 representing the $36,000 deposit less the difference between the original sale price of the contract with the Pirnies (D) plus some additional enhancements made to sell the property. On appeal, the Kutzins (P) were awarded the entire deposit. The Pirnies (D) appealed from this judgment and the appellate court reinstated the trial court's ruling.

ISSUE: Is a seller entitled to retain the entire deposit in excess of actual damages when a buyer breaches a contract that does not contain a liquidated damages or forfeiture clause?

HOLDING AND DECISION: (Clifford, J.) No. A seller is not entitled to retain the entire deposit when a buyer breaches a contract that does not contain a liquidated damages or forfeiture clause. Although the common law was that where the buyer of real property makes a partial payment but fails to fulfill the contract, he may not recover the payment even if the seller profits by the default. This view has been increasingly rejected. The Restatement (Second) of Contracts advises a contrary result so as not to allow the seller more than fair compensation for the injury and so as not to impose a forfeiture on the buyer. Accordingly, prior case law adhering to the common law is overruled and the Restatement approach (when a buyer breaches and proves that the deposit exceeds the seller's actual damages, the buyer may recover the difference) is adopted. This holding applies only in the absence of a liquidated damages provision. The trial court's original damages award is reinstated.

▶ ANALYSIS

The court took the opportunity presented here to overturn prior law based on the common law principle that allowed the buyer to retain the deposit regardless of actual damages. The court did acknowledge that there was existing and valid case law requiring that the deposit be in excess of 10%, which was not the case here, but chose to simply site the contrary case law and proceed with its ruling adopting the Restatement's approach.

■═■

Quicknotes

CONTRACT DAMAGES Monetary compensation awarded by the court to a party as the result of a breach of contract by another party.

FORFEITURE CLAUSE A clause providing for the loss of property or a right without compensation therefor.

LIQUIDATED DAMAGES An amount of money specified in a contract representing the damages owed in the event of breach.

■═■

CHAPTER 9

An Introduction to Interpretation

Quick Reference Rules of Law

Lucy v. Zehmer

Purchaser of farm (P) v. Owners of farm (D)

Va. Sup. Ct. App., 196 Va. 493, 84 S.E.2d 516 (1954).

NATURE OF CASE: Action for specific performance of a land sale contract.

FACT SUMMARY: Zehmer (D) claimed his offer to sell his farm to Lucy (P) was made in jest.

🏛 RULE OF LAW
If a person's words and acts, judged by a reasonable standard, manifest a certain intent, it is immaterial what may be the real but unexpressed state of that person's mind.

FACTS: Zehmer (D) and his wife (D) contracted to sell their 471-acre farm to Lucy (P) for $50,000. Zehmer (D) contended that his offer was made in jest while the three of them were drinking and that Zehmer (D) only desired to bluff Lucy (P) into admitting he did not have $50,000. Lucy (P) appeared to have taken the offer seriously by discussing its terms with Zehmer (D), rewriting it to enable Mrs. Zehmer (D) to sign also, by providing for title examination, and by taking possession of the agreement. Lucy (P) offered $5 to bind the deal and the next day sold a one-half interest to his brother (P) in order to raise money.

ISSUE: Does the law impute to a person an intention corresponding to the reasonable meaning of his words and acts?

HOLDING AND DECISION: (Buchanan, J.) Yes. The existence of an offer depends upon the reasonable meaning to be given the offeror's acts and words. For the formation of a contract, the mental assent of the parties is not required. If the words and acts of one of the parties have but one reasonable meaning, his undisclosed intention is immaterial except when an unreasonable meaning which he attaches to his manifestations is known to the other party. Accordingly, one cannot say he was merely jesting when his conduct and words would warrant reasonable belief that a real agreement was intended. Reversed and remanded.

▌ANALYSIS

Note that it is not what is said, but how it is heard and reasonably understood. Mutual assent of the parties is required for the formation of a contract, but mental assent is not. Where one party can reasonably believe from the other party's acts and words that a real agreement is intended, the other party's real but unexpressed intention is immaterial. Mutual assent is an objective determination based upon what a reasonable man would believe. An offer is an expression of will or intention creating a power of acceptance upon the offeree. If the offer to sell the farm had been for a price of $50, the court could judge the ridiculousness of the offer in determining whether a reasonable man would believe it to be serious.

Quicknotes

MUTUAL ASSENT A requirement of a valid contract that the parties possess a mutuality of assent as manifested by the terms of the agreement and not by a hidden intent.

OFFER A proposed promise to undertake performance of an action, or to refrain from acting, that is to become binding upon acceptance by the offeree.

Raffles v. Wichelhaus

Cotton seller (P) v. Buyer (D)

Ct. of Exchequer, 2 Hurl. & C. 906 (1864).

NATURE OF CASE: Appeal from demurrer.

FACT SUMMARY: After Raffles (P) contracted to sell Wichelhaus (D) cotton from a ship called the Peerless arriving from Bombay, another ship called the Peerless arrived with the cotton.

🏛 RULE OF LAW
A contract may not be formed where there is no consensus between the parties as to the meaning of the terms of the contract.

FACTS: Raffles (P) contracted to sell Wichelhaus (D) 125 bales of cotton. The cotton was to arrive from Bombay on a ship called the Peerless. The cotton arrived from Bombay on a different ship called the Peerless. Wichelhaus (D) refused to buy the cotton. Raffles (P) sued Wichelhaus (D) for breach of contract. Wichelhaus (D) moved for a demurrer.

ISSUE: May a contract be formed where there is no consensus between the parties as to the meaning of the terms of the contract?

HOLDING AND DECISION: (Per curiam) No. A contract may not be formed where there is no consensus between the parties as to the meaning of the terms of the contract. There is nothing in this contract to show that any particular ship called the Peerless was meant, but a latent ambiguity arose when two ships called the Peerless arrived from Bombay. Parol evidence was given that showed that Raffles (P) meant one Peerless and Wichelhaus (D) the other. That being so, there was no consensus of the parties and, therefore, no binding contract. Judgment for Wichelhaus (D).

▶ ANALYSIS

Judge Holmes commenting on the famous decision stated: "By the theory of our language, while other words may mean different things, a proper name means one person or thing and no other .... In theory of speech your name means you and my name means me, and the two names are different. They are different words .... In the use of common names and words a plea of different meaning from that adopted by the court would be bad, but here the parties have said different things and never have expressed a contract." Holmes, The Theory of Legal Interpretation, 12 Harv. L. Rev. 417, 418 (1889).

Quicknotes

DEMURRER The assertion that the opposing party's pleadings are insufficient and that the demurring party should not be made to answer.

LATENT AMBIGUITY Language capable of more than one interpretation that seems clear on its face, but the introduction of extrinsic evidence proves it to have a different meaning.

Frigaliment Importing Co. v. B.N.S. Intern. Sales Corp.

Buyer (P) v. Seller (D)

190 F. Supp. 116 (S.D.N.Y. 1960).

NATURE OF CASE: Action for breach of warranty of a contract for the sale of goods.

FACT SUMMARY: Frigaliment (P) ordered a large quantity of "chicken" from BNS (D), intending to buy young chicken suitable for broiling and frying, but BNS (D) believed, in considering the weights ordered at the prices fixed by the parties, that the order could be filled with older chicken, suitable for stewing only, and termed "fowl" by Frigaliment (P).

🏛 **RULE OF LAW**
The party who seeks to interpret the terms of the contract in a sense narrower than their everyday use bears the burden of persuasion to so show, and if that party fails to support its burden, it faces dismissal of its complaint.

FACTS: Frigaliment (P), a Swiss corporation, and BNS (D), a New York corporation, made two almost identical contracts for the sale of chicken by the latter to the former as follows: U.S. fresh frozen chicken, Grade A, government inspected, eviscerated, all wrapped and boxed suitably for export, 75,000 lbs. 2½–3 lbs. at $33.00 per 100 lbs. and 25,000 lbs. 1½–2 lbs. at $36.50 per 100 lbs. The second contract was the same except for 25,000 lbs. less of the heavier chicken and a price of $37.00 per 100 lbs. for the lighter birds. BNS (D), which was new to the poultry business, believed any kind of chicken could be used to fill the order including stewing chickens. Most of the order for heavier birds was filled with stewers as that was the only way BNS (D) could make a profit on the contract.

ISSUE: Did Frigaliment support its burden of persuasion that the word "chicken" should be used in its narrower sense so as to exclude stewing chicken?

HOLDING AND DECISION: (Friendly, J.) No. Frigaliment (P) failed to support its burden. While cables leading up to negotiations were predominantly in German, the use of the English word "chicken" as meaning "young chicken" rather than the German word "Huhn" meaning broilers and stewers lost its force when BNS (D) asked if any kind of chickens were wanted to which an affirmative answer meaning "Huhn" was given. BNS (D), being new to the chicken trade, the other party must show the other's acceptance of the trade use of a term. Frigaliment (P) failed to offer such proof. There was conflicting evidence anyway as to the trade use of the word "chicken." BNS's (D) price of $33.00 per 100 lbs. for the larger birds was $2.00 to $4.00 less than for broilers. Frigaliment (P) could not say that the price appeared reasonable because it was closer to the $35.00 broiler price than the $30.00 stewer price. BNS (D) could be expected not to sell at a loss. While the evidence is generally conflicting, overall it appeared that BNS (D) believed it could comply by supplying stewing chicken. This did conform with one dictionary meaning, with the definition in the department of animal regulations to which at least there was a contractual reference, and with some trade usage. This evidence must be relied upon as the contract language itself could not settle the question here. Judgment dismissing the complaint shall be entered.

▶ *ANALYSIS*

In determining the intent of the parties the court will turn first to the language of the contract to see whether the meaning of the ambiguous term can be understood. If this is unsuccessful, the court must look to other evidence. Under Restatement 1st, § 235, certain guidelines aid in determining meaning. First, the ordinary meaning of language throughout the country is given to words unless circumstances show that a different meaning is applicable. Also, all circumstances surrounding the transaction may be taken into consideration. Also, if after consideration of all factors, it is still uncertain what meaning should be given, a reasonable, lawful, and effective meaning to all manifestations of intention is preferred to an interpretation which leaves a part of such unreasonable, unlawful, or ineffective. Restatement 1st, § 236(a). Even so, the principal apparent purpose of the parties should be given greater weight in determining the meaning to be given.

■=■

Quicknotes

AMBIGUITY Language that is capable of more than one interpretation.

WARRANTY An assurance by one party that another may rely on a certain representation of fact.

■=■

Embry v. Hargadine, McKittrick Dry Goods Co.

Employee (P) v. Rehiring employer (D)

Mo. Ct. App., 127 Mo. App. 383, 105 S.W. 777 (1907).

NATURE OF CASE: Action to enforce renewal of employment contract.

FACT SUMMARY: Embry (P) was allegedly rehired by Hargadine-McKittrick (D) after his employment contract had expired. Hargadine-McKittrick (D) denied the rehiring.

🏛 RULE OF LAW
The secret feelings, intentions, or beliefs of a party will not affect the formation of a contract if his words and acts indicate that he intends to enter into a binding agreement.

FACTS: Embry (P) was working for Hargadine-McKittrick (D) under a written employment contract. After its expiration, Embry (P) approached McKittrick (D) and demanded a new contract or he would immediately quit. According to Embry (P), McKittrick (D) agreed to rehire him. Embry (P) was terminated in February of the next year. He brought suit to recover the amount due him under the contract. McKittrick (D) swore that the conversation never took place and that Embry (P) had not been rehired. The judge instructed the jury that even if the conversation occurred as related by Embry (P), to form a contract both parties must have intended to enter into a binding agreement. The jury found against Embry (P). He appealed on the basis that the judge's instruction was incorrect; that if McKittrick (D) conveyed by word and deed his intent to rehire Embry (P), a binding contract was formed regardless of McKittrick's (D) secret intention.

ISSUE: Will a hidden, undisclosed intention affect the formation of a contract?

HOLDING AND DECISION: (Goode, J.) No. If the other party reasonably relies on the promise, an undisclosed intention will not affect the formation of a binding contract. Therefore, the trial judge's instructions were erroneous. If the jury reasonably believed that McKittrick (D) had promised to rehire Embry (P), it is immaterial whether McKittrick (D) meant his promise or not. It is obvious that Embry (P) believed a valid contract had been formed because he remained on the job. His reliance was reasonable since McKittrick (D) was the president of the company and had the authority to rehire him. Therefore, the case must be remanded for a new trial since it cannot be determined on what basis the jury found for McKittrick (D). The same holding applies where a reasonable person would interpret the meaning of a conversation as the formation of a binding contract. The fact that McKittrick (D) did not intend to rehire Embry (P) is immaterial if the natural interpretation of the conversation is that he was being rehired. Again, McKittrick's (D) undisclosed intent is immaterial. Reversed and remanded.

▶ ANALYSIS

In order to analyze the manifest intentions of the parties, there are several standards of interpretation which may be applied to their words. First, there is the general accepted meaning of the terms used. Then, there is the meaning of the term according to trade or custom. Finally, there is the meaning the parties may have assigned to the term in the course of past dealings. By utilizing these methods, a court attempts to determine what the parties thought they were doing and to give effect to their legitimate expectations.

■━■

Quicknotes

RELIANCE Dependence on a fact that causes a party to act or refrain from acting.

■━■

MCC-Marble Ceramic Center, Inc. v. Ceramica Nuova d'Agostino

Buyer (P) v. Seller (D)

144 F.3d 1384 (11th Cir. 1998).

NATURE OF CASE: Appeal from summary judgment for defendant in international breach of contract action.

FACT SUMMARY: MCC (P) sought not to be bound by the terms written on the reverse side of a contract which its agent, Monzon, signed, and which were in the Italian language.

🏛 RULE OF LAW
The plain language of the CISG requires an inquiry into a party's subjective intent as long as the other party was aware of that intent.

FACTS: Monzon, MCC's (P) agent, signed a contract while in Italy. Above the signature line was a provision incorporating the terms located on the reverse side of the form. The contract's terms were in the Italian language and Monzon neither spoke nor read Italian. MCC (P) brought suit against D'Agostino (D) for alleged breach of its requirements contract, and D'Agostino (D) responded that it was under no obligation to fill MCC's (P) orders because MCC (P) had defaulted on payment for prior shipments. D'Agostino (D) relied on the pre-printed terms of the contracts to support its position. MCC (P) submitted affidavits stating that the parties subjectively intended not to be bound by the terms on the reverse of the order form, but the magistrate judge held that the affidavits did not raise an issue of material fact regarding the interpretation of the terms of the written contract, and the district court accepted his recommendation to grant summary judgment on behalf of D'Agostino (D). MCC (P) appealed, claiming that the Convention on International Sale of Goods (CISG), which governed the case, required consideration of the parties' subjective intent when they memorialized the terms of their agreement.

ISSUE: Does the plain language of the CISG require an inquiry into a party's subjective intent as long as the other party was aware of that intent?

HOLDING AND DECISION: (Birch, J.) Yes. The plain language of the CISG requires an inquiry into a party's subjective intent as long as the other party was aware of that intent. The CISG governs international contracts for the sale of goods. The magistrate judge erred by applying the parol evidence rule in derogation of the CISG. MCC (P) has raised an issue of material fact concerning the parties' subjective intent to be bound by the terms on the reverse of the pre-printed contract, precluding summary judgment. Reversed and remanded.

▶ ANALYSIS

The court reasoned that a reasonable finder of fact could disregard testimony that sophisticated merchants signed a contract without intending to be bound as simply too incredible to believe. Nevertheless, the affidavits raised an issue for the jury to consider. In this case both parties acknowledged a subjective intent not to be bound by the terms of the pre-printed contract.

■══■

Quicknotes

AFFIDAVIT A declaration of facts written and affirmed before a witness.

BREACH OF CONTRACT Unlawful failure by a party to perform its obligations pursuant to contract.

PAROL EVIDENCE RULE Doctrine precluding parties to an agreement from introducing evidence of prior or contemporaneous agreements in order to repudiate or alter the terms of a written contract.

REQUIREMENTS CONTRACT An agreement pursuant to which one party agrees to purchase all his required goods or services from the other party exclusively for a specified time period.

SUBJECTIVE STANDARD A standard that is based on the personal belief of an individual.

SUMMARY JUDGMENT Judgment rendered by a court in response to a motion by one of the parties, claiming that the lack of a question of material fact in respect to an issue warrants disposition of the issue without consideration by the jury.

■══■

Mayol v. Weiner Companies, Ltd.

Purchaser of real property (P) v. Agent/seller of real property (D)

III. Ct. App, 4th Dist., 98 III. App. 3d 985, 425 N.E.2d 45 (1981).

NATURE OF CASE: Action for breach of contract.

FACT SUMMARY: Mayol (P) refused to proceed with the purchase of real property from Weiner (D) that was "subject to tenant's rights" once Mayol (P) discovered that the tenant had a right to purchase the property.

🏛 RULE OF LAW
An ambiguous contract term that is understood differently by the parties will not be construed against a party not at fault for the misunderstanding.

FACTS: Somers hired Weiner (D) to help sell a rental property occupied by a tenant. Weiner showed the property to Mayol (P) who signed a contract to purchase the property that included a provision that delivery of the property was "subject to tenant's rights." When Mayol (P) subsequently discovered that the tenant had a right of purchase, Mayol (P) refused to continue with the purchase and sued for return of the deposit. The trial court determined that the "subject to tenant's rights" language was ambiguous and therefore subject to interpretation through extrinsic evidence and considered the contract to mean that Mayol (P) intended to purchase the property subject to the right of the tenant to purchase the property. The trial court awarded Weiner (D) the deposit as liquidated damages. Mayol (P) appealed.

ISSUE: Will an ambiguous contract term that is understood differently by the parties be construed against a party who is not at fault for the misunderstanding?

HOLDING AND DISPOSITION: (Trapp, J.) No. An ambiguous contract term that is understood differently by the parties will not be construed against a party not at fault for the misunderstanding. The phrase "subject to tenant's rights" is ambiguous and therefore the parties' intent as shown by intrinsic evidence controls. Here, although Mayol (P) knew there was a lease, Mayol (P) had no reason to know that among the rights at issue was the tenant's right to purchase the property. Mayol (P) did not receive a copy of the lease until after the contract was signed and Weiner (D) had no reason to believe that Mayol (P) would know that the lease contained an option to purchase. According to the Restatement (Second) of Contracts, § 21(a) (19), there is not a contract where the parties' intent does not coincide on a material term unless one of the parties is more at fault than the other. The trial court's decision is reversed. Mayol (P) is entitled to return of the escrowed deposit.

▶ ANALYSIS

Extrinsic evidence as to the parties' intent is considered only after a determination is made that the material term is ambiguous. Although the phrase "subject to tenant's rights" is not ambiguous on its face, a right to purchase would not typically be found among the rights of a tenant. Thus, it is the unusual nature of the right that renders the phrase ambiguous. Here, greater fault for the misunderstanding cannot be placed on Mayol (P) and, therefore, the trial court's interpretation of the ambiguous term against Mayol (P) was against the manifest weight of the evidence. This ruling is an example of the evolution of contract law from a strict interpretation of the terms of the contract toward an approach that gives weight to the subjective intent of the parties.

■■■

Quicknotes

AMBIGUOUS TERMS Contract terms that are capable of being understood to have more than one interpretation.

BREACH OF CONTRACT Unlawful failure by a party to perform its obligations pursuant to contract.

EXTRINSIC EVIDENCE Evidence that is not contained within the text of a document or contract, but which is derived from the parties' statements or the circumstances under which the agreement was made.

LIQUIDATED DAMAGES An amount of money specified in a contract representing the damages owed in the event of breach.

■■■

Haines v. City of New York

Land developer (P) v. City (D)

N.Y. Ct. App., 41 N.Y.2d 769, 364 N.E.2d 820 (1977).

NATURE OF CASE: Action to compel performance.

FACT SUMMARY: An action was brought to require New York (D) to build a new sewage treatment plant for the benefit of additional users of the system.

🏛 RULE OF LAW
Where no duration is specified, the court may determine the intentions of the parties in order to ascertain the proposed term of the contract.

FACTS: The City of New York (D), pursuant to a statutory authorization, entered into a contract to construct a sewage system consisting of a plant, sewer mains, and laterals. All construction costs and subsequent maintenance, operation, and repair were to be borne by the City (D). The contract was executed in 1924. By the 1970s, the flow through the plant was at its maximum capacity. Any increase in usage would render the purification treatment nugatory and would interfere with the quality of the water leaving the treatment plant. Haines (P) sought approval to develop his land into a subdivision. The City (D) refused permission on the ground that the sewage plant could not handle the increased flow. Haines (P) brought suit alleging that the City's (D) obligation under the contract was perpetual and that it was obligated to construct additional plants under it if usage required.

ISSUE: Where a contract does not contain a clause specifying its duration, may the courts determine the parties' intent in order to ascertain the term and scope of the contract?

HOLDING AND DECISION: (Gabrielli, J.) Yes. Unless a contract specifically states that it is to be perpetual, no such intention will be presumed. Where no duration is specified, the court must inquire into the intentions of the parties and the facts surrounding the execution of the contract to ascertain the term intended by them. Where duration can be fairly and reasonably fixed by implication, a contract will not be deemed terminable at will. Where no duration is specified, it will normally be presumed that the parties intended it to continue for a reasonable time. Under the circumstances herein, this would be until the City (D) no longer needed or desired the water purity that the plant was designed to ensure. The City (D), however, obligated itself to build only one plant and to expand it for future needs. The City (D) cannot be required to build additional plants under the agreement or to reduce the water purity requirement to handle additional needs. Judgment for the City (D). Judgment, after modified, affirmed.

▶ ANALYSIS

Contracts of agency or employment are deemed terminable at will where no duration is specified. *Clark Paper & Mfg. Co. v. Stenacher*, 236 N.Y. 312. A contract will never be deemed to be perpetual in duration absent a clear, unequivocal promise in the contract. *Mitler v. Freideberg*, 32 Misc. 2d 78. Rather, as was held in *Haines*, the court will attempt to determine the intention of the parties. 1 Williston, Contract § 38.

Spaulding v. Morse

Trustee for son (P) v. Father (D)

Mass. Sup. Jud. Ct., 322 Mass. 149, 76 N.E.2d 137 (1947).

NATURE OF CASE: Action to enforce a divorce settlement.

FACT SUMMARY: Pursuant to a divorce settlement, Morse (D) agreed to pay $1,200 a year in trust for the maintenance and education of his son. Morse (D) stopped paying when his son was drafted.

🏛 RULE OF LAW
In order to determine whether or not the occurrence of an event suspends or terminates the obligation to perform under a contract, it is necessary to consider the intentions of the parties, their circumstances, and the purpose of the contract.

FACTS: As part of a divorce settlement agreement, Morse (D) agreed to pay $1,200 a year into a trust for the maintenance and education of his son. If, after high school, the son entered college, Morse (D) was to pay $2,200 per year for no more than four years. After high school, the son was immediately drafted. Morse (D) refused to pay the trustee, Spaulding (P), the $1,200. The trial court held that Morse (D) must continue to pay the $1,200 until the son entered college or reached his majority. Morse (D) appealed, contending that such a construction of the divorce settlement was not consistent with the true meaning of the contract.

ISSUE: Is it necessary to examine all of the factors surrounding a contract as well as its express terms in order to determine whether or not a subsequent event relieves a party of his duty to perform?

HOLDING AND DECISION: (Dolan, J.) Yes. In order to determine whether or not the occurrence of an event suspends or terminates the obligation to perform under a contract, it is necessary to consider the intention of the parties, their circumstances, and the purposes of the contract. A particular end may be implied from an instrument in its entirety as well as from its express language and terms. As applied to the facts before us, it is evident that the trust fund was instituted to provide for the son's education and maintenance. The trust instrument specifically provided that payments should be made for as long as the mother maintained and educated the son to the satisfaction of the trustee, Spaulding (P). The son is now subject to the maintenance and control of the army. He is not being educated. Neither of the main objectives of the trust is capable of being satisfied. Since the purposes of the agreement cannot be fulfilled, Morse (D) is relieved of his duty to perform. Judgment reversed and final decree ordered.

▶ ANALYSIS

In *Lawson v. Martin Timber Co.,* 238 La. 467 (1959), a contract provided that there would be a one-year extension to an agreement to remove timber from Lawson's land if there was high water during the contract term. Martin Timber removed lumber after the contract had expired. There had been high water during the period, but the evidence showed that all of the timber could easily have been cut during the contract period despite the high water. The court found for Martin on the basis of the express terms of the contract. The dissent urged that the intent of the parties should govern and that the clause was obviously to protect Martin only in the event that high water interfered with his ability to harvest within the contract term. On rehearing, the position of the dissent was adopted and Lawson prevailed, the court holding that the late harvest was unjustified in light of the original intentions of the parties in inserting the contingency clause.

■■■

Quicknotes

CONTINGENT Based on the uncertain happening of another event.

PAROLE EVIDENCE RULE Doctrine precluding parties to an agreement from introducing evidence of prior or contemporaneous agreements in order to repudiate or alter the terms of a written contract.

TRUST The holding of property by one party for the benefit of another.

■■■

Foxco Industries, Ltd. v. Fabric World, Inc.

Seller of knitted fabric (P) v. Buyer of knitted fabric (D)

595 F.2d 976 (5th Cir. 1979).

NATURE OF CASE: Appeal from evidentiary ruling in action for breach of contract.

FACT SUMMARY: In action for breach of contract between Fabric World (D) and Foxco (P), the trial court admitted into evidence, over Fabric World's (D) objection, the standards of the Knitted Textile Association regarding the definition of the term "first quality" goods.

🏛 **RULE OF LAW**
Evidence of customary and trade usage of terms is admissible at trial to explain or supplement terms in a contract.

FACTS: Foxco (P) entered into a contract with Fabric World (D) to manufacture and deliver fabrics identified in the contact as "first quality" goods. "First quality" was not a defined term in the contract. Volatility in the textile market prompted Fabric World (D) to cancel its order just prior to completion of the manufacturing process. After Foxco (P) refused the cancellation and threatened to seek cover damages, Fabric World (D) agreed to proceed under the contract but threatened to reject the shipment as not conforming to "first quality" goods if it contained even one flaw. Believing that this level of quality was unachievable given the size of the order, Foxco (P) did not deliver the material and sold the goods elsewhere. At trial, the court admitted into evidence, over Fabric World's (D) objection, the definition of "first quality" goods utilized by the Knitted Textile Association. On appeal, Fabric World (D) argued that the use of the Knitted Textile Association standards to explain the contract term was in error because Fabric World (D) was not a member of the Association and the standards were a custom and usage of which Fabric World (D) had no knowledge.

ISSUE: Is evidence of customary and trade usage admissible at trial to explain or supplement terms in the contract?

HOLDING AND DESCISION: (Tjoflat, J.) Yes. The trial court's ruling admitting into evidence the standards of the Knitted Textile Association was not in error. Although there is no direct evidence that Fabric World (D) was on notice that the industry standards would apply to its contract with Foxco (P), under U.C.C. § 2-202 and the Alabama code, customary and trade usage terms are incorporated into the contract and unless carefully negated become an element of the contract terms. Here, the Knitted Textile Association standards could qualify as trade usages and were therefore admissible. Affirmed.

▶ **ANALYSIS**

The issue on appeal is limited to the evidentiary ruling, and is concerned only with whether it was error for the trial court to admit the industry standards into evidence. The standards of the Knitted Textile Association are extrinsic or parol evidence. Under U.C.C. § 2-202, terms of the contract may not be contradicted by extrinsic evidence but may be explained or supplemented by usages of the trade. Thus, had the contract defined the term "first quality" goods, extrinsic evidence would not have been admissible.

■━■

Quicknotes

EXTRINSIC EVIDENCE Evidence that is not contained within the text of a document or contract, but which is derived from the parties' statements or the circumstances under which the agreement was made.

PAROL EVIDENCE Evidence given verbally; extraneous evidence.

■━■

The Mechanics of the Bargain— Offer and Revocation

Quick Reference Rules of Law

Lonergan v. Scolnick

Interested property buyer (P) v. Property seller (D)

Cal. Ct. App., 129 Cal. App. 2d 179, 276 P.2d 8 (1954).

NATURE OF CASE: Specific performance or damages.

FACT SUMMARY: Lonergan (P) made inquiries concerning property which Scolnick (D) had advertised in a newspaper. He received a form letter describing the land and a second letter which responded to questions he had asked. Scolnick (D) sold the property to someone else.

🏛 RULE OF LAW
There can be no contract unless the minds of the parties have met and mutually agreed upon some specific thing.

FACTS: Lonergan (P) made inquiries concerning property which Scolnick (D) had advertised in a newspaper. Scolnick (D) sent him a form letter describing the property. On April 7, 1952, Lonergan (P) wrote Scolnick (D), asking him for a legal description of the property and whether a certain bank would be a satisfactory escrow agent. Scolnick (D) wrote back on April 8th, stating that Lonergan (P) would have to act fast, inasmuch as Scolnick (D) expected to have a buyer in the next week. Lonergan (P) responded on April 14th that he would proceed immediately to have escrow opened. On April 12th, Scolnick (D) sold the property to someone else.

ISSUE: Can there be a contract where the minds of the parties have not met and mutually agreed upon some specific thing?

HOLDING AND DECISION: (Barnard, J.) No. There can be no contract unless the minds of the parties have met and mutually agreed upon some specific thing. This agreement is usually evidenced by one party making an offer which is accepted by the other. However, if from a promise or manifestation of intention, or from existing circumstances, the person to whom the promise or manifestation is addressed knows or has reason to know that the person making it does not intend it to constitute an expression of fixed purpose until he has given a further expression of assent, no offer has been made. Such was the case here. The newspaper ad was merely a request for an offer. The form letter sent by Scolnick (D) contained no definitive offer, and his letter of April 8th added nothing which caused previous communications to ripen into an offer. In fact, it stated that he expected a buyer within the week, indicating that he intended to sell to the first-comer. Lonergan's (P) letter on April 15th stating that he was opening escrow, therefore, could not have created a contract between the parties since there had been no offer. Affirmed.

▶ ANALYSIS

In *Fairmount Glass Works v. Crunden-Martin Woodenware Co.*, 106 Ky. 659, 51 S.W. 196 (1899), the plaintiff inquired as to the defendant's lowest price on 10 loads of Mason jars. The reply was "$4.50 and $5.00 for immediate acceptance." The defendant refused to fill plaintiff's subsequent order. The court held that defendant's reply "was not a quotation of prices, but a definite offer to sell." In *Harvey v. Facey*, A.C. 552 (1893), plaintiff telegraphed defendant, "Will you sell us Bumper Hall Pen? Telegraph lowest price." The defendant replied, "Lowest price for Bumper Hall Pen £900." Plaintiff responded, "We agree to buy Bumper Hall Pen for £900." The court held that there was no contract.

■=■

Quicknotes

ACCEPTANCE Assent to the specified terms of an offer, resulting in the formation of a binding agreement.

DAMAGES Monetary compensation that may be awarded by the court to a party who has sustained injury or loss to his or her person, property or rights due to another party's unlawful act, omission or negligence.

ESCROW A written contract held by a third party until the conditions therein are satisfied, at which time it is delivered to the obligee.

MEETING OF THE MINDS A requirement of a valid contract that the parties possess a mutuality of assent as manifested by the terms of the agreement and not by a hidden intent; enforceability of the contract is limited to those terms to which the parties assented.

OFFER A proposed promise to undertake performance of an action, or to refrain from acting, that is to become binding upon acceptance by the offeree.

SPECIFIC PERFORMANCE An equitable remedy whereby the court requires the parties to perform their obligations pursuant to a contract.

■=■

Lefkowitz v. Great Minneapolis Surplus Store

Advertising responder (P) v. Store (D)

Minn. Sup. Ct., 251 Minn. 188, 86 N.W.2d 689 (1957).

NATURE OF CASE: Action to recover damages for breach of contract.

FACT SUMMARY: Surplus Store (D) advertised one fur stole on a "first-come-first-served" basis but would not sell the stole to Lefkowitz (P) who accepted the alleged offer.

🏛 **RULE OF LAW**
A newspaper advertisement (for the sale of an article) which is clear, definite and explicit, and leaves nothing to negotiation is an offer, acceptance of which will create a binding contract.

FACTS: Surplus Store (D) published the following advertisement in a Minneapolis newspaper: "SATURDAY 9 A.M. 2 BRAND NEW PASTEL MINK 3-SKIN SCARFS Selling for $89.50 Out they go Saturday. Each . . . $1.00 1 BLACK LAPIN STOLE Beautiful, worth $139.50 . . . $1.00. FIRST COME FIRST SERVED." Lefkowitz (P) was the first to present himself on Saturday and demanded the Lapin Stole for one dollar. The Surplus Store (D) refused to sell to him because of a "house rule" that the offer was intended for women only. Lefkowitz (P) sued the Surplus Store (D) and was awarded $138.50 as damages. Surplus Store (D) appealed.

ISSUE: May a newspaper advertisement constitute an offer such that acceptance will complete a contract?

HOLDING AND DECISION: (Murphy, J.) Yes. The test of whether a binding obligation may originate in advertisements addressed to the public is "whether the facts show that some performance was promised in positive terms in return for something requested." Whether an advertisement is an offer or merely an invitation for offers depends on the legal intention of the parties and the surrounding circumstances. Where an offer is clear, definite and explicit, and leaves nothing open for negotiation, it constitutes an offer such that acceptance of it will create a contract. With respect to the Lapin fur, Surplus Store's (D) advertisement was such an offer. As to Surplus Store's (D) alleged "house rule," while an advertiser has the right at any time before acceptance to modify his offer, he does not have the right, after acceptance, to impose new or arbitrary conditions not contained in the published offer. Affirmed.

▶ **ANALYSIS**

Although most advertisements for goods at a certain price are held not to be offers, the present case presents an interesting exception to that rule. Restatement of 2nd § 5 (Illustration No. 1) indicates that the basis of the court's decision is that the words "First come first served" create language of promise which is ordinarily lacking in advertisement for the sale of goods. Probably it was this factor in conjunction with the statement of quantity (to wit, one), which motivated the court. CAVEAT: The Uniform Commercial Code has dealt a blow to the present court's insistence that nothing be left open for negotiation [see U.C.C. § 2-204(3)].

◾━◾

Quicknotes

ACCEPTANCE Assent to the specified terms of an offer, resulting in the formation of a binding agreement.

OFFER A proposed promise to undertake performance of an action, or to refrain from acting, that is to become binding upon acceptance by the offeree.

◾━◾

Akers v. J.B. Sedberry, Inc.

Employees (P) v. Employer company (D)

Tenn. Ct. App., 39 Tenn. App. 633, 286 S.W.2d 617, *cert. denied*, Tenn. Sup. Ct. (1955).

NATURE OF CASE: Action for damages for breach of contract.

FACT SUMMARY: Sedberry's (D) president had not responded to an offer of resignation by Akers (P), an employee under contract, during the conversation in which it took place, but she later sent him a telegram attempting to accept his offer.

> ## 🏛 RULE OF LAW
> Ordinarily, an offer made by one to another in a face-to-face conversation is deemed to continue only to the close of the conversation and cannot be accepted thereafter.

FACTS: Both Akers (P) and Whitsitt (P) had five-year employment contracts with Sedberry (D). During a face-to-face conversation with Sedberry's (D) president and primary stockholder, Mrs. Sedberry, the two men said that to show their good faith they would offer to resign on a 90-day notice, provided they were paid according to their contracts for that period. Mrs. Sedberry said nothing about accepting the offer but proceeded to discuss business matters (including friction between the new manager and the two employees). However, four days later, Mrs. Sedberry sent telegrams attempting to accept the offer of resignation. She contended that she had not wanted to respond to the offer until she had a chance to talk with her manager. Akers (P) and Whitsitt (P) brought suits to recover damages for breach of contract. Sedberry (D) appealed judgments awarding both the requested recovery.

ISSUE: Does an offer made in a face-to-face conversation continue only until the end of the conversation?

HOLDING AND DECISION: (Felts, J.) Yes. Ordinarily, an offer made by one to another in a face-to-face conversation is deemed to continue only to the close of their conversation and cannot be accepted thereafter. This is the natural consequence of the rule that an offer must be accepted within the time fixed by the terms of the offer itself or, if no time is fixed, within a reasonable time. What is a reasonable time is a question of fact, depending on the nature of the contract proposed, the usages of business, and other circumstances of the case. In the case at hand, Mrs. Sedberry did not accept the offer made by the time the conversation in which it was made ended. Furthermore, by her conduct, she led the others to believe she had rejected it. Thus, her later attempt to accept it was futile. Assignments of error overruled, judgment affirmed, and causes remanded.

▶ ANALYSIS

According to Restatement, Second, Contracts § 41(3), "unless otherwise indicated by the language or the circumstances, . . . an offer sent by mail is seasonably accepted if an acceptance is mailed any time before midnight on the day on which the offer is received." The ability to accept all other offers terminates at the time specified or at the end of a reasonable time. § 41(1).

Quicknotes

MAILBOX RULE Common law rule that acceptance of an offer is binding upon dispatch at which time an enforceable contract is formed so long as it complies with the requirements for acceptance.

OFFER A proposed promise to undertake performance of an action, or to refrain from acting, that is to become binding upon acceptance by the offeree.

Ardente v. Horan

Prospective home buyer (P) v. Homeowners (D)

R.I. Sup. Ct., 117 R.I. 254, 366 A.2d 162 (1976).

NATURE OF CASE: Action to specifically enforce an agreement.

FACT SUMMARY: Ardente (P) asserted that he had accepted the Horans' (D) offer to sell their home and that a contract had thus been formed, but the Horans (D) insisted he had made only a counteroffer.

RULE OF LAW
An acceptance which is equivocal or upon condition or with a limitation is a counteroffer and requires acceptance by the original offeror before a contractual relationship can exist.

FACTS: The Horans (D) offered their home for sale, whereupon Ardente (P) made a $250,000 bid that was communicated to them through their attorney. The attorney advised Ardente (P) that the bid was acceptable to the Horans (D) and prepared a purchase and sale agreement that was forwarded for Ardente's (P) signature to his attorney. Ardente (P) executed the agreement after investigating certain title conditions. His attorney sent it to the Horans (D) along with a $20,000 check and a letter from Ardente's (P) attorney stating his client's concern that certain items remain with the real estate as they would be difficult to replace (dining room set and tapestry in dining room, fireplace fixtures, and sun parlor furniture). It stated, "I would appreciate your confirming that these items are a part of the transaction." The Horans (D) refused to include the items and did not sign the agreement, which their attorney returned along with the check. Ardente (P) filed an action for specific performance, arguing that a contract had been formed. In granting summary judgment for the Horans (D), the court held the aforementioned letter was a conditional acceptance amounting to a counteroffer which was not accepted by the Horans (D).

ISSUE: Is a conditional acceptance treated as a counteroffer which must itself be accepted?

HOLDING AND DECISION: (Doris, J.) Yes. To be effective, an acceptance must be definite and unequivocal. An acceptance which is equivocal or upon condition or with a limitation is a counteroffer and requires acceptance by the original offeror before a contract arises. However, an acceptance may be valid despite conditional language if the acceptance is clearly independent of the condition. Ardente's (P) acceptance was not clearly independent of the condition and thus operated as a counteroffer that was not accepted by the Horans (D). Thus, no contract was formed. Affirmed and remanded.

ANALYSIS

Restatement, Second, Contracts § 39, Comment (b) indicates that an offeree can state he is holding the offer under advisement but if the offeror desires to close the bargain immediately, he makes a counteroffer. In this way, the original offer remains open for its original term, but the counteroffer is nonetheless introduced. Thus, the counteroffer does not kill the original offer.

Quicknotes

ACCEPTANCE Assent to the specified terms of an offer, resulting in the formation of a binding agreement.

SPECIFIC PERFORMANCE An equitable remedy whereby the court requires the parties to perform their obligations pursuant to a contract.

SUMMARY JUDGMENT Judgment rendered by a court in response to a motion by one of the parties, claiming that the lack of a question of material fact in respect to an issue warrants disposition of the issue without consideration by the jury.

Dickinson v. Dodds

Buyer of land (P) v. Seller of land (D)

Ct. App., Chancery Div., 2 Ch. Div. 463 (1876).

NATURE OF CASE: Action for specific performance of a contract for the sale of real property.

FACT SUMMARY: On June 10, 1874, Dodds (D) gave a writing to Dickinson (P) giving the latter until 9 a.m., June 12, 1874, to accept Dodds's (D) offer to purchase his land and buildings upon it for £800. On the afternoon of June 11, 1874, Dodds (D) sold the same property to Allan (D) for £800 and had accepted a £40 deposit.

🏛 **RULE OF LAW**
An offer may be withdrawn by an indirect revocation where the offeree receives reliable information from a third party that the offeror has engaged in conduct indicative to a reasonable man that the offer was withdrawn.

FACTS: On June 10, 1874, Dodds (D) gave Dickinson (P) a writing that stated that the former agreed to sell his land and buildings upon it to the latter for £800, the offer to be left open until June 12, 1874, 9 a.m. Dickinson (P) decided to accept on the morning of June 11, 1874, but did not immediately convey his acceptance, believing he had until the next morning. That afternoon, one Berry informed Dickinson (P) that Dodds (D) had decided to sell the property to Allan (D). Dickinson (P) went to Dodds's (D) mother-in-law's home, where he was staying, and left his acceptance there, but it never got to Dodds (D). The next morning at 7 a.m., Berry, as Dickinson's (P) agent, attempted to give a copy of the acceptance to Dodds (D) who said it was too late. On June 11, 1874, the day before, Dodds (D) had sold the property to Allan (D) for £800 and had accepted a £40 deposit.

ISSUE: Was there adequate revocation of the offer?

HOLDING AND DECISION: (James, L.J.) Yes. The writing was not an agreement to sell, but an offer. Both parties had not yet agreed to go through with the deal. There was no consideration given for the promise. The promise was not binding, so Dodds (D) was free to do whatever he wanted to do before receiving an acceptance from Dickinson (P). There did not have to be an express and actual withdrawal of the offer. From the circumstances, Dickinson (P) knew that Dodds (D) had changed his mind; it was clear from his statements and actions. Accordingly, there was no meeting of the minds between the two parties and no contract. Bill dismissed.

▌ *ANALYSIS*

It is seen that an indirect revocation may arise through a third party or by the circumstances. The First Restatement stated that the doctrine of indirect revocation should be limited to the sale of land and chattels but Restatement 2d, § 42, now holds oppositely. There is always a problem as to what information is reliable. The information must be true and put a reasonable man acting in good faith to inquiry. But what if the offeree hears reliably that the offeror has made the same offer to a second person? Grismore believes that a reasonable man would conclude that since he was given no notice of revocation, that the offeror is willing to run the risk of two open offers.

■=■

Quicknotes

MEETING OF THE MINDS A requirement of a valid contract that the parties possess a mutuality of assent as manifested by the terms of the agreement and not by a hidden intent; enforceability of the contract is limited to those terms to which the parties assented.

OFFER A proposed promise to undertake performance of an action, or to refrain from acting, that is to become binding upon acceptance by the offeree.

REVOCATION The cancellation or withdrawal of some authority conferred or an instrument drafted, such as the withdrawal of a revocable contract offer prior to the offeree's acceptance.

SPECIFIC PERFORMANCE An equitable remedy whereby the court requires the parties to perform their obligations pursuant to a contract.

■=■

Ragosta v. Wilder

Property buyer (P) v. Property seller (D)

Vt. Sup. Ct., 156 Vt. 390, 592 A.2d 367 (1991).

NATURE OF CASE: Appeal from a judgment ordering specific performance in relation to the conveyance of a piece of real property.

FACT SUMMARY: Wilder (D) offered to sell a piece of real property to Ragosta (P) contingent on Ragosta's (P) meeting Wilder (D) at his bank with the purchase amount before November 1, but on October 8, Wilder (D) informed Ragosta (P) that he had decided not to sell the property after all.

🏛 RULE OF LAW
Where an offer invites an offeree to accept by rendering a performance, an option contract is created when the offeree tenders or begins the invited performance.

FACTS: Ragosta (P) mailed a letter to Wilder (D), along with a deposit check, offering to purchase a property Wilder (D) had for sale. Ragosta (P) then began arrangements to obtain the necessary financing. Wilder (D) returned the check but offered to sell the property for a certain sum at any time up until November 1, if Ragosta (P) would appear with Wilder (D) at his bank with the designated sum, providing the property had not been sold to another buyer. On October 8, Wilder (D) informed Ragosta (P) that he would not sell the property after all. Ragosta (P) appeared at the bank with the purchase price, but Wilder (D) did not appear. Ragosta (P) brought suit, seeking specific performance. The trial court, holding that Wilder (D) could not revoke his offer on October 8 because Ragosta (P), in reliance, had already begun performance by arranging financing, ordered specific performance. Wilder (D) appealed.

ISSUE: Where an offer invites an offeree to accept by rendering a performance, is an option contract created when the offeree tenders or begins the invited performance?

HOLDING AND DECISION: (Peck, J.) Yes. Where an offer invites an offeree to accept by rendering a performance, an option contract is created when the offeree tenders or begins the invited performance. What is begun or tendered must be part of the actual performance invited in order to preclude revocation. However, in this case, since Wilder (D) received no consideration, his promise to keep the offer open was not enforceable. Moreover, Ragosta's (P) attempt to seek financing does not constitute consideration. Ragosta (P) began to seek financing even before Wilder (D) made a definite offer to sell the property. Whatever detriment he suffered was not in exchange for Wilder's (D) promise. Ragosta (P) was merely engaged in preparation for performance but never tendered or even began to tender the purchase price. Wilder's (D) offer was never accepted, and no contract was ever created. Reversed and remanded.

▶ ANALYSIS

As can be seen by the above case, offers not supported by consideration or detrimental reliance can be revoked at will by the offeror, even if he has promised not to revoke for a specified period of time. An offeror may terminate an offer by directly communicating the revocation to the offeree or by indirect means, for example, through a reliable third party. General offers made by publication may be terminated by publishing the revocation by comparable means.

Quicknotes

CONSIDERATION Value given by one party in exchange for performance, or a promise to perform, by another party.

CONVEYANCE The transfer of property, or title to property, from one party to another party.

DETRIMENTAL RELIANCE Action by one party, resulting in loss, that is based on the conduct or promises of another.

OPTION CONTRACT A contract pursuant to which a seller agrees that property will be available for the buyer to purchase at a specified price and within a certain time period.

REVOCATION The cancellation or withdrawal of some authority conferred or an instrument drafted, such as the withdrawal of a revocable contract offer prior to the offeree's acceptance.

SPECIFIC PERFORMANCE An equitable remedy whereby the court requires the parties to perform their obligations pursuant to a contract.

Drennan v. Star Paving Co.

School construction company (P) v. Paving subcontractor (D)

Cal. Sup. Ct., 51 Cal. 2d 409, 333 P.2d 757 (1958).

NATURE OF CASE: Appeal of an award of damages for breach of contract.

FACT SUMMARY: Drennan (P) sued Star (D) to recover damages when Star (D) could not perform the paving work at the price quoted in its subcontracting bid.

🏛 RULE OF LAW
Reasonable reliance on a promise binds an offeror even if there is no other consideration.

FACTS: In formulating a bid to the Lancaster School District, Drennan (P), a general contractor, solicited bids for subcontracting work. Star (P), a paving company, submitted the lowest paving bid, and Drennan (P) used that bid in formulating its bid to the school district. Using Star's (D) subcontracting bid of $7,131.60, Drennan (P) was awarded the general contract. Star (D) then told Drennan (P) that it made a mistake and could not do the work for less than $15,000. Star (D) refused to do the work, and Drennan (P) found a substitute company that did the work for $10,948.60. Drennan (P) sued Star (D) for the difference, claiming that Drennan (P) had reasonably relied on Star's (D) offer. Star (D) claimed that it had made a revocable offer. The trial court ruled in favor of Drennan (P) on the grounds of promissory estoppel, and Star (D) appealed.

ISSUE: Does reasonable reliance on a promise bind the offeror if there no other consideration?

HOLDING AND DECISION: (Traynor, J.) Yes. Reasonable reliance on a promise binds the offeror even if there is no other consideration. Section 90 of the Restatement of Contracts provides that when a promise is made that induces action or forbearance of the promisee, the promisor is bound if injustice would result from nonenforcement. In the case of a unilateral offer, the offeror is bound to the promise if it produces reasonable reliance. Star (D) made a promise to Drennan (P) of a certain price. Star's (D) bid was the lowest, and Drennan (P) reasonably relied on it in formulating its bid and winning the contract. As a result, Drennan (P) was obligated to do the work at the price quoted and even had to put up a bond. Star (D) should have known such a result would occur if Star's (D) bid was accepted. The absence of consideration is not fatal to Star's (D) initial promise, as Drennan (P) substantially changed its position in reliance on Star (D). Injustice can only be avoided by the enforcement of Star's (D) subcontracting promise. Affirmed.

▶ ANALYSIS

Such reasonable reliance cases are often called firm offers. Firm offers can sometimes be implied promises to hold an offer open and have received criticism on the grounds that one party (the subcontractor) is bound while the other party (the general contractor) is not. Nonetheless, the modern trend is to enforce such promises.

■═■

Quicknotes

DAMAGES Monetary compensation that may be awarded by the court to a party who has sustained injury or loss to his or her person, property or rights due to another party's unlawful act, omission or negligence.

IRREVOCABLE OFFER An offer that may not be retracted by the promisor without the assent of the offeree.

PROMISSORY ESTOPPEL A promise that is enforceable if the promisor should reasonably expect that it will induce action or forbearance on the part of the promisee, and does in fact cause such action or forbearance, and it is the only means of avoiding injustice.

RELIANCE Dependence on a fact that causes a party to act or refrain from acting.

UNILATERAL CONTRACT An agreement pursuant to which a party agrees to act, or to forbear from acting, in exchange for performance on the part of the other party.

■═■

CHAPTER 12

The Mechanics of the Bargain— Modes of Acceptance

Quick Reference Rules of Law

Klockner v. Green

Son (P) v. Executor of stepmother's estate (D)

N.J. Sup. Ct., 54 N.J. 230, 254 A.2d 782 (1969).

NATURE OF CASE: Action to enforce an oral contract.

FACT SUMMARY: Klockner (P) maintained that his stepmother, Green's (D) decedent, had promised to provide for him in her will in return for his services but did not do so.

🏛 RULE OF LAW
When an offeror requests an act as consideration for a unilateral contract, one who does that act with the intent of accepting the offer brings an enforceable contract into being.

FACTS: Klockner (P) and his daughter had a close relationship with his stepmother, both performing numerous services for her after Klockner's (P) father died. The stepmother approached her attorney, Green (D), saying that she wanted to leave her real property to Klockner (P) and her personal property to his daughter. A will of that nature was drawn up but never executed. Subsequently, Klockner's (P) stepmother told him she wanted to compensate him for being so helpful and that if he would agree to continue to look after her and continue to let his daughter visit her, she would leave her real property to him and the balance of the estate to his daughter. The stepmother again called Green (D) and had him draw up such a will, but she left it unexecuted due to her belief that a will was a premonition of death. She thereafter became suddenly ill and died. Klockner (P) brought suit against the executor of her estate, Green (D), to enforce the oral contract he alleged had existed obligating her to bequeath her real property to him and her personal property to his daughter. Both the trial and appellate division held for Green (D) on the ground that Klockner (P) and his daughter had testified that they would have continued to perform the services for decedent even without her promise of compensation.

ISSUE: Is a contract formed when one does the act requested by the offeror with the intent of accepting the offer?

HOLDING AND DECISION: (Schettino, J.) Yes. A contract comes into existence when, with the intent of accepting the offer, one does the act the offeror requested as consideration for a unilateral contract. It is not necessary that the performance of the act be induced solely by the offer of compensation. Thus, the fact that Klockner (P) also may have been motivated by other feelings is inconsequential. A contract was clearly formed here. Reversed and remanded.

▶ ANALYSIS

In a case like this, the offeror automatically knows that the performance constituting acceptance of the offer is under way. However, in those cases where the offeree has reason to know that the offeror has no adequate means of learning of his performance, he must use reasonable diligence to notify the offeror of such within a reasonable time.

■■■

Quicknotes

ACCEPTANCE Assent to the specified terms of an offer, resulting in the formation of a binding agreement.

CONSIDERATION Value given by one party in exchange for performance, or a promise to perform, by another party.

ORAL CONTRACT A contract that is not reduced to written form.

UNILATERAL CONTRACT An agreement pursuant to which a party agrees to act, or to forbear from acting, in exchange for performance on the part of the other party.

■■■

Carlill v. Carbolic Smoke Ball Co.

Influenza sufferer (P) v. Smoke ball company (D)

Ct. App., 1 Q.B. 256 (1893).

NATURE OF CASE: Damages for breach of contract.

FACT SUMMARY: The Carbolic Smoke Ball Co. (D) advertised a reward to any person contracting influenza after using the Carbolic Smoke Ball but refused to pay such reward to Carlill (P) when she caught the influenza after using the ball.

🏛 RULE OF LAW
An advertised reward to anyone who performs certain conditions specified in the advertisement is an offer, and the performance of such conditions is an acceptance which creates a valid contract.

FACTS: The Carbolic Smoke Ball Co. (D) advertised, in various newspapers, a reward to any person who contracted influenza, colds, or any disease caused by taking cold after having used the Carbolic Smoke Ball three times daily for two weeks according to printed directions on each ball. Carlill (P) used the ball as directed but still caught the influenza. Thereafter, Carlill (P) brought an action against the Carbolic Smoke Ball Co. (D) to recover damages for breach of contract. After Carlill (P) was awarded damages in the amount of the original advertised reward, the Carbolic Smoke Ball Co. (D) brought this appeal.

ISSUE: When a company advertises a reward to anyone who performs certain conditions and someone performs such conditions, has a valid contract been formed?

HOLDING AND DECISION: (Lindley, L.J.) Yes. An advertised reward to anyone who performs certain conditions specified in the advertisement is an offer, and the performance of such conditions is an acceptance which creates a valid contract. Furthermore, since such an advertisement requests deeds, not words, an offeree need not give notice that he is going to perform the required deeds. Here, the advertisement clearly offered a reward to anyone who performed certain specified conditions. As such, when Carlill (P) performed these conditions she was entitled to the reward. Furthermore, there is no basis to the Carbolic Smoke Ball Co.'s (D) contention that there was no consideration for its promise. Any acceptance of the Company's (D) offer benefited it by stimulating sales of the smoke ball, and, furthermore, Carlill (P) was inconvenienced by using the ball. Appeal dismissed.

▶ ANALYSIS

This case illustrates a case in which an advertisement is considered an offer (i.e., when there is no problem as to quantity because the ad specifies a reward to anyone who uses the product). The ordinary advertisement, though, which states than an item has been reduced in price, is not considered an offer because no quantity of the item is specified. Instead, such advertisements are generally held to represent only an intention to sell or a preliminary proposal inviting offers. Note, also, that this case illustrates the general rule that no notice is required before performance of an act specified in a unilateral contract. There are three different views, though, regarding notice after such performance: (1) no notice is required unless requested by the offeror; (2) notice is required if the offeree knows that the offeror has no adequate means of learning of the performance within a reasonable time; and (3) notice is always required.

■═■

Quicknotes

ACCEPTANCE Assent to the specified terms of an offer, resulting in the formation of a binding agreement.

NOTICE Communication of information to a person by an authorized person or an otherwise proper source.

OFFER A proposed promise to undertake performance of an action, or to refrain from acting, that is to become binding upon acceptance by the offeree.

UNILATERAL CONTRACT An agreement pursuant to which a party agrees to act, or to forbear from acting, in exchange for performance on the part of the other party.

■═■

Bishop v. Eaton

Lender (P) v. Guarantor of loan (D)

Mass. Sup. Jud. Ct., 161 Mass. 496, 37 N.E. 665 (1894).

NATURE OF CASE: Action on a guarantee contract.

FACT SUMMARY: Eaton (D), who had offered to guarantee Bishop's (P) assumption of a note made by Eaton's (D) brother, claimed that he never received notice of Bishop's (P) acceptance which had been properly mailed.

🏛 RULE OF LAW
A guarantor who had made an offer to a unilateral contract will not be discharged of his obligation where communication by letter is naturally to be expected and the offeree has posted notice of his performance.

FACTS: In December 1886, Eaton (D), a resident of Nova Scotia, wrote Bishop (P), a resident of Illinois, a letter in which he offered to reimburse Bishop (P) for any money Bishop (P) might lend Eaton's (D) brother. In January 1887, Bishop (P) signed as surety a promissory note payable by the brother to a third person. Bishop (P) mailed notification of this to Eaton (D), but although the letter had the correct postage and was properly addressed, Eaton (D) would later claim that he never received it. In August 1889, during a personal interview, Eaton (D) asked Bishop (P) to assume the note still outstanding and reiterated his promise of reimbursement. In October 1891, Bishop (P) paid the note and then sought to collect from Eaton (D). Eaton (D), however, denied the existence of any guarantee contract entered into with Bishop (P) since he had no prior notice that Bishop (P) had accepted his offer.

ISSUE: Is a person who has made an offer to a unilateral guarantee contract by mail bound by his offer if the offeree properly mails notice of his performance but the offeror never receives the letter?

HOLDING AND DECISION: (Knowlton, J.) Yes. Ordinarily, an offeror in a unilateral contract becomes bound when the offeree performs the requested act; no notice of performance is required. However, where the act is of such a kind that knowledge of it will not quickly come to the promisor, the promisee is bound to give him notice of his acceptance within a reasonable time after doing that which constitutes the acceptance. Where an act fulfilling an offer of guarantee is performed, the kind of notice required depends upon the nature of the transaction, the situation of the parties, and the inferences to be drawn from their previous dealings. In the present case, Eaton (D), having made the guarantee offer to an out-of-state resident by letter, must have contemplated that notification would be by return mails. After assisting Eaton's (D) brother to get the money as Eaton (D) had requested,

Bishop (P) did all he was required to do when he seasonably sent Eaton (D) a letter by mail informing him of what had been done. New trial granted.

▶ ANALYSIS

According to the Restatement, Second, Contracts, § 56: "(1) Where an offer invites an offeree to accept by rendering a performance, no notification is necessary to make such an acceptance effective unless the offer requests such a notification." However, the rule is different where the offeree has "reason to know that the offeror has no adequate means of learning of the performance with reasonable promptness and certainty."

Quicknotes

ACCEPTANCE Assent to the specified terms of an offer, resulting in the formation of a binding agreement.

GUARANTOR A party who agrees to be liable for the debt or default of another.

NOTICE Communication of information to a person by an authorized person or an otherwise proper source.

PROMISSORY NOTE A written promise to tender a stated amount of money at a designated time and to a designated person.

SURETY A party who guarantees payment of the debt of another party to a creditor.

UNILATERAL CONTRACT An agreement pursuant to which a party agrees to act, or to forbear from acting, in exchange for performance on the part of the other party.

International Filter Co. v. Conroe Gin, Ice & Light Co.

Water purification company (P) v. Purchasing company (D)

Tex. Comm. App., 277 S.W. 631 (1925).

NATURE OF CASE: Action for damages for breach of contract.

FACT SUMMARY: Filter (P) offered a water purifier to Conroe (D) by letter, stating that there would be a contract when Conroe's (D) acceptance was approved by Filter's (P) executive officer at its Chicago office. This was done, but Conroe (D) revoked its order claiming no contract existed.

🏛 RULE OF LAW
As the offeror is in control of his offer, he may specify the type of acceptance which is required and can dispense with the requirement of its communication.

FACTS: Filter (P), through its traveling salesman, submitted to Conroe (D) a letter offering a water purification system and that a contract for purchase would arise when Conroe's (D) order was received and approved by an executive officer of Filter (P) in its Chicago office. On the same day, Conroe (D) communicated its order which was approved by Engel, Filter's (P) President and Vice President. Filter (P) then sent an acknowledgment of Conroe's (D) order and requested Conroe (D) to send a water sample so the purifier could be properly adjusted before shipment. Two weeks later, Conroe (D) revoked its order, and Filter (P) sued. The trial court entered a verdict for Conroe (D) and the court of appeals affirmed.

ISSUE: Was notice of acceptance of Conroe's (D) order required to be communicated by Filter (P) to Conroe (D)?

HOLDING AND DECISION: (Nickels, J.) No. Engel's endorsement of the order was an approval by an executive officer at Filter's (P) Chicago office. The paper then became a contract as notice of acceptance was not required under the terms of the offer. A prompt order was required, and it was expressly stated that a contract would arise upon approval by Filter's (P) executive officer in Chicago. Even though notice of acceptance was not required, Filter's (P) letter of acknowledgment and request for a water sample sufficiently communicated acceptance anyway. The form of the notice of acceptance can be quite different from the acceptance itself. It was quite clear that Filter (P) intended to ship the system and would not have so intended unless it had accepted the order. Reversed and remanded.

▶ ANALYSIS

Generally, when an offer looks to a bilateral contract, the offeree's promise must be communicated to the offeror.

But as the offeror is the "master" of his offer, he can specify the type of acceptance required, and can dispense with the requirement of a communication altogether. Restatement (Second) of Contracts, § 57(a), does not follow this case and requires that the offeree exercise "reasonable diligence to notify the offeror of acceptance or that the offeror will receive an acceptance seasonally." Usually, however, notification of acceptance does not have to be given if it is made clear by the course of events that it has been given.

Quicknotes

ACCEPTANCE Assent to the specified terms of an offer, resulting in the formation of a binding agreement.

BILATERAL CONTRACT An agreement pursuant to which each party promises to undertake an obligation, or to forbear from acting, at some time in the future.

Polaroid Corp. v. Rollins Environmental Services (NJ), Inc.

Camera company (P) v. Waste disposal service (D)

Mass. Sup. Jud. Ct., 416 Mass. 684, 624 N.E.2d 959 (1993).

NATURE OF CASE: Appeal from judgment granting declaratory relief and indemnification for costs.

FACT SUMMARY: Polaroid (P) brought an action against Rollins (D) seeking indemnification for liability incurred in cleaning up hazardous waste spills at a temporary storage facility.

🏛 RULE OF LAW
When an offeree accepts the offeror's services without expressing any objection to the offer's essential terms, the offeree has manifested assent to those terms.

FACTS: In early 1976, Polaroid (P) and Rollins (D) entered into an agreement whereby Rollins (D) agreed to perform waste disposal services for Polaroid (P). Polaroid (P) gave Rollins (D) a copy of Polaroid's (P) "Supplemental General Conditions for Chemical Waste Disposal Services" and informed Rollins (D) that agreement to the supplemental conditions was an essential condition to any contract between the parties. Rollins (D) made several changes and then both parties signed the supplemental conditions. The agreement stated that Rollins (D) would indemnify Polaroid (P) for any losses arising from services performed by Rollins (D) or its employees. Throughout the course of the business relationship, Rollins (D) often stored Polaroid's (P) waste materials at a facility in Bridgeport until they were able to process the waste. Several spills occurred at the facility and the Environmental Protection Agency (EPA) notified Polaroid (P) that they would be held potentially liable if the waste could be traced to their shipments. Polaroid (P) brought suit when Rollins (D) refused to indemnify them for fines paid for the Bridgeport spills. The trial court concluded that the indemnification contract required Rollins (D) to indemnify Polaroid (P) for all liability and loss for releases of hazardous waste at the Bridgeport site. Rollins (D) appealed.

ISSUE: When an offeree accepts the offeror's services without expressing any objection to the offer's essential terms, has the offeree manifested assent to those terms?

HOLDING AND DECISION: (Lynch, J.) Yes. When an offeree accepts the offeror's services without expressing any objection to the offer's essential terms, the offeree has manifested assent to those terms. Rollins (D) incorrectly argues that it did not accept the indemnification language for every order because it did not return an acknowledgement of acceptance with each purchase order. There was no requirement that the only means of acceptance of the terms of the order was by written acknowledgement, and the circumstances justify the assumption that Rollins' (D) silence indicated assent. Because of the ongoing nature of the parties' relationship, the fact that Rollins (D) routinely completed performance of the orders constitutes acceptance of all of the contract's terms, including the indemnity clause. Affirmed.

▶ ANALYSIS

This case presents an exception to the general rule that silence does not constitute acceptance. The rationale is that it is unfair to be put in the position of not knowing that you have formed a contract. However, where there is an ongoing relationship between the parties, or where an offeree consciously retains goods tendered under the terms of an explicit offer, then the risk that one party does not know about the contract does not exist.

■■■

Quicknotes

COURSE OF DEALING Previous conduct between two parties to a contact which may be relied upon to interpret their actions.

ESSENTIAL TERMS Terms without which a contract may not be entered.

DECLARATORY RELIEF A judgment of the court establishing the rights of the parties.

INDEMNIFICATION Reimbursement for losses sustained or security against anticipated loss or damages.

■■■

Holman Erection Co. v. Orville E. Madsen & Sons, Inc.

Subcontractor (P) v. General construction contractor (D)

Minn. Sup. Ct., 330 N.W.2d 693 (1983).

NATURE OF CASE: Appeal from summary denial of damages for breach of contract.

FACT SUMMARY: In Holman's (P) suit against Madsen (D) for breach of contract on a public construction contract, Holman (P) contended that Madsen (D) had accepted Holman's (P) sub-bid on a wastewater treatment project and had thus formed a binding contract which it breached by awarding the subcontract to a different company.

RULE OF LAW
A contract between a general contractor and a subcontractor is not formed when the general submits a bid on a construction project and lists the subcontractor as the proposed subcontractor for one aspect of the project, as required by the awarding authority.

FACTS: Madsen (D) decided to bid on the general contract to build a wastewater treatment facility. Madsen (D) sent bid invitations to potential subcontractors, including Holman (P). Holman (P) made Madsen (D) a bid which Madsen (D) took over the telephone. The bid was received 2–3 hours before the general bid was due. Holman (P) also submitted bids to six other general contractors that were bidding on the same project. Madsen (D) utilized Holman's (P) bid in preparing its bid for the general contract, as the awarding authority required general contractors to list all proposed subcontractors on their prime bids. Madsen (D) was awarded the contract and awarded a subcontract to a company other than Holman (P). Holman (P) sued Madsen (D), contending that Madsen (D) had accepted Holman's (P) sub-bid on the project and had thus formed a binding contract, which it breached by awarding the subcontract to a different company. Madsen (D) moved for summary judgment and the court granted it, finding that no contract had been made. Holman (P) appealed.

ISSUE: Is a contract between a general contractor and a subcontractor formed when the general submits a bid on a construction project and lists the subcontractor as the proposed subcontractor for one aspect of the project as required by the awarding authority and the general later wins the contract and awards the subcontract to a different subcontractor?

HOLDING AND DECISION: (Yetka, J.) No. A contract between a general contractor and a subcontractor is not formed when the general submits a bid on a construction project and lists the subcontractor as the proposed subcontractor for one aspect of the project as required by the awarding authority. While commentators have urged that a general contractor be bound to a listed subcontractor upon the mere listing or use of the subcontractor's bid in the general bid, the court does not adopt the reasoning. Binding general contractors to subcontractors because a particular bid was listed in the general bid or was utilized in making the bid would remove a considerable degree of needed flexibility. Here, the project was a public project and regulations required that an effort be made to use minority contractors. When Madsen (D) began to put the project together, it was forced to juggle the subcontracts in order to comply with Minnesota regulations. The subcontractor chosen instead of Holman (P) qualified as a minority business and offered to supply materials and supplies not included in Holman's (P) bid. If Madsen (D) was bound to the bids listed in its prime bid, there is a possibility that the contract would have been lost due to failure to comply with regulations. Such an outcome would clearly have been inappropriate. Affirmed.

ANALYSIS

The general contractor makes his bids after gathering and evaluating a number of subcontract calls. Once the general wins the prime contract from the awarding authority, he is bound to his own bid. For the subcontractor to be able to refuse to perform would subject the general to a financial detriment.

Quicknotes

SUBCONTRACTOR A contractor who enters into an agreement with a principal contractor, or other subcontractor, to perform all or a part of a contract.

Phillips v. Moor

Owner of barn (P) v. Hay buyer (D)

Me. Sup. Jud. Ct., 71 Me. 78 (1880).

NATURE OF CASE: Action on assumpsit.

FACT SUMMARY: After seller (P), pursuant to an agreement with buyer (D), in which all the material terms had been settled, tendered to the buyer (D) the hay, the hay was accidentally destroyed.

🏛 RULE OF LAW
When the terms of sale are agreed on and the bargain is struck, and everything that the seller has to do with the goods is complete, the contract of sale becomes absolute without actual payment or delivery, and the property and risk of accident to the goods vest in the buyer.

FACTS: Moor (D), by letter, negotiated with Phillips's (P) guardian for the purchase of a quantity of hay in Phillips's (P) barn. Moor (D), whose men had pressed the hay, agreed to pay at a certain rate if the terms of sale could not be agreed on. In return, Phillips's (P) guardian agreed to accept in writing Moor's (D) price-offer, if satisfactory, upon receipt of it, and if unsatisfactory, to send Moor (D) money for whatever pressing he had done. On June 14th, Moor (D) examined the hay after it had been pressed, and on June 15th mailed a final offer which was not received by Phillips's (P) guardian until later that day. On June 20th, Phillips's (P) guardian wrote Moor (D) that although he was in hopes that Moor (D) might have offered more, "you can take the hay at your offer, and when you get it hauled in, if you can pay $10 I would like to have you do it, if the hay proves good enough for the price." Moor (D) received this letter, said nothing, and three days later the barn burned down and the hay was destroyed. Phillips's (P) guardian sued for the price of the hay, and Moor (D) counterclaimed.

ISSUE: Where all the terms of a sale contract are complete, is the contract binding on the buyer in the absence of actual payment or delivery?

HOLDING AND DECISION: (Barrows, J.) Yes. The risk of accident to the goods vests in the buyer when the bargain is struck, and the seller has done everything with respect to the goods that he could do. At that point, even though there has been no actual payment or delivery, the property is the buyer's. In the present case, all the hay was sold, Moor (D) had determined its quality, the price was fixed, and Moor (D) had been told he could cart the hay away. As for the contention that Phillips's (P) guardian's acceptance of Moor's (D) offer had not been made within a reasonable time, since he arguably had promised an immediate acceptance or rejection, it is without merit.

Even assuming that Moor (D), expecting a prompt acceptance, had the right to retract his offer, he quite simply did not do so. Moor (D) let two days elapse after receiving the letter of acceptance during which time he could have sought to retract his offer. Yet he permitted Phillips's (P) guardian to consider it sold, and, thus, Moor (D) did not act in good faith. Judgment for plaintiff.

▶ ANALYSIS

Where neither party to a contract for the sale of goods is in breach, and the contract does not expressly allocate the risk of loss, U.C.C. § 2-509(3) provides that "the risk of loss passes to the buyer on his receipt of the goods if the seller is a merchant; otherwise, the risk passes to the buyer on tender of delivery."

Quicknotes

ACTION IN ASSUMPSIT Action to recover damages for breach of an oral or written promise to perform or pay pursuant to a contract.

COUNTERCLAIM An independent cause of action brought by a defendant to a lawsuit in order to oppose or deduct from the plaintiff's claim.

MATERIAL TERMS Terms without the existence of which a contract would not have been entered.

REVOCATION The cancellation or withdrawal of some authority conferred or an instrument drafted, such as the withdrawal of a revocable contract offer prior to the offeree's acceptance.

RISK OF LOSS Liability for damage to or loss of property that is the subject matter of a contract for sale.

Vogt v. Madden

Sharecropper (P) v. Landlord (D)

Idaho Ct. App., 110 Idaho 6, 713 P.2d 442 (1985).

NATURE OF CASE: Appeal from judgment for plaintiff for breach of an alleged contract.

FACT SUMMARY: Vogt (P) claimed that Madden (D) had agreed that Vogt (P) could continue to sharecrop on his land.

🏛 RULE OF LAW
Silence and inaction do not constitute an acceptance of an offer.

FACTS: Vogt (P) and Madden (D) discussed continuing a sharecropping agreement. When Madden (D) leased the property to another party for the 1981 crop year, Vogt (P) sued for damages. The jury concluded, despite Madden's (D) testimony to the contrary, that a sharecrop agreement existed between the parties for the year 1981, and awarded damages for breach of contract. Madden (D) appealed, claiming the previous dealings between the parties involved an express oral agreement for sharecropping the farm, and that his failure to reject the offer could not be considered to have been an acceptance.

ISSUE: Do silence and inaction constitute an acceptance of an offer?

HOLDING AND DECISION: (Walters, C.J.) No. Silence and inaction do not constitute an acceptance of an offer. Silence may serve as an acceptance only where the offeree takes the benefit of the offered services knowing they were offered with the expectation of compensation, where the offeror has stated that assent may be manifested by silence, or where, because of previous dealings, it is reasonable that the offeree should notify the offeror if he does not intend to accept. None of these exceptions apply to the facts of this case. Reversed.

▶ ANALYSIS

Vogt (P) alleged that the exception for prior dealings should apply. The court found, however, that the previous dealings were inapposite. The previous dealings only resulted in a contract when both parties had expressly agreed.

■══■

Quicknotes

ACCEPTANCE Assent to the specified terms of an offer, resulting in the formation of a binding agreement.

BREACH OF CONTRACT Unlawful failure by a party to perform its obligations pursuant to contract.

CONTRACT An agreement pursuant to which a party agrees to act, or to forbear from acting, in exchange for performance on the part of the other party.

OFFER A proposed promise to undertake performance of an action, or to refrain from acting, that is to become binding upon acceptance by the offeree.

■══■

Cole-McIntyre-Norfleet Co. v. Holloway

Seller of meal (D) v. Country store owner (P)

Tenn. Sup. Ct., 141 Tenn. 679, 214 S.W. 817, 7 A.L.R. 1683 (1919).

NATURE OF CASE: Action for failure to deliver purchased goods.

FACT SUMMARY: Seller (D) notified buyer (P) 60 days after buyer (P) had, through one of seller's (D) agents, placed an order for meals that it had rejected his order.

RULE OF LAW
Delay in communicating action as to the acceptance of an offer may amount to an acceptance itself.

FACTS: A salesman for Cole-McIntyre-Norfleet Co. (D) stopped at Holloway's (P) country store once a week to take orders for goods. On March 26, 1917, this salesman solicited from Holloway (P) an order for some barrels of meal. The meal could be ordered out by Holloway (P) anytime before July 31. The contract also provided that it was not binding until accepted by Cole (D) at its head office. On May 26, while at the head office, Holloway (P) told Cole (D) to begin shipment of the meal on his contract. Cole (D) informed Holloway (P) that it did not accept his order of March 26. During the period between the time Holloway (P) placed his order and the time he was notified of its rejection, the price of meal had risen sharply. Holloway (P) thereupon sued Cole (D) for failure to deliver the meal as ordered.

ISSUE: May a delay in communicating action as to the acceptance or rejection of an offer amount to an acceptance itself?

HOLDING AND DECISION: (Landsden, C.J.) Yes. Particularly when the subject of a contract, either in its nature or by virtue of conditions of the market, will become unmarketable by delay, delay in notifying the other party of his decision to an acceptance by the offeree will be construed as amounting to an acceptance. To hold otherwise would allow a seller to place his goods on the market, solicit orders, and yet hold the other party to the contract while he reserves time to himself to see if the contract will be profitable. While some cases have held that mere delay in accepting or rejecting an offer cannot make an agreement, these cases have involved either a suit for damages on an executed contract or a situation where the parties had never dealt with one another or were not dealing in due course at the time of the order. In the present case, the delay was some 60 days in length. Cole (D), through its salesman, had weekly opportunities to inform Holloway (P) of its rejection of his order and, of course, could always notify him by mail or wire. Cole's (D) delay was, therefore, unreasonable and it is liable to Holloway (P). Writ and petition to rehear denied.

ANALYSIS

Restatement, Second, Contracts, § 72(1) provides: "Where an offeree fails to reply to an offer, his silence and inaction operates as an acceptance . . . (b) where the offeror has stated or given the offeree reason to understand that assent may be manifested by silence or inaction, and the offeree in remaining silent and inactive intends to accept the offer . . . (c) where, because of previous dealings or otherwise, it is reasonable that the offeree should notify the offeror if he does not intend to accept."

Quicknotes

ACCEPTANCE Assent to the specified terms of an offer, resulting in the formation of a binding agreement.

REJECTION The refusal to accept the terms of an offer.

CHAPTER 13

Implied-in-Law and Implied-in-Fact Contracts; Unilateral Contracts Revised

Quick Reference Rules of Law

Nursing Care Services, Inc. v. Dobos

Nursing service (P) v. Patient (D)

Fla. Dist. Ct. App., 4th Dist., 380 So. 2d 516 (1980).

NATURE OF CASE: Appeal from judgment that disallowed compensation for certain nursing care services.

FACT SUMMARY: Dobos (D) asserted that she was not obligated to pay for medical assistance because she had never asserted to the services.

🏛 **RULE OF LAW**
Where services are rendered by one person for another that are knowingly and voluntarily accepted, the law presumes that such services are given and received in expectation of being paid for, and they will imply a promise to pay what they are reasonably worth.

FACTS: Mary Dobos (D) was admitted to the hospital with an abdominal aneurysm. Her doctor believed her condition was very serious and ordered twenty-four-hour nursing care from Nursing Care Services, Inc. (P). Dobos (D) received two weeks of in-hospital nursing care, forty-eight hours of postrelease care, and two weeks of at-home care. The total bill came to $3,723.90, but Dobos (D) disputed the bill. She claimed that she never signed a written contract nor orally consented to liability for the cost of the nursing services and believed that perhaps Medicare would cover the costs. Nursing Services (P) filed suit to compel payment, but the trial court held that they were only entitled to payment for the forty-eight-hour postrelease care because Dobos's (D) daughter admitted to consenting to it. As to the other services, the court found that there were insufficient communications to let Dobos (D) know that she would be held responsible for the services. Nursing Services (P) appealed.

ISSUE: Where services are rendered by one person for another and are knowingly and voluntarily accepted, will the law presume that such services are given and received in expectation of being paid for and that they imply a promise to pay what they are reasonably worth?

HOLDING AND DECISION: (Hurley, J.) Yes. Where services are rendered by one person for another and are knowingly and voluntarily accepted, the law presumes that such services are given and received in expectation of being paid for and that they will imply a promise to pay what they are reasonably worth. Contracts implied in law are imposed on the grounds of justice and equity. The most common areas in which recovery will be granted are for work performed or services rendered. However, this is subject to the limitation that the person for whose benefit they were rendered either requested the service or knowingly and voluntarily accepted the benefits.

Dobos (D) was gravely ill, and it is unclear whether she understood or intended that compensation be paid. However, there was never any question as to the propriety of the services she received, and it would be unconscionable to deny Nursing Services (P) recovery. Just because Dobos (D) mistakenly believed that Medicare would cover the bills, she is not absolved of liability. Remanded with instructions to enter judgment for Nursing Services (P) in the amount of $3,723.90 plus interest and court costs.

▶ **ANALYSIS**

The court also made reference to the tremendous increase in malpractice lawsuits. In light of this fact, Dobos's (D) doctor and Nursing Services (P) would subject themselves to tremendous liability if they simply stopped rendering services to Dobos (D) because they had not yet received payment. Therefore, for public policy reasons, enforcing an implied-in-law contract is the appropriate remedy.

■■■■

Quicknotes

IMPLIED-AT-LAW CONTRACT Refers to constructive conditions which set forth the order of performance of certain aspects of the agreement in the event that the express terms of the bargain have not specified such conditions.

IMPLIED PROMISE A promise inferred by law from a document as a whole and the circumstances surrounding its implementation.

QUASI-CONTRACT An implied contract created by law to prevent unjust enrichment.

SERVICE CONTRACT A written agreement to perform maintenance and/or repair service on a product for a specified duration.

■■■■

Day v. Caton

Brick wall builder (P) v. Neighbor (D)

Mass. Sup. Jud. Ct., 119 Mass. 513 (1876).

NATURE OF CASE: Action on a contract to recover the value of one-half of a party wall built upon and between adjoining estates.

FACT SUMMARY: Day (P) erected a valuable party wall between his and his neighbor's (D) land, but the neighbor (D), who knew of the construction and said nothing, refused to pay for one-half of the wall's construction.

🏛 RULE OF LAW

If a party voluntarily accepts and avails himself of valuable services rendered for his benefit, when he has the option to accept or reject them, even if there is no distinct proof that they were rendered by his authority or request, a promise to pay for them may be inferred.

FACTS: Day (P) claimed he had an express agreement with the adjacent landowner, Caton (D), that in return for Day's (P) construction of a brick party wall upon and between their adjoining properties, Caton (D) would pay him one-half the value for the wall. When Caton (D) denied that any express agreement had ever been reached concerning payment for the party wall, Day (P) sued to enforce the alleged agreement.

ISSUE: When one stands by in silence and sees valuable services rendered upon his real estate by the erection of a structure, may such silence, coupled with the knowledge on his part that the party rendering the service expects payment in return, be treated as evidence tending to show an agreement to pay for it?

HOLDING AND DECISION: (Devens, J.) Yes. Where one person knows that another is conferring a valuable benefit on him with expectation of payment and allows him to do so without objection, then a jury may infer a promise of payment. Silence may be interpreted as assent in the face of facts which fairly call upon one to speak. The question is one for the jury. Exceptions overruled.

▶ ANALYSIS

Section 72(1)(a) of the Restatement, Second, Contracts is in accord with the present decision. However, where one family member renders services to another family member, the presumption is that the services were made without expectation of payment. This is a rebuttable presumption.

Quicknotes

SERVICE CONTRACT A written agreement to perform maintenance and/or repair service on a product for a specified duration.

UNJUST ENRICHMENT The unlawful acquisition of money or property of another for which both law and equity require restitution to be made.

Bastian v. Gafford

Builder (P) v. Property owner (D)

Idaho Sup. Ct., 98 Idaho 324, 563 P.2d 48 (1977).

NATURE OF CASE: Action to foreclose a material-man's lien.

FACT SUMMARY: Bastian (P) contended there had been an implied-in-fact contract requiring Gafford (D) to pay him for his services in drafting plans for a building to be constructed, but the trial court entered judgment for Gafford (D) on the ground that Gafford (D) had not been unjustly enriched.

🏛 RULE OF LAW
Although unjust enrichment is necessary for recovery based upon quasi-contract, it is irrelevant to a contract implied in fact.

FACTS: Gafford (D) had asked Bastian (P) if he would be interested in constructing an office building on some property Gafford (D) owned in Twin Falls, Idaho. Subsequent to several discussions between the parties, Bastian (P) orally agreed to construct the building and began drafting the plans therefor. They were substantially completed by the time Gafford (D) contacted First Federal to obtain construction financing. First Federal informed him that it required a firm bid by the contractor and would not finance the project on a cost-plus basis. When Bastian (P) indicated he would construct the building only on a cost-plus basis, Gafford (D) proceeded to hire another architect to prepare a second set of plans and another contractor to construct the building using those plans. Bastian (P) then filed a materialman's lien on the property (in the amount of $3,250) for goods and services he had rendered in preparing plans. In bringing an action to foreclose the lien, he alleged that there had been an implied-in-fact contract to compensate him for his services. The trial court entered judgment for Gafford (D) on the ground that he had not been unjustly enriched, having received no benefit from Bastian's (P) plans because he did not use them in constructing the building.

ISSUE: Is unjust enrichment irrelevant to whether one can recover under an implied-in-fact contract?

HOLDING AND DECISION: (Donaldson, J.) Yes. While it is necessary for recovery based upon quasi-contract, unjust enrichment is irrelevant to a contract implied in fact. Thus, for Bastian (P) to recover under the theory that there was an implied-in-fact contract to compensate him for his services, it is not necessary that Gafford (D) either used the plans or derived any benefit from them. It is enough if he requested and received them under circumstances which imply an agreement that he pay for Bastian's (P) service. Reversed and remanded for a new trial.

▶ ANALYSIS

The object in enforcing a contract under the theory that it is implied in fact is to enforce the parties' intention to form a contract. Thus, all the elements required for formation, including offer and acceptance, must be present, whether by implication from the conduct of the parties or otherwise. However, recovery based on quasi-contract is often imposed despite the parties' intent and in the absence of these elements.

■=■

Quicknotes

IMPLIED-AT-LAW CONTRACT Refers to constructive conditions which set forth the order of performance of certain aspects of the agreement in the event that the express terms of the bargain have not specified such conditions.

MATERIALMAN'S LIEN A lien enforceable pursuant to statute in structures and/or improvements constructed in order to secure payment for the value of materials furnished.

QUASI-CONTRACT An implied contract created by law to prevent unjust enrichment.

UNJUST ENRICHMENT The unlawful acquisition of money or property of another for which both law and equity require restitution to be made.

■=■

Wagenseller v. Scottsdale Memorial Hospital

Terminated employee (P) v. Supervisor (D)

Az. Sup. Ct., en banc, 147 Ariz. 370, 710 P.2d 1025 (1985).

NATURE OF CASE: Appeal of summary judgment dismissing action for wrongful termination.

FACT SUMMARY: Wagenseller (P) allegedly was fired for refusing to join her supervisor in committing acts of indecent exposure during a camping trip.

🏛 RULE OF LAW
An employer may terminate an at-will employee for good cause or no cause but not for cause contrary to public policy.

FACTS: Wagenseller (P) worked at Scottsdale Memorial Hospital (D). Her supervisor was Smith (D). According to Wagenseller (P), her relationship with Smith (D) began to deteriorate when, on a camping trip, Wagenseller (P) refused to join in a skit wherein the participants "mooned" the audience. Wagenseller (P) alleged that this led to her termination. She sued Smith (D) and the Hospital (D). The trial court entered summary judgment dismissing the action, holding that, as an at-will employee, Wagenseller (P) could be fired for any reason. The court of appeals affirmed. The Arizona Supreme Court granted review.

ISSUE: May an employer terminate an at-will employee for any cause?

HOLDING AND DECISION: (Feldman, J.) No. An employer may terminate an at-will employee for good cause or no cause but not for cause contrary to public policy. Originally, the doctrine of at-will employment gave employers the right to terminate for any reason. Increasingly, courts have recognized that this area of law involves a balancing of the employer's interest in its ability to manage itself against society's interest in a stable work force and the prevention of acts contrary to public policy. When an employer fires an employee for reasons inimical to public policy, society is hurt. Therefore, the proper balance is to permit an employer to fire for no cause or good cause but not for "bad" cause. As to what defines public policy, the enactments of the legislature are a point of departure. To permit an employer to fire an employee for refusing to break a law would certainly be contrary to the policy expressed in that law. Here, "mooning" arguably constitutes indecent exposure, which is a violation of the criminal code. Wagenseller (P) may not be fired for refusing to violate this law, and, therefore, this action must be tried on the merits. Summary judgment of the trial court affirmed, decision of the court of appeals vacated, and case remanded.

▶ ANALYSIS

The court considered two other theories presented by Wagenseller (P). The first involved her contention that her firing was contrary to procedures outlined in the employment manual, which was part of an implied-in-fact contract. The court agreed that she should be permitted to litigate this. The court rejected, however, her contention that every employment relationship contained an implied-at-law covenant of good faith. This, said the court, would essentially abrogate the at-will doctrine, which it declined to do.

Quicknotes

EMPLOYEE AT WILL An employee who works pursuant to the agreement that either he or his employer may terminate the employment relationship at any time and for any cause.

GOOD CAUSE Sufficient justification for failure to perform an obligation imposed by law.

IMPLIED-AT-LAW CONTRACT Refers to constructive conditions which set forth the order of performance of certain aspects of the agreement in the event that the express terms of the bargain have not specified such conditions.

PUBLIC POLICY Policy administered by the state with respect to the health, safety and morals of its people in accordance with common notions of fairness and decency.

SUMMARY JUDGMENT Judgment rendered by a court in response to a motion made by one of the parties, claiming that the lack of a question of material fact in respect to an issue warrants disposition of the issue without consideration by the jury.

WRONGFUL TERMINATION Unlawful termination of an individual's employment.

Preliminary Negotiations, Indefiniteness, and the Duty to Bargain in Good Faith

Quick Reference Rules of Law

Academy Chicago Publishers v. Cheever

Publisher (P) v. Widow of author (D)

Ill. Sup. Ct., 144 Ill. 2d 24, 161 Ill. Dec. 335, 578 N.E.2d 981 (1991).

NATURE OF CASE: Appeal of an action to determine the validity of a publishing contract.

FACT SUMMARY: Academy Chicago Publishers (P) filed suit against Mary Cheever (D), the widow of author John Cheever, when she changed her mind after agreeing to the publishing of an anthology of her husband's short stories.

RULE OF LAW
In order for a valid contract to be formed, an offer must be so definite as to its material terms, or require such definite terms in the acceptance, that the promises and performances to be rendered by each party are reasonably certain.

FACTS: The widow of author John Cheever, Mary Cheever (D), entered into an agreement with Academy Chicago Publishers (ACP) (P) for the publication of a collection of John Cheever's short stories that had never before been published in a single anthology. However, many terms in the agreement were left unresolved including the date the final anthology would be delivered to ACP (P), the date the collection would published, the price it would sell for, the length of the book, and the stories it would contain. After ACP (P) had procured and delivered some sixty stories to Cheever (D) to review and sent her an advance payment, she informed ACP (P) in writing that she objected to the publication of the book and attempted to return her advance. ACP (P) filed suit seeking a declaratory judgment compelling Cheever's (D) compliance with the agreement. The trial court entered judgment for ACP (P), and the appellate court affirmed.

ISSUE: In order for a valid contract to be formed, must an offer be so definite as to its material terms, or require such definite terms in the acceptance, that the promises and performances to be rendered by each party are reasonably certain?

HOLDING AND DECISION: (Heiple, J.) Yes. In order for a valid contract to be formed, an offer must be so definite as to its material terms, or require such definite terms in the acceptance, that the promises and performances to be rendered by each party are reasonably certain. Although a contract may be enforced even though some contract terms may be missing or unresolved, if the essential terms are so uncertain that there is no basis for deciding whether the agreement has been made or broken, then there is no contract. The pertinent language of the agreement lacks the definite and certain essential terms required for the formation of an enforceable contract and does not provide the court with a means of determining the intent of the parties. It is not the role of the court to decide which stories should be included in the anthology. The trial court incorrectly supplied minimum compliance terms to the agreement to find that there was an enforceable contract. Reversed.

ANALYSIS

Neither the common law nor the U.C.C. will imply terms where the parties were silent after a conscious or overt attempt at agreement. Furthermore, at common law, an attempt to leave a present term open to be agreed upon later leads to the failure of the contract. However, the U.C.C. is more flexible when the parties leave the price open for later determination as long as the other essential elements are clearly defined.

Quicknotes

DECLARATORY JUDGMENT An adjudication by the courts which grants not relief but is binding over the legal status of the parties involved in the dispute.

MATERIAL TERMS OF CONTRACT A fact without the existence of which a contract would not have been entered.

OFFER A proposed promise to undertake performance of an action, or to refrain from acting, that is to become binding upon acceptance by the offeree.

Channel Home Centers v. Grossman

Mall space lessee (P) v. Mall purchaser (D)

795 F.2d 291 (3d Cir. 1986).

NATURE OF CASE: Appeal from judgment finding contract unenforceable.

FACT SUMMARY: After Mr. and Mrs. Grossman (D) began the process of acquiring a mall, they obtained a letter of intent from Channel (P) to be a tenant of the mall after Grossman's (D) acquisition.

🏛 **RULE OF LAW**
Parties may be bound by a letter of intent to negotiate in good faith where both parties manifest an intention to be bound, the terms are sufficiently definite to be enforced, and there is consideration.

FACTS: Grossman (D) wanted to acquire a mall. Grossman (D) acquired Channel's (P) signature on a letter of intent to become a lessee in the mall to help secure financing for Grossman's (D) acquisition. In exchange for Channel's (P) signing the letter, Grossman (D) signed a letter of intent promising to withdraw Channel's (P) proposed store from the rental market and to negotiate a lease with Channel (P). However, after Channel (P) expended over $25,000 in connection with the proposed lease agreement, Grossman (D) rented the store to another tenant. Channel (P) sued Grossman (D), contending that Grossman's (D) conduct violated its letter of intent and constituted a breach of contract. The court ruled that Grossman's (D) letter of intent was unenforceable for lack of consideration. Channel (P) appealed.

ISSUE: May parties be bound by a letter of intent to negotiate in good faith where both parties manifest an intention to be bound, the terms are sufficiently definite to be enforced, and there is consideration?

HOLDING AND DECISION: (Becker, J.) Yes. Parties may be bound by a letter of intent to negotiate in good faith where both parties manifest an intention to be bound, the terms are sufficiently definite to be enforced, and there is consideration. Here, the letter of intent provided that to induce Channel (P) to proceed with the leasing of the store, Grossman (D) would withdraw the store from the rental market. Both parties intended the promise to be binding. Channel (P) made extensive preparations to perform the terms of the lease, obtaining measurements for renovations and developing marketing plans. Grossman's (D) promise to withdraw the store from the rental market was sufficiently definite to be specifically enforced. Sufficient consideration flowed to each party from the other's performance. Channel's (P) execution of the letter was valid consideration for Grossman's (D) return promise to negotiate in good faith. Reversed and remanded.

▶ **ANALYSIS**

In *A/S Apothekernes Laboratorium for Specialpraeparater v. I.M.C. Chemical Group, Inc.*, 873 F.2d 155 (7th Cir. 1989), the court disagreed with the court's holding in the principal case. The court stated, "The purpose and function of a preliminary letter of intent is not to bind the parties to their ultimate contractual objective. Instead, it is only to provide the initial framework from which the parties might later negotiate a final agreement, if the deal works out."

Quicknotes

CONSIDERATION Value given by one party in exchange for performance, or a promise to perform, by another party.

LETTER OF INTENT A written draft embodying the proposed intent of the parties and which is not enforceable or binding.

MUTUALITY OF OBLIGATION Requires that both parties to a contract are bound or else neither is bound.

Teachers Insurance and Annuity Association of America v. Tribune Co.

Lending institution (P) v. Borrower (D)

670 F. Supp. 491 (S.D.N.Y. 1987).

NATURE OF CASE: Contract dispute concerning the nature of a commitment letter.

FACT SUMMARY: Tribune Co. failed to negotiate after receiving a commitment letter from Teachers Insurance and Annuity Association of America (TIAA).

RULE OF LAW
A binding preliminary commitment obligates both sides to negotiate in good faith toward the conclusion of a final agreement.

FACTS: To raise cash for the operation of its newspaper and other purposes, the Tribune Co. (D) decided to sell the News Building. Thus, the Tribune Co. arranged to sell the News Building to LaSalle Partners in a complex three-party transaction whereby LaSalle Partners would pay for the News Building by giving the Tribune Co. a mortgage note assured by a mortgage and the Tribune Co. would borrow from a lending institution an amount of money equal to the mortgage note. The complex nature of the transaction was driven by tax motives and accounting. By setting off its debt to the lending institution against the mortgage note, the Tribune Co. hoped to eliminate both its debt and the mortgage from its balance sheet. Of six lending institutions solicited for the loan, only TIAA issued a commitment letter within the limited time requested by the Tribune Co. Attached to the commitment letter was a two–page term sheet covering all the pertinent economic terms of the transaction. The Tribune Co. later closed the sale of the building to LaSalle Partners, but due to a drop in interest rates and Tribune Co.'s concerns that TIAA might not let it use offset accounting, the Tribune Co. failed to negotiate further with TIAA. As a result, TIAA brought the present suit.

ISSUE: Did any obligations arise out of TIAA's commitment letter?

HOLDING AND DECISION: (Leval, J.) Yes. The commitment letter constituted a binding preliminary agreement obligating the Tribune Company to negotiate the open issues in good faith. The exchange of letters between the Tribune Company and TIAA constituting the commitment evidenced an intent that the commitment letter be binding. The open issues in the commitment letter included rights of approval and promises to prepare and execute certain documents in a manner satisfactory to the opposing party. Neither of these open issues serves to nullify or override the earlier acknowledgement by both parties that the commitment letter be treated as a binding agreement. Further, the two–page term sheet covered all the important economic terms of the transaction. All that remained open for negotiation were relatively minor terms. The fact that these minor terms were left open by the commitment letter does not compel the conclusion that the parties did not intend to be bound. The existence of open issues and the failure of the parties to satisfy the condition of execution is chargeable to Tribune Co. Judgment granted to the plaintiff

ANALYSIS

Contractual liability arises from consent to be bound or the manifestation of consent. Thus, determining assent in preliminary negotiations such as the commitment letter at issue in *Teachers Insurance and Annuity Association of America v. Tribune Co.* is of utmost importance to the question of breach.

Quicknotes

BREACH The violation of an obligation imposed pursuant to contract or law, by acting or failing to act.

Hoffman v. Red Owl Stores, Inc.

Grocery store purchaser (P) v. Supermarket company (D)

Wis. Sup. Ct., 26 Wis. 2d 683, 133 N.W.2d 267 (1965).

NATURE OF CASE: Appeal from award of damages.

FACT SUMMARY: Hoffman (P) was assured by an agent of the Red Owl Stores, Inc. (D) that if he took certain steps he would obtain a supermarket franchise, but, after taking these steps at great expense, Hoffman (P) did not receive the franchise.

RULE OF LAW
Under the doctrine of promissory estoppel, as stated in § 90 of Restatement 1, Contracts, "A promise which the promisor should reasonably expect to induce action or forbearance of a definite and substantial character on the part of the promisee and which does induce such action or forbearance is binding if injustice can be avoided only by enforcement of the promise."

FACTS: An agent of the Red Owl Stores, Inc. (D) promised Hoffman (P) that Red Owl (D) would establish him in a supermarket store for the sum of $18,000. In reliance upon this promise, and upon the recommendations of the agent, Hoffman (P) purchased a grocery store to gain experience. Thereafter, upon further recommendations of the agent, Hoffman (P) sold his grocery store fixtures and inventory to Red Owl (D), before the profitable summer months started, and paid $1,000 for an option on land for building a franchise outlet. After moving near this outlet, Hoffman (P) was told that he needed $24,100 for the promised franchise. After Hoffman (P) acquired this amount, most of it through a loan from his father-in-law, he was told that he needed an additional $2,000 for the deal to go through. Finally, after acquiring the additional $2,000, Hoffman (P) was told he would be established in his new store as soon as he sold a bakery store which he owned. After doing this, though, Red Owl (D) told Hoffman (P) that in order to enhance his credit rating he must procure from his father-in-law a statement that the funds acquired from him were an outright gift and not a loan. In response, Hoffman (P) sued for damages to recover income which he lost and expenses which he incurred in reliance upon the promises of Red Owl (D). After an award of damages for Hoffman (P), Red Owl (D) appealed.

ISSUE: When a promisor makes a promise which he should reasonably expect to induce action on the part of the promisee and which does induce such action, can he be estopped from denying the enforceability of that promise?

HOLDING AND DECISION: (Judge not listed in casebook excerpt.) Yes. Under the doctrine of promissory estoppel, as stated in § 90 of Restatement 1, Contracts,

"A promise which the promisor should reasonably expect to induce action or forbearance of a definite and substantial character on the part of the promisee and which does induce such action or forbearance is binding if injustice can be avoided only by enforcement of the promise." Of course, such damages as are necessary to prevent injustice can be awarded under the doctrine of promissory estoppel instead of specific performance. Furthermore, an action based upon promissory estoppel is not equivalent to a breach of contract action, and, therefore, the promise does not have to "embrace all essential details of a proposed transaction between promisor and promisee so as to be the equivalent of an offer that would result in a binding contract between the parties if the promisee were to accept the same." Here, therefore, it is not important that no final construction plans, etc., were ever completed. It is instead important that Hoffman (P) substantially relied to his detriment on Red Owl's (D) promise and that Red Owl (D) should have reasonably foreseen such reliance. Therefore, Hoffman (P) is entitled to those damages which are necessary to prevent injustice. He is entitled to losses resulting from selling his bakery, from purchasing the option on land for a franchise, from moving near the franchise outlet, and from selling his grocery store fixtures and inventory. Hoffman's (P) reasonable damages from selling his grocery store fixtures and inventory, though, do not include any future lost profits, since he only purchased the grocery store temporarily to gain experience (i.e., he is only entitled to any loss measured by the difference between the sales price and fair market value). Affirmed.

▶ ANALYSIS

This case illustrates the doctrine of promissory estoppel. At common law, such doctrine afforded protection to any party threatened with "substantial economic loss" after taking "reasonable steps in foreseeable reliance upon a gratuitous promise." The Restatement Second, though, does not require that the promise be gratuitous or that the reliance be "substantial." It only requires reasonable, foreseeable reliance upon any promise. Note that an action under the doctrine of promissory estoppel is not equivalent to an action for breach of contract, and, therefore, no consideration is necessary to make the promise binding. Furthermore, the promise upon which a person reasonably relies will be enforced specifically or by damages whenever the court decides that the interests of justice would be served by such enforcement.

Continued on next page.

Quicknotes

PROMISSORY ESTOPPEL A promise that is enforceable if the promisor should reasonably expect that it will induce action or forbearance on the part of the promisee, and does in fact cause such action or forbearance, and it is the only means of avoiding injustice.

RELIANCE Dependence on a fact that causes a party to act or refrain from acting.

SPECIFIC PERFORMANCE An equitable remedy whereby the court requires the parties to perform their obligations pursuant to a contract.

The Parol Evidence Rule and the Interpretation of Written Contracts

Quick Reference Rules of Law

Mitchill v. Lath

Property buyer (P) v. Seller (D)

N.Y. Ct. App., 247 N.Y. 377, 160 N.E. 646, 68 A.L.R. 239 (1928).

NATURE OF CASE: Action for specific performance.

FACT SUMMARY: Mitchill (P) bought some property from Lath (D) pursuant to a full and complete written sales contract. She sought to compel Lath (D) to perform on his parol agreement to remove an icehouse on neighboring property.

🏛 RULE OF LAW
An oral agreement is permitted to vary a written contract only if it is collateral in form, does not contradict express or implied conditions of the written contract, and consists of terms which the parties could not reasonably have been expected to include in the written contract.

FACTS: Mitchill (P), through a contract executed by her husband, bought some property from Lath (D). The written contract of sale was completely integrated. Lath (D) then made an oral agreement with Mitchill (P) that in consideration of her purchase of the property, he would remove an icehouse which he maintained on neighboring property and which Mitchill (P) found objectionable.

ISSUE: Will an oral agreement which is not collateral, which contradicts express or implied conditions of a written contract, or which consists of terms which the parties could reasonably have been expected to embody in the original writing be permitted to vary a written contract?

HOLDING AND DECISION: (Andrews, J.) No. An oral agreement is permitted to vary a written contract only if it is collateral in form, does not contradict express or implied conditions of the written contract, and consists of terms which the parties could not reasonably have been expected to include in the original writing. Here, the parol agreement does not meet these requirements since it is closely related to the subject of the written contract. It could also be said to contradict the conditions of the written contract. The fact that the written contract was made with her husband while the oral agreement was made with Mitchill (P) herself is not determinative since the deed was given to her and it is evidence that she, and not her husband, was the principal in the transaction. Reversed and the complaint dismissed.

DISSENT: (Lehman, J.) Even when it's complete, a written contract only covers a limited field. This contract was for the conveyance of a piece of property, and would not cover a prior agreement involving obligations related to another piece of property. While the majority is correct that three conditions must exist before an oral agreement may be proven to increase the obligation shown by the

written agreement, in this case the oral agreement meets the third condition, contrary to what the majority holds. The question that must be answered, and which the majority did not answer, is whether or not an agreement to remove the icehouse from one parcel as an inducement for the purchase of another would be embodied in the contract for the conveyance of the other parcel. The promise by the defendants to remove the icehouse from other land was not connected to their obligation to convey, except that one agreement would not have been made unless the other was also made. Though complete on its face with regard to the conveyance, the contract does not show that it was intended to embody negotiations or agreements associated with the removal of the icehouse from another parcel, which is a matter only loosely bound to the conveyance.

▶ ANALYSIS

U.C.C. § 2-202 provides, "Terms with respect to which the writings of the parties agree or which are set forth in a writing intended by the parties as a final expression of their agreement may not be contradicted by evidence of any prior agreement or of a contemporaneous oral agreement but may be explained or supplemented by course of dealing or usage of trade, or by course of performance, and by evidence of consistent additional terms unless the court finds the writing to have been intended as a complete and exclusive statement of the terms of the agreement." The section, according to the official commentator, conclusively rejects any assumption that, because a writing is final in some respects, it is to be interpreted as including all matters agreed upon by the parties.

Quicknotes

BATTLE OF THE FORMS Refers to the exchange of forms, pursuant to a contract for the sale of goods, between a buyer and seller.

COLLATERAL AGREEMENT An agreement that is made prior to or contemporaneous with a written agreement, which is admissible in evidence as long as it is consistent with the written document.

PAROL EVIDENCE RULE Doctrine precluding parties to an agreement from introducing evidence of prior or contemporaneous agreements in order to repudiate or alter the terms of a written contract.

SPECIFIC PERFORMANCE An equitable remedy whereby the court requires the parties to perform their obligations pursuant to a contract.

Masterson v. Sine

Ranch grantees (P) v. Ranch owners (D)

Cal. Sup. Ct., 68 Cal. 2d 222, 65 Cal. Rptr. 545, 436 P.2d 561 (1968).

NATURE OF CASE: Action for declaratory relief to establish a right to enforce an option.

FACT SUMMARY: Dallas and Rebecca Masterson (D) owned a ranch as tenants in common and conveyed it to Medora and Lu Sine (P) by grant deed reserving an option to purchase the ranch back within 10 years—by February 25, 1968—or the same consideration as was paid for the ranch plus the depreciation value of any improvements the Sines (P) might have added. When Dallas went bankrupt, Rebecca (D) sought to establish her right to enforce the option.

🏛 RULE OF LAW
Evidence of oral collateral agreements should be excluded only when the fact finder (the court) is likely to be misled.

FACTS: Dallas Masterson and his wife, Rebecca Masterson (D), owned a ranch as tenants in common. On February 25, 1958, they conveyed by grant deed the ranch to his sister and her husband, Medora and Lu Sine (P), reserving an option to repurchase the ranch within 10 years from the date of conveyance for the consideration paid by the Sines (P) plus depreciation value of any improvements as allowed under U.S income tax regulations. Dallas Masterson went bankrupt. Rebecca Masterson (D) and Dallas Masterson's trustee in bankruptcy (D) sought to establish their right to enforce the option. Parol evidence was admitted to clarify the meaning of the option.

ISSUE: Was the option provision too uncertain to be enforced so that parol evidence should not have been admitted as to clarify its meaning?

HOLDING AND DECISION: (Traynor, C.J.) No. Parol evidence was necessary to clarify the terms of the option which expressly stated an intention to reserve an option. However, it was error of the trial court to exclude extrinsic evidence that the option was personal to the grantors and, therefore, nonassignable. When a written contract is a complete and full embodiment of the agreement's terms, parol evidence cannot be used to add to or vary terms. When only part of the agreement is complete, the same rule applies to that part, but parol evidence can be shown to prove elements as to the remainder not reduced to writing. It must be determined whether the parties intended the written agreement to be the complete and full embodiment of the terms. However, this rule has not been applied consistently. A parol evidence rule must take into consideration the problems of human memory being less accurate than a writing and the possibility of fraud. Accordingly, evidence of oral collateral agreements should

be excluded only when the fact finder is likely to be misled. Under Restatement 1st, § 240(1)(b), parol evidence of a collateral agreement is permitted if such an agreement is shown as might naturally be made as a separate agreement by parties situated as were parties to the written contract. Or from an opposite standpoint which is even more liberal, if the additional terms are such that, if agreed upon, they would certainly have been included, then parol evidence is not admissible, U.C.C. § 2-202. Here, the option clause did not explicitly provide that it contained the complete agreement. The deed does not speak to assignability. Nothing showed that the parties had any warnings as to the disadvantages of failing to put the whole agreement in the deed. Therefore, it appeared that collateral agreements might naturally be made as a separate agreement. The judgment must be reversed to permit parol evidence on the issue of assignability of the option.

DISSENT: (Burke, J.) Parol evidence should not be permitted to contradict the terms of this written agreement. To hold that parol evidence is admissible where the collateral oral agreement might naturally have been made as a separate agreement by the parties under the particular agreement is too uncertain and confusing. The holding permits a bankrupt to deceive his creditors by testifying to nonassignability which he failed to state in the writing so as to keep the ranch out of the hands of the trustee. This appears to be evidence which would mislead the fact finder.

▶ ANALYSIS

In this case, California opts for the more liberal approach to the parol evidence rule as supported by Professor Corbin. Here, the California court under Mr. Chief Justice Traynor found that when any rule of law is riddled with exceptions and decisions about it are difficult to reconcile, litigation is stimulated rather than reduced. The tendency toward liberalizing the admission of parol evidence is based upon the trial court judge's having control over the testimony and his determining when it would appear that proffered testimony is perjured. The more liberal rule is supposed to remove the problems found in the restrictive rule favored by Williston which finds the intent of the parties in their writing only. In the extreme, this would disallow oral testimony as to intent whenever a writing exists thereby possibly defeating the true intent of the parties.

■=■

Continued on next page.

Quicknotes

ASSIGNMENT OF RIGHTS The transfer of a party's interest or rights in property.

COLLATERAL AGREEMENT An agreement that is made prior to or contemporaneous with a written agreement, which is admissible in evidence as long as it is consistent with the written document.

PAROL EVIDENCE RULE Doctrine precluding parties to an agreement from introducing evidence of prior or contemporaneous agreements in order to repudiate or alter the terms of a written contract.

TENANTS IN COMMON Two or more people holding an interest in property, each with equal right to its use and possession; interests may be partitioned, sold, conveyed, or devised.

U.C.C. § 2-202 Provides that terms of a writing cannot be contradicted by evidence of prior or contemporaneous oral agreements.

Hunt Foods and Industries, Inc. v. Doliner

Food company (P) v. Prospective purchaser of assets (D)

N.Y. App. Div., 1st Dept., 26 A.D.2d 41, 270 N.Y.S.2d 937 (1966).

NATURE OF CASE: Appeal of a motion for summary judgment for specific performance.

FACT SUMMARY: Doliner (D) claimed he had an oral understanding that Hunt's (P) option was only to be exercised if he solicited an outside offer for a higher price, but when negotiations broke down, Hunt (P) sought to exercise the option.

🏛 RULE OF LAW
The parol evidence rule bars the introduction of evidence of a prior or contemporaneous oral agreement that contradicts a written memorandum intended as the final agreement between the parties.

FACTS: Hunt Foods and Industries (P) negotiated with Doliner (D) to buy certain assets, and when negotiations recessed because of failure to agree to certain terms, Hunt Foods and Industries, Inc. (P) demanded and obtained an unconditional written option to purchase at a fixed price. Doliner (D) claimed he obtained an oral understanding that the option was to be used only in the event that he solicited an outside offer for a higher price. When negotiations broke down for failure to reach an agreement, the written option was exercised. Doliner (D) refused tender. Hunt Foods and Industries, Inc. (P) sued for specific performance.

ISSUE: Does the parol evidence rule bar the introduction of all prior or contemporaneous oral agreements where there is a written memorandum intended as the final agreement between the parties?

HOLDING AND DECISION: (Steuer, J.) Yes. Though terms in a written memorandum intended as a final agreement may not be contradicted by evidence of any prior or contemporaneous oral agreement, the oral agreement here, though clearly additional, must be "inconsistent" with the written memoranda to be subject to the prohibitions of the parol evidence rule. "Inconsistent" means that it negates a term of the writing. It must negate the writing factually, making the coexistence of the written and oral agreements impossible—not just implausible. Motion for summary judgment denied and judgment reversed.

▶ ANALYSIS

The rule of this case was based on U.C.C. § 2-202. The official comment to that section notes three points which are "definitely" rejected: (1) that the premise that construction of the language should be by rules of law rather than by the commercial context in which it was used; (2) that it should be assumed that because there is a writing which is final on some matters, it includes all matters agreed upon; and (3) that the court must find the language ambiguous before admitting oral evidence of trade usage (U.C.C. § 1-205) or course of performance (U.C.C. § 2-208).

■═■

Quicknotes

FOUR CORNERS The express terms of a written document.

OPTION A contract pursuant to which a seller agrees that property will be available for the buyer to purchase at a specified price and within a certain time period.

PAROL EVIDENCE RULE Doctrine precluding parties to an agreement from introducing evidence of prior or contemporaneous agreements in order to repudiate or alter the terms of a written contract.

SPECIFIC PERFORMANCE An equitable remedy whereby the court requires the parties to perform their obligations pursuant to a contract.

SUMMARY JUDGMENT Judgment rendered by a court in response to a motion by one of the parties, claiming that the lack of a question of material fact in respect to an issue warrants disposition of the issue without consideration by the jury.

U.C.C. § 2-202 Provides that terms of a writing cannot be contradicted by evidence of prior or contemporaneous oral agreements.

■═■

Steuart v. McChesney

Owner of property (P) v. Prospective purchaser (D)

Pa. Sup. Ct., 498 Pa. 45, 444 A.2d 659 (1982).

NATURE OF CASE: Appeal from judgment denying specific performance.

FACT SUMMARY: Mr. and Mrs. Steuart (D) executed an agreement granting to Mr. and Mrs. McChesney (P) a right of first refusal to purchase Steuart's (D) property.

🏛 RULE OF LAW
If the words of a contract are clear and unambiguous, the intent is to be discovered only from the express language of the agreement.

FACTS: Steuart (D) owned a parcel of real property. Steuart (D) and McChesney (P) executed an agreement which granted McChesney (P) a right of first refusal over Steuart's (D) property. The right of first refusal stated that: "the ... McChesneys (P) may exercise the right to purchase said premises at a value equivalent to market value of the premises according to the assessment rolls as maintained by the county ... the date of valuation shall be that the ... Steuarts (D) notify ... McChesneys (P), in writing of the existence of a Bona Fide Purchaser." Nine years after execution of the agreement, Steuart (D) received offers of $30,000 and $35,000 to purchase their property. Steuart (D) notified McChesney (P) of the offers, and McChesney (P) exercised their right of first refusal by tendering $7,820, the assessed value of the property, to Steuart (D). After Steuart (D) refused to tender the property, McChesney (P) sued Steuart (D) for specific performance. The trial court held that the assessed value was intended merely to serve as a mutual protective minimum price for the premises rather than the controlling price and granted McChesney (P) a right to purchase the property for $35,000, the third party offer. On appeal, the superior court reversed, holding that the plain language of the agreement required that assessed market value, alone, should determine the exercise price. Steuart (D) appealed.

ISSUE: If the words of a contract are clear and unambiguous, must the intent be discovered only from the express language of the agreement?

HOLDING AND DECISION: (Flaherty, J.) Yes. If the words of a contract are clear and unambiguous, the intent is to be discovered only from the express language of the agreement. Here, the language of the Right of First Refusal, viewed in context, is express and clear and is therefore not in need of interpretation by reference to extrinsic evidence. The plain meaning is that if during Steuart's (D) lifetime, a bona fide purchaser for value makes an offer, McChesney (P) may purchase the property

at a price equivalent to the assessed value on the county assessment rolls. Affirmed.

DISSENT: (Roberts, J.) Here, where Steuart (D) received bona fide offers of $30,000 and $35,000 for the property, there can be no doubt that the actual value of Steuart's (D) property was at least four times greater than the value according to the outdated assessment on the county tax rolls. It would be the height of unfairness to grant McChesney's (P) decree for specific performance at a price based on a nine-year-old valuation.

▶ ANALYSIS

In *Amoco Production Co. v. Western Slope Gas Co.,* 754 F.2d 303 (10th Cir. 1985), the court stated that: "Under the U.C.C., the lack of facial ambiguity in the contract language is basically irrelevant to whether extrinsic evidence ought to be considered by the court as an initial matter. A judge first must consider the circumstances and purposes surrounding the making of the writing before he or she can determine whether or not it is in fact ambiguous."

Quicknotes

BONA FIDE PURCHASER A party who purchases property in good faith and for valuable consideration without notice of a defect in title.

EXTRINSIC EVIDENCE Evidence that is not contained within the text of a document or contract but which is derived from the parties' statements or the circumstances under which the agreement was made.

SPECIFIC PERFORMANCE An equitable remedy whereby the court requires the parties to perform their obligations pursuant to a contract.

RIGHT OF FIRST REFUSAL Allows one to meet the terms of a proposed contract before it is executed.

Pacific Gas & Electric Co. v. G.W. Thomas Drayage & Rigging Co.

Steam turbine owner (P) v. Repair company (D)

Cal. Sup. Ct., 69 Cal. 2d 33, 69 Cal. Rptr. 561, 442 P.2d 641 (1968).

NATURE OF CASE: Action for damages for breach of a contract.

FACT SUMMARY: Thomas (D) contracted to repair Pacific's (P) steam turbine and to perform work at its own risk and expense and to indemnify Pacific (P) against all loss and damage. Thomas (D) also agreed to procure not less than $50,000 insurance to cover liability for injury to property. When the turbine rotor was damaged, Pacific (P) claimed it was covered under that policy, while Thomas (D) said it was only to cover injury to property of third persons.

🏛 **RULE OF LAW**
The test of admissibility of extrinsic evidence to explain the meaning of a written instrument is not whether it appears to the court to be plain and unambiguous on its face but whether the offered evidence is relevant to prove a meaning to which the language of the instrument is reasonably susceptible.

FACTS: Thomas (D) contracted to replace the upper metal cover on Pacific's (P) steam turbine and agreed to perform all work "at [its] own risk and expense" and to "indemnify" Pacific (P) against all loss, damage, expense, and liability connected with performance of the contract. Thomas (D) agreed to obtain not less than $50,000 insurance to cover liability for injury to property. Pacific (P) was to be an additional named insured, but the policy was to contain a cross-liability clause extending the coverage of Pacific's (P) property. During the work, the cover fell, damaging the exposed rotor in the amount of $25,144.51. Thomas (D), during trial, offered to prove that its conduct under similar contracts entered into with Pacific (P) showed that the indemnity clause was meant to cover injury to third person's property only, not to Pacific's (P).

ISSUE: Was Thomas's (D) offered evidence relevant to proving a meaning to which the language of the instrument was susceptible?

HOLDING AND DECISION: (Traynor, C.J.) Yes. While the trial court admitted that the contract was "the classic language for a third party indemnity provision" it held that the plain language of the contract would give a meaning covering Pacific's (P) damage. However, this admission by the court clearly shows the ambiguous nature of the agreement and the need for extrinsic evidence in order to clarify the intentions of the parties. Extrinsic evidence for the purpose of showing the intent of the parties could be excluded only when it is feasible to determine the meaning of the words from the instrument alone.

Rational interpretation requires at least an initial consideration of all credible evidence to prove the intention of the parties. Reversed.

▶ **ANALYSIS**

This case strongly disapproves of the "plain meaning rule" which states that if a writing appears clear and unambiguous on its face, the meaning must be determined from the "four corners" of the writing without considering any extrinsic evidence at all. The trial court applied this rule. However, the rule, while generally accepted but widely condemned, would exclude evidence of trade usage, prior dealings of the parties, and even circumstances surrounding the creation of the agreement. U.C.C. § 2-202 expressly throws out the plain meaning rule. Instead, it allows use of evidence of a course of performance or dealing to explain the writing "unless carefully negated." Here, Chief Justice Traynor greatly expanded the admission of extrinsic evidence to show intent. When he says it should not be admitted only when it is feasible "to determine the meaning the parties gave to the words from the instrument alone," he is saying in all practicality that extrinsic evidence to show intent should be admissible in just about any case and that rarely will the instrument be so exact as to clearly show intent.

Quicknotes

EXTRINSIC EVIDENCE Evidence that is not contained within the text of a document or contract but which is derived from the parties' statements or the circumstances under which the agreement was made.

FOUR CORNERS The express terms of a written document.

INDEMNIFICATION Reimbursement for losses sustained or security against anticipated loss or damages.

PLAIN LANGUAGE RULE Rule that the meaning of a document should be construed in accordance with the ordinary meaning of the language used.

TRADE USAGE A course of dealing or practice commonly used in a particular trade.

U.C.C. § 2-202 Provides that terms of a writing cannot be contradicted by evidence of prior or contemporaneous oral agreements.

Nanakuli Paving and Rock Co. v. Shell Oil Co.

Asphalt buyer (P) v. Oil Company (D)

664 F.2d 772 (9th Cir. 1981).

NATURE OF CASE: Appeal from judgment notwithstanding verdict in breach of contract action.

FACT SUMMARY: Shell (D) refused to give Nanakuli (P) price protection for asphalt Shell (D) sold Nanakuli (P) for Nanakuli's (P) paving construction business.

RULE OF LAW
An agreement means the bargain of the parties in fact as found in the contract language or by implication from other circumstances including course of dealing, trade usage, or course of performance.

FACTS: Nanakuli (P) and Shell (D) entered into a five-year contract under which Nanakuli (P) agreed to buy asphalt from Shell (D) for use in Nanakuli's (P) paving construction business. The contract gave Nanakuli (P) a reliable supplier so that it could compete on equal terms with its competitors and gave Shell (D) the potential to drastically expand its asphalt sales in Hawaii. The contract provided that the asphalt would be sold to Nanakuli (P) at Shell's (D) price for the asphalt at the time of its delivery for sale to all buyers. Nanakuli (P) sued Shell (D) for breach of contract arguing that notwithstanding this price term, Nanakuli (P) was entitled to price protection under both trade usage and course of performance doctrines and that Shell (D) had breached its agreement by failing to give such protection. The jury awarded Nanakuli (P) damages. On appeal, the district court granted Shell's (D) motion for judgment notwithstanding the verdict. Nanakuli (P) appealed.

ISSUE: Does an agreement mean the bargain of the parties in fact as found in the contract language or by implication from other circumstances including course of dealing, trade usage, or course of performance?

HOLDING AND DECISION: (Hoffman, J.) Yes. An agreement means the bargain of the parties in fact as found in the contract language or by implication from other circumstances including course of dealing, trade usage, or course of performance. The most important of these additional criteria is the actual performance of the parties. Here, Shell (D) afforded Nanakuli (P) protection on two separate occasions prior to the alleged breach. As far as trade usage evidence is concerned, the evidence is overwhelming that all suppliers to the asphalt paving trade protected customers under the same type of circumstances that were present here. Reversed and remanded with instructions to enter final judgment.

CONCURRENCE: (Kennedy, J.) The opinion should not be interpreted as permitting juries to import price protection from a concept of good faith that is not based on well-established custom and usage or other objective standards of which the parties had clear notice.

ANALYSIS

One commentator has stated that: "Some of the Article Two provisions on the formation of contracts have not only radically altered sales law but have influenced the . . . Restatement (Second) of Contracts as well. . . . Section 1-201 (11) defines 'contract' as the 'total legal obligation which results from the parties' agreement,' and § 1-201(3) defines 'agreement' to mean 'the bargain of the parties in fact as found in their language or by implication from other circumstances including course of dealing or usage of trade or course of performance as provided in the Act.'" (J. J. White & R. Summers, Uniform Commercial Code 27-28 (3d practitioner's ed. 1988)).

Quicknotes

AMBIGUOUS TERMS Contract terms that are capable of more than one interpretation.

COURSE OF DEALING Previous conduct between two parties to a contact which may be relied upon to interpret their actions.

COURSE OF PERFORMANCE Previous conduct between two parties to a contact which may be relied upon to interpret their actions.

JUDGMENT N.O.V. A judgment entered by the trial judge reversing a jury verdict if the jury's determination has no basis in law or fact.

TRADE USAGE A course of dealing or practice commonly used in a particular trade.

Contract Formation in a Form-Contract Setting

Quick Reference Rules of Law

Gardner Zemke Co. v. Dunham Bush, Inc.

DOE contractor (P) v. Air-conditioning supplier (D)

N.M. Sup. Ct., 115 N.M. 260, 850 P.2d 319 (1993).

NATURE OF CASE: Appeal of an action for breach of contract based on the rules governing form contracts.

FACT SUMMARY: Gardner Zemke (P) filed suit against Dunham Bush (D) for breach of contract alleging that a warranty disclaimer on the back of an acknowledgment form is not binding by silence.

🏛 RULE OF LAW
Where clauses on confirming forms sent by both parties conflict, each party must be assumed to object to a clause of the other, and the contract then consists of the terms originally expressly agreed to and terms on which the confirmations agree.

FACTS: Gardner Zemke (P), as the general contractor on a Department of Energy (DOE) project, ordered air-conditioning equipment from Dunham Bush (D) to be used in connection with the project. The order contained a one-year manufacturer's warranty provision and the requirement that the units comply with the specifications attached to the order. Dunham Bush (D) responded with its preprinted acknowledgment form containing extensive warranty disclaimers and a provision stating that silence was deemed acquiescence to the terms of the agreement. Neither party addressed the discrepancies in the forms exchanged and proceeded with the transaction. Several months after the units were installed, the DOE notified Gardner Zemke (P) of problems with two of the units, and they in turn contacted Dunham Bush (D) for on-site warranty repairs. Dunham Bush (D) informed Gardner Zemke (P) that prior to service they would need a purchase order from the DOE as payment for the repair services. Gardner Zemke (P) rejected the proposal asserting that DOE had a warranty to cover the repairs, and DOE eventually hired an independent contractor at a cost of $24,245. DOE then withheld $20,000 from its contract with Gardner Zemke (P), and Gardner Zemke (P) filed suit against Dunham Bush (D) for breach of contract. The trial court found that the acknowledgment form sent by Dunham Bush (D) was a counteroffer that Gardner Zemke (P) accepted by silence, so they were therefore not covered by warranty or entitled to damages. On appeal, Gardner Zemke (P) argued that the trial court erred in finding that the acknowledgment was a counteroffer.

ISSUE: Where clauses on confirming forms sent by both parties conflict, must each party be assumed to object to a clause of the other conflicting with one on the confirmation sent by himself?

HOLDING AND DECISION: (Franchini, J.) Yes. Where clauses on confirming forms sent by both parties conflict, each party must be assumed to object to a clause of the other and the contract then consists of the terms originally expressly agreed to and terms on which the confirmations agree. Furthermore, whether an acceptance is made expressly conditional on assent to different or additional terms is dependent on the commercial context of the transaction. This requires consideration of both parties' activities during the making of the bargain and, when available, relevant evidence of the course of performance. These are questions of fact to be determined on remand. Remanded.

▶ ANALYSIS

U.C.C. § 2-207, which encompasses the rule of this case, has been one of the most controversial provisions and derivations from the common law. The common law requires a mirror-image acceptance, and anything else is deemed to be a rejection terminating the outstanding offer. While the U.C.C. aimed to temper that harsh result and create a bargain where the common law would not, this attempt has often led to more questions than answers.

■━■

Quicknotes

BATTLE OF THE FORMS Refers to the exchange of forms, pursuant to a contract for the sale of goods, between a buyer and seller.

COUNTEROFFER A statement by the offeree which has the legal effect of rejecting the offer and of proposing a new offer to the offeror.

U.C.C. § 2-207 Provides that a definite expression of acceptance sent within a reasonable time operates as an acceptance even though it states terms additional to or different from those offered, unless acceptance is expressly made conditional on assent to the additional terms.

■━■

Diamond Fruit Growers, Inc. v. Krack Corp.

Tubing supplier (D) v. Cooling unit manufacturer (P)

794 F.2d 1440 (9th Cir. 1986).

NATURE OF CASE: Appeal from award of indemnity on a written contract.

FACT SUMMARY: Metal-Matic (D) contended that it effectively disclaimed responsibility to Krack (P) for incidental damages caused by its defective tubing by including such disclaimers in its sales receipt.

🏛 RULE OF LAW
U.C.C. § 2-207 holds that the exchange of differing purchase orders constitutes a binding contract only as to those portions upon which the writings agree.

FACTS: Over the course of many years, Krack (P) ordered tubing from Metal-Matic (D) pursuant to purchase orders sent by both parties. The purchase orders sent by Metal-Matic (D) contained a disclaimer of liability to Krack (P) for any incidental damages caused by any defect in the tubing. Krack's (P) purchase order did not contain this provision. Diamond sued Krack (P) for damages to fruit caused by a toxic leak in the tubing. Krack (P) filed a third-party complaint against Metal-Matic (D), who defended on the basis of the disclaimer. The trial court denied Metal-Matic's (D) motion for directed verdict. The jury held Metal-Matic (D) 30% responsible, and it appealed, after unsuccessfully moving for judgment n.o.v.

ISSUE: Is the exchange of purchase orders between merchants a binding agreement as to those provisions on which the orders agree?

HOLDING AND DECISION: (Wiggins, J.) Yes. U.C.C. § 2-207 holds that the exchange of differing purchase orders constitutes a binding contract only as to those portions upon which the orders agree. This is changed only upon an affirmative acquiescence to the terms of the differing order. In this case, while some discussions occurred concerning the disclaimer, no affirmative adoption occurred on the part of Krack (P). As a result, the disclaimer was not agreed to and did not become a part of the contract. Affirmed.

▌ ANALYSIS

U.C.C. § 2-207 represents a statutory departure from the common law mirror image rule where any slight deviation from the offer constituted a rejection. Differing orders can constitute an agreement but only on like terms. This rule is consistent with public policy because neither party gets its way merely because it sent the last form.

Quicknotes

BATTLE OF THE FORMS Refers to the exchange of forms, pursuant to a contract for the sale of goods, between a buyer and seller.

DIRECTED VERDICT A verdict ordered by the court in a jury trial.

DISCLAIMER Renunciation of a right or interest.

JUDGMENT N.O.V. A judgment entered by the trial judge reversing a jury verdict if the jury's determination has no basis in law or fact.

MIRROR-IMAGE RULE The common law rule that for acceptance to be effective the offeree must accept each and every term of the offer.

INDEMNITY The duty of a party to compensate another for damages sustained.

U.C.C. § 2-207 Provides that a definite expression of acceptance sent within a reasonable time operates as an acceptance even though it states terms additional to or different from those offered, unless acceptance is expressly made conditional on assent to the additional terms.

ProCD, Inc. v. Zeidenberg

Software manufacturer (P) v. Purchaser (D)

86 F.3d 1447 (7th Cir. 1996).

NATURE OF CASE: Appeal from an order in favor of defendant in a case alleging breach of the terms of a shrinkwrap or end-user license.

FACT SUMMARY: When Zeidenberg (D), a customer, bought and then resold the data compiled on its CD-ROM software disk, ProCD (P) sued for breach of contract.

🏛 **RULE OF LAW**
A buyer accepts goods when, after an opportunity to inspect, he fails to make an effective rejection.

FACTS: ProCD (P) compiled information from over 3,000 telephone directories into a computer database which it sold on CD-ROM disks. Every box containing the disks declared that the software came with restrictions stated in an enclosed license. This license, which was encoded on the CD-ROM disks as well as printed in the manual, and which appeared on a user's screen every time the software ran, limited use of the application program and listings to non-commercial purposes. Zeidenberg bought a ProCD (P) software package but decided to ignore the license and to resell the information in the database. Zeidenberg (D) also made the information from ProCD's (P) database available over the Internet for a price, through his corporation. ProCD (P) sued for breach of contract. The district court found that placing the package of software on the shelf was an "offer," which the customer "accepted" by paying the asking price and leaving the store with the goods. A contract includes only those terms which the parties have agreed to and one cannot agree to secret terms. Thus, the district court held that buyers of computer software need not obey the terms of shrinkwrap licenses. Such licenses were found to be ineffectual because their terms did not appear on the outsides of the packages. ProCD (P) appealed.

ISSUE: Does a buyer accept goods when, after an opportunity to inspect, he fails to make an effective rejection?

HOLDING AND DECISION: (Easterbrook, J.) Yes. A buyer accepts goods when, after an opportunity to inspect, he fails to make an effective rejection under § 2-602 of the Uniform Commercial Code. A vendor, as master of the offer, may invite acceptance by conduct, and may propose limitations on the kind of conduct that constitutes acceptance. ProCD (P) proposed a contract that a buyer would accept by using the software after having an opportunity to read the license at leisure. Zeidenberg (D) did this, since he had no choice when the software splashed the license across his computer screen and would not let him proceed without indicating acceptance. The license was an ordinary contract accompanying the sale of products and was therefore governed by the common law of contracts and the Uniform Commercial Code. Transactions in which the exchange of money precedes the communication of detailed terms are common. Buying insurance and buying a plane ticket are two common examples. ProCD (P) extended an opportunity to reject if a buyer should find the license terms unsatisfactory. Zeidenberg (D) inspected the package, tried out the software, learned of the license, and did not reject the goods. Reversed and remanded.

▶ **ANALYSIS**

The sale of information contained in computer databases presented new challenges to courts. Some courts found that the sale of software was the sale of services, rather than of goods. This case treated the sale of software as a sale of goods governed by Article 2 of the U.C.C.

Quicknotes

CD-ROM Compact disc read only memory.

INSPECTION OF GOODS The examination of goods, which are the subject matter of a contract for sale, for the purpose of determining whether they are satisfactory.

REJECTION The refusal to accept the terms of an offer.

SHRINKWRAP LICENSE Terms of restriction packaged inside a product.

U.C.C. § 2-602 Provides that a rejection after an opportunity to inspect may be effective unless the buyer manifests acceptance in the manner invited by the offeror.

Chateau des Charmes Wines Ltd. v. Sabaté USA Inc.

Cork purchaser (P) v. Cork supplier (D)

328 F. 3d 528 (9th Cir. 2003).

NATURE OF CASE: Appeal from dismissal of action for breach of contract.

FACT SUMMARY: Sabaté (D), who supplied corks to Chateau des Charmes (Charmes) (P) pursuant to an oral contract, later attempted to enforce additional terms that were contained in invoices accompanying shipments of the corks.

🏛 RULE OF LAW
Forum selection clauses contained in invoices corresponding to shipments do not become part of a valid oral contract under the United Nations Convention on Contracts for the International Sale of Goods (C.I.S.G.).

FACTS: Canadian company Charmes (P) orally contracted with Sabaté (D), a U.S. company, to purchase wine corks. Sabaté (D) shipped corks from France to Charmes (P) on several occasions. Invoices corresponding to the shipments contained forum selection clauses specifying that all disputes be adjudicated in France. Charmes (P) later decided that the corks were defective and brought suit against Sabaté (D) in California federal district court, which dismissed the action on grounds that the forum selection clauses were valid. Charmes (D) appealed.

ISSUE: Are forum selection clauses enforceable in an action on a valid oral contract between international parties where the clauses were not part the oral contract but were contained in invoices corresponding to shipments of goods?

HOLDING AND DESCISION: (Per curiam) No. Under the C.I.S.G., Sabaté's (D) forum selection clauses in the invoices do not become part of the contract. International sales contracts are governed by the C.I.S.G., which does not require that a valid contract be evidenced by a writing. As there was sufficient agreement between Sabaté (D) and Charmes (P) regarding the kind, quantity and price of the cork to be supplied, a binding contract was formed. Under the C.I.S.G., such a contract may be modified by the parties merely by agreement. Here, however, forum selection is a material provision and there is no indication that Charmes (P) agreed to the new terms. Therefore, Sabaté (D) could not unilaterally alter the contract. The federal district court's dismissal of the action was an abuse of discretion. Reversed and remanded.

▶ ANALYSIS

The requirements for formation of a contract under the C.I.S.G. are less stringent than under the Uniform Commercial Code which would require the contract between Sabaté (D) and Charmes (P) to be evidenced by a writing. In the absence of such a writing, the court adhered strictly to terms discussed by the parties when forming the contract. Indeed, the court took note of the fact that Sabaté (D) sent several separate invoices containing the forum selection clauses, but did not consider this to be sufficient to add the terms because the original telephone conversations establishing the contract anticipated that there would be multiple shipments.

■▬■

Quicknotes

BREACH OF CONTRACT Unlawful failure by a party to perform its obligations pursuant to contract.

FORUM SELECTION CLAUSE Provision contained in a contract setting forth the particular forum in which the parties would resolve a matter if a dispute were to arise.

■▬■

Specht v. Netscape Communications Corp.

User (P) v. Software program provider (D)

306 F.3d 17 (2d Cir. 2002).

NATURE OF CASE: Motion to compel arbitration.

FACT SUMMARY: Specht (P) downloaded from the Internet free software from Netscape Communications (D). When an issue arose as to Specht's (P) use of the software, Netscape (D) moved to compel arbitration.

🏛 **RULE OF LAW**
Where consumers are urged to download free software, mere reference to the existence of license terms on a submerged screen does not place consumers on inquiry notice or constructive notice of terms.

FACTS: Specht (P) downloaded from the Internet free software from Netscape Communications (D). Specht (P) then brought suit against Netscape (D), alleging that usage of the software transmitted to Netscape (D) private information about the user's file transfer activity on the Internet in violation of federal statute. Netscape (D) moved to compel arbitration, arguing that Specht's (P) downloading of the Netscape (D) software constituted acceptance of the compulsory arbitration provision contained in the online licensing agreement.

ISSUE: Where consumers are urged to download free software, does mere reference to the existence of license terms on a submerged screen place consumers on inquiry notice or constructive notice of terms?

HOLDING AND DECISION: (Sotomayor, J.) No. Mere reference to the existence of license terms on a submerged screen does not place consumers on inquiry notice or constructive notice of terms. The download webpage screen was printed in such a manner that it tended to conceal the fact that it was an express acceptance of Netscape's (D) rules and regulations. There is no reason to assume that viewers will scroll down to subsequent screens simply because screens are there. Specht (P) was responding to an offer that did not carry an immediate visible notice of the existence of license terms or require unambiguous manifestations of assent to those terms. The uncontested evidence revealed that Specht (P) was unaware that Netscape (D) intended to attach license terms to the use of the downloaded software. The district court's denial of the motion to compel arbitration is affirmed.

▶ *ANALYSIS*

As noted by the court in *Specht*, when products are "free" and users are invited to download them in the absence of reasonably conspicuous notice that they are about to bind themselves to contract terms, the transactional circum-

stances cannot be fully analogized to those "in the paper world" of arm's-length bargaining.

■■■

Quicknotes

CONSTRUCTIVE NOTICE Knowledge of a fact that is imputed to an individual who was under a duty to inquire and who could have learned of the fact through the exercise of reasonable prudence.

INQUIRY NOTICE The communication of information that would cause an ordinary person of average prudence to inquire as to its truth.

■■■

Register.com, Inc. v. Verio, Inc.

Registrar of Internet domains (P) v. Website designer (D)

356 F.3d 393 (2d Cir. 2004).

NATURE OF CASE: Appeal from order granting injunctive relief.

FACT SUMMARY: Verio (D) used an automated program to make repeated requests for information from Register.com (Register) (P) regarding recent registration of Internet domain names. Register's (P) automated response to each the request was accompanied by a heading conditioning the release of information on the information not being used to solicit business. Verio (D) used the information obtained from Register (P) to solicit business.

🏛 RULE OF LAW

Conditions on the use of information provided over the Internet that are communicated after the information has been delivered are enforceable where the information is provided in response to multiple automated inquiries and the receiver has knowledge of the condition through prior dealings with the provider.

FACTS: Registrar (P) is a registrar of Internet domain names pursuant to an agreement with ICANN (an organization authorized to govern the Internet domain name system). The agreement requires Register (P) to publish certain information about its clients. This publication took the form of an automated response to received queries that contained the requested information, along with a heading that conditioned the release of the information on the recipient not using the information to solicit business. Verio (D) established an automated inquiry process that made multiple requests for information about Register's (P) clientele. Verio (D) then used the information it obtained from Register (P) in its e-mail, telephone and direct mail marketing. Register (P) filed suit and moved for a preliminary injunction which was entered by the district court. Verio (D) appealed.

ISSUE: Are conditions on the use of information provided over the Internet that are communicated after the information has been delivered enforceable?

HOLDING AND DESCISION: (Leval, J.) Yes. Where the information is provided in response to multiple automated inquiries and the receiver has knowledge of the condition through prior dealing with the provider, the conditions are enforceable. Because Verio (D) had made numerous requests, it was well aware of the conditional nature of the information supplied by Register (P). One cannot repeatedly avail oneself of an opportunity and repeatedly claim to be ignorant of the conditional nature

of the offer presented by the opportunity. Verio (D) chose to continue its automated inquiry program after it knew Register (P) was conditioning the release of the information on Verio (D) not using it in its marketing. By continuing to request the information, Verio (D) accepted to offer of the contract and the terms contained in the response. Affirmed.

▶ ANALYSIS

The court takes pains to distinguish this case from other situations unique to Internet commerce, specifically, where an "I agree" icon is used to establish the conditional terms and where the conditional terms are contained on a Web page that was not necessarily seen by the user. Here, the fact that there could be no doubt that Verio (D) was aware of the condition was dispositive.

◼︎━◼︎

Quicknotes

INJUNCTIVE RELIEF A court order issued as a remedy, requiring a person to do, or prohibiting that person from doing, a specific act.

◼︎━◼︎

Interpretation and Unconscionability in a Form-Contract Setting

Quick Reference Rules of Law

Sardo v. Fidelity & Deposit Co.

Jewelry stock owner (P) v. Insurer (D)

N.J. Ct. of Errors & App., 100 N.J. Eq. 332, 134 A. 774 (1926).

NATURE OF CASE: Suit to reform an insurance policy.

FACT SUMMARY: Sardo (P) requested Fidelity (D) to issue an insurance policy covering his jewelry. The policy issued covered money and securities but not jewelry.

🏛 RULE OF LAW
A written contract for insurance will not be reformed for mistake unless the mistake was mutual and each party was under the same misconception as to the terms of the written instrument.

FACTS: Sardo (P) went to a Fidelity & Deposit Co. (D) agent to obtain theft insurance on his jewelry stock. The agent requested Fidelity (D) to issue a policy covering Sardo's (P) jewelry. After negotiations with Sardo (P), through its agents, Fidelity (D) issued a policy which covered money and securities but did not cover jewelry. The agent read the policy but concluded that "money and securities" included jewelry. Sardo (P) did not read the policy but assumed that it covered jewelry and paid his premium. Subsequently, Sardo's (P) store was robbed and a large amount of jewelry was stolen. The policy defines "securities" as only such bonds, checks, coupons, notes, and bills as are negotiable.

ISSUE: Can a written contract for insurance be reformed for mistake where there is evidence of a unilateral mistake but no evidence that the company was under the same misconception as the insured?

HOLDING AND DECISION: (Kays, J.) No. In order to reform an insurance policy or other written contract in the absence of fraud, it must appear that the minds of the parties have met, that a mutual mistake has been made, and that the misconception was mutual. There is no evidence here which would indicate that a mutual mistake had been made or that Fidelity (D) intended to issue any other policy than the policy which it issued. The most that can be said is that it was the agent's opinion that the policy covered jewelry. However, this opinion was never expressed to Sardo (P), and even if it had been it would not bind Fidelity (D). Judgment for Sardo (P) is therefore reversed.

▶ ANALYSIS

The majority view is that where an applicant states his interest in certain property and distinctly asks for insurance on it, and the agent agrees to comply with his request but adopts a form which does not cover that interest, equity will reform the contract so as to make it cover the interest sought to be protected. For example, where an agent has knowledge of all the facts relating to the ownership of a car sought to be insured and also has instructions as to who is to be covered by the party, but through the agent's mistake a person intended to be insured is not named in the policy, that policy will be reformed to conform to the agreement between the parties. In *Sardo* the court did not look to the agreement between the parties. In *Sardo* the court looked to the intention of the insurance company rather than to the intention of its agent.

Quicknotes

FRAUD A false representation of facts with the intent that another will rely on the misrepresentation to his detriment.

REFORMATION A correction of a written instrument ordered by a court to cause it to reflect the true intentions of the parties.

UNILATERAL MISTAKE Occurs when only one party to an agreement makes a mistake and is generally not a basis for relief by rescission or reformation.

Weaver v. American Oil Co.

Station lessee (D) v. Oil company (P)

Ind. Sup. Ct., 257 Ind. 458, 276 N.E.2d 144 (1971).

NATURE OF CASE: Personal injury action.

FACT SUMMARY: Weaver (D) signed an indemnification agreement holding the lessor, American Oil (P), harmless for its negligence.

🏛 RULE OF LAW
Where there is no showing of a voluntary knowing and understanding release of rights, and there is unequal bargaining power and the clause is grossly unfair, the court may find it unconscionable.

FACTS: Weaver (D) leased an American Oil (P) station. As part of the standardized contract, in small print and without a heading, there was a clause under which Weaver (D) agreed to indemnify American (P) for its negligent acts. The clause was never explained to Weaver (D), and it was never even established that he had read the contract or was otherwise aware of the clause. An American (P) employee negligently sprayed Weaver (D) and an assistant with gasoline, causing them to be burned and injured on the leased premises. American (P) sought a declaratory judgment to determine Weaver's (D) liability for the injuries under the clause. Weaver (D) alleged that the clause was unconscionable.

ISSUE: Where there is no showing of a valid waiver of normal rights, is a highly unreasonable contract clause imposed by a party with superior bargaining power unconscionable?

HOLDING AND DECISION: (Arterburn, C.J.) Yes. Unconscionability may be found where a party in a superior bargaining position exploits the unequal position to impose highly unfair and unreasonable terms on the other party. A court may find that such a grossly unfair use of bargaining power is unconscionable. This is not to say that parties may not voluntarily, knowingly, and intelligently accept such clauses. However, it is the burden of the party attempting to enforce the clause to show such a waiver. Here, Weaver (D) had little formal education, and the clause was in fine print and was not titled. No one ever explained the clause to him, and there is no showing that he even read the contract. In such cases, a lessor in a dominant position such as American (P) cannot be allowed to enforce such an unfair clause to produce an unconscionable result. Judgment of trial court reversed to be entered for the appellant.

⏵ ANALYSIS

While the law will not normally relieve a party from a business mistake, where one party has taken advantage of another's necessities and disadvantage to obtain an unfair advantage, and the other party has, owing to his condition, encumbered himself with a heavy liability or an onerous obligation for the sake of a small or inadequate present gain, the courts are prone to grant relief. *Stiefler v. McCullough*, 97 Ind. App. 123, 174 N.E. 823 (1933).

Quicknotes

DECLARATORY JUDGMENT A judgment of court establishing the rights of the parties.

INDEMNIFICATION Reimbursement for losses sustained or security against anticipated loss or damages.

UNCONSCIONABILITY Rule of law whereby a court may excuse performance of a contract, or of a particular contract term, if it determines that such term(s) are unduly oppressive or unfair to one party to the contract.

WAIVER The intentional or voluntary forfeiture of a recognized right.

Darner Motor Sales v. Universal

Car sales agency (P) v. Insurer (D)

Ariz. Sup. Ct., en banc, 140 Ariz. 383, 682 P.2d 388 (1984).

NATURE OF CASE: Appeal of an action for damages regarding Insurance coverage.

FACT SUMMARY: Darner Motors (P) brought suit against Universal (D) when an individual who rented a car from Darner (P) struck a pedestrian and Universal (D) disputed the amount of coverage under Darner's (P) policy.

RULE OF LAW
The terms of a standardized form contract may be superseded by separately negotiated or added terms, are construed against the contract's draftsman, and are subject to the overriding obligation of good faith and the power of the court to refuse to enforce an unconscionable contract or term.

FACTS: Darner (P), a car sales and leasing agency, purchased an insurance policy from Universal (D) for liability coverage for Darner (P) and its lessees. Darner also purchased an umbrella policy that contained a greater amount of coverage than the regular policy. Darner (P) received the copy of the policy, which was so lengthy that the owner of Darner (P) never read it. Furthermore, when Darner (P) had a concern about the amounts of coverage, the representative at Universal (D) told them not to worry about the coverage limits. Darner (P) rented a car to Dwayne Crawford, who severely injured a pedestrian. Crawford filed suit against Darner (P) alleging that the coverage should have been higher, so Darner (P) called Universal (D) to provide additional coverage. When Universal (D) refused to do so, asserting that the policy clearly provided different levels of coverage for lessees, Darner (P) filed a third-party complaint against Universal (D). The trial court granted Universal's (D) motion for summary judgment, and the court of appeals affirmed.

ISSUE: May the terms of a standardized form contract be superseded by separately negotiated or added terms, construed against the contract's draftsman, and subject to the overriding obligation of good faith and the power of the court to refuse to enforce an unconscionable contract or term?

HOLDING AND DECISION: (Feldman, J.) Yes. The terms of a standardized form contract may be superseded by separately negotiated or added terms, are construed against the contract's draftsman, and are subject to the overriding obligation of good faith and the power of the court to refuse to enforce an unconscionable contract or term. This rule, encompassed in Restatement (Second) of Contracts § 211, will hopefully provide more leverage to a consumer contracting with an insurance company as well as greater uniformity and predictability of results. In addition, the parol evidence rule does not necessarily prevent establishing the true terms of the agreement. Therefore, applying this rule, the fact finder might properly find that Darner (P) was justified in relying on Universal's (D) assurances of higher coverage. Decision of the court of appeals vacated and trial court's summary judgment reversed.

ANALYSIS

This rule for interpretation of standardized contracts recognizes the modern commercial practice of business entities in using automated equipment to effect a large volume of transactions. It serves to protect individuals who do not negotiate every term in a form contract. However, this standard does not provide a defense for those who fail to read a contract that was negotiated in detail.

Quicknotes

PAROL EVIDENCE RULE Doctrine precluding parties to an agreement from introducing evidence of prior or contemporaneous agreements in order to repudiate or alter the terms of a written contract.

UNCONSCIONABILITY Rule of law whereby a court may excuse performance of a contract, or of a particular contract term, if it determines that such term(s) are unduly oppressive or unfair to one party to the contract.

CHAPTER 18

Mistake

Quick Reference Rules of Law

Donovan v. RRL Corp.

Car buyer (P) v. Car dealership (D)

Cal. Sup. Ct., 26 Cal. 4th 261, 109 Cal. Rptr. 2d 807, 27 P.3d 702 (2001).

NATURE OF CASE: Review of appeal in action for breach of contract.

FACT SUMMARY: Donovan (P) attempted to purchase a used Jaguar automobile from dealership RRL (D) at an erroneously advertised price.

🏛 RULE OF LAW
Rescission of a contract for unilateral mistake of fact is authorized where enforcement would be unconscionable and the party in error acted in good faith.

FACTS: RRL (D), a car dealer, placed a newspaper advertisement offering to sell a particular used Jaguar automobile. Due to the newspaper's typographical and proofreading errors, as well as the dealership's failure to catch the mistake, the advertisement listed the vehicle at a price 32 percent lower than intended. RRL (D) discovered the mistake when Donovan (P) tendered the advertised price and the dealer refused to complete the transaction. Donovan (P) brought suit and the trial court entered judgment for RRL (D), finding that the publishing of the lower sales offer was not made in bad faith. The appellate court reversed, finding sufficient evidence in the record on appeal to find the dealer negligent and relying in part on a Vehicle Code statute making it unlawful for a dealer not to sell at the advertised price while the vehicle remains unsold and the advertisement has not expired.

ISSUE: Is rescission of a contract for unilateral mistake authorized where enforcement would be unconscionable and the party seeking rescission made an honest mistake?

HOLDING AND DECISION: (George, C.J.) Yes. Rescission of an otherwise binding contract is available to a party who honestly makes a mistake of material fact and where enforcing the contract would be unconscionable. Because Donovan (P) had no reason to know of and did not cause the erroneous advertisement, RRL (D) must show: (1) a mistake of fact that (2) was material and (3) was not a risk taken on by RRL (D) and (4) that the effect of enforcing the contract would be unconscionable. As Donovan (P) necessarily concedes that the error was material, the determining issues are whether RRL (D) bore the risk of the error and whether the resulting contract would be unconscionable. Although, in extreme cases, the fault of a party could preclude rescission based on unilateral mistake of fact, such cases involve bad faith which is not present here. Because it was an honest mistake, it would not be reasonable to allocate risk of the error to RRL (D). Furthermore, enforcement of an error that would result in

a 32 percent loss on the part of RRL (D) would be unconscionable. Reversed.

▶ ANALYSIS

The ruling turns on the question of whether the dealership's failure to adequately proofread the advertisement before publication was conduct sufficient to allocate to RRL (D) the risk of the error so as to bar RRL (D) from seeking rescission based on unilateral mistake. For the court of appeals, the Vehicle Code (placing strict standards on car dealerships) was enough to tip the scales in favor of Donovan (P). By defining the allocation of risk in such a way that the "good faith" of the party in error is taken into consideration, the Supreme Court of California pushed the balance back toward rescission.

■■■

Quicknotes

BREACH OF CONTRACT Unlawful failure by a party to perform its obligations pursuant to contract.

GOOD FAITH An honest intention to abstain from taking advantage of another.

MATERIAL MISTAKE A mistake as to a factual assumption upon which an action or contract is based, and which may be an adequate defense to a criminal prosecution or a cause for voiding or reforming a contract.

RESCISSION The canceling of an agreement and the return of the parties to their positions prior to the formation of the contract.

UNILATERAL MISTAKE A mistake or misunderstanding as to the terms of a contract made by one party which is generally not a basis for relief by rescission or reformation.

■■■

Travelers Ins. Co. v. Bailey

Insurance company (P) v. Life insurance applicant (D)

Vt. Sup. Ct., 124 Vt. 114, 197 A.2d 813 (1964).

NATURE OF CASE: Action for reformation of an insurance policy.

FACT SUMMARY: Travelers (P) made a mistake in transcribing the information in Bailey's (D) application for a life insurance policy and erroneously issued a policy with too-large annuity provisions.

🏛 RULE OF LAW
Where it is established beyond a reasonable doubt that there was a specific contractual agreement between the parties and a subsequent erroneous rendition of the terms of the agreement in a material particular, the party penalized by the error is entitled to reformation if there has been no prejudicial change of position by the other party while ignorant of the mistake.

FACTS: Bailey (D) applied for a life insurance policy, but Travelers (P) inserted the correct descriptive information on the wrong policy form when the application was accepted and the policy was being prepared at its home office. As a result, the policy that was issued in 1931 stated an annuity obligation to pay $500 per month for life, after age 65, 100 months certain. Bailey (D) had applied for an annuity obligation of $500 per year for life, after age 65, 10 years certain and paid premium commensurate with that coverage. The actual policy did not come into Bailey's (D) possession for the first time until the middle of 1961, at which point he took it to Travelers (P) and made inquiry about the annuity provisions. Travelers (P) was thereafter unsuccessful in getting Bailey (D) to accept its tender of a policy amended to reflect the originally desired annuity terms, and it brought suit for reformation of the original policy on the basis of mistake. When such reformation was permitted, Bailey (D) appealed.

ISSUE: Can the party penalized by an erroneous rendition of the terms of an agreement obtain reformation of the contract?

HOLDING AND DECISION: (Barney, J.) Yes. Once it is proven beyond a reasonable doubt that there was a specific contractual agreement between the parties and that a subsequent erroneous rendition of the terms of the agreement in a material particular occurred, the party penalized by the error is entitled to reformation if there has been no prejudicial change of position by the other party while he was ignorant of the mistake. If a prejudicial change has occurred and can equitably be taken into account and adjusted for in the decree, reformation may be possible even then. It is clear that such a mistake occurred here and that no prejudicial change of position arose to prevent reformation. Affirmed.

▶ ANALYSIS

The traditional view was that "mutuality" of mistake in expression was necessary for reformation to be proper. Rescission of the contract was considered the proper remedy for unilateral mistake. This and other cases evidence a new trend away from such a strict stance and toward a broader basis for reformation that does not make this often confusing distinction.

■══■

Quicknotes

MUTUAL MISTAKE A mistake by both parties to a contract, who are in agreement as to what the contract terms should be, but the agreement as written fails to reflect that common intent; such contracts are voidable or subject to reformation.

REFORMATION A correction of a written instrument ordered by a court to cause it to reflect the true intentions of the parties.

UNILATERAL MISTAKE Occurs when only one party to an agreement makes a mistake and is generally not a basis for relief by rescission or reformation.

■══■

Sherwood v. Walker

Purchaser of cow (P) v. Cow owner (D)

Mich. Sup. Ct., 66 Mich. 568, 33 N.W. 919 (1887).

NATURE OF CASE: Action of replevin for a cow.

FACT SUMMARY: The Walkers (D), having sold a cow to Sherwood (P) in the mistaken belief that it was barren, refused to deliver it.

> ## 🏛 RULE OF LAW
> Where the parties to a contract for the sale of personal property are mutually mistaken as to a material fact which affects the substance of the whole consideration, the contract is unenforceable.

FACTS: The Walkers (D) agreed to sell Sherwood (P) a certain cow, "Rose 2nd of Aberlone," for a price of $850. At the time the contract was entered into, the Walkers (D) indicated their belief that the animal was barren. To this, Sherwood (P) replied that he thought she could be made to breed but that he believed she was not with calf. The cow was not weighed at the time. When the Walkers (D) discovered that the cow was pregnant, and could have been sold for up to $1,000, they refused to deliver it, whereupon Sherwood (P) brought an action of replevin.

ISSUE: Does a mutual mistake of a material, underlying fact afford a basis for rescission of a contract for the sale of personal property?

HOLDING AND DECISION: (Morse, J.) Yes. Where the thing actually delivered or received is different in substance from the thing bargained for and intended to be sold, there is no contract. However, the mutual mistake must not only be as to some material fact but must also affect the substance of the whole consideration. Here, the mistake was as to a crucial, material fact. The parties would not have made the contract if they knew that the cow was capable of breeding. A barren cow is a different creature than a breeding one. The cow was sold for beef, when in fact she had considerable value as a breeder. As a result, there was no contract formed. Reversed and new trial granted.

DISSENT: (Sherwood, J.) There was no "mutual" mistake here since Sherwood (P) believed the cow would breed. Regardless, no conditions were attached to the sale by either party.

▶ ANALYSIS

The court's interpretation of the facts in this case suggests the difficulties inherent in ascertaining all the surrounding circumstances in mistaken assumption analysis. As a result, many commentators have suggested an alternative approach. Following the cue of U.C.C. § 2-615, these commentators have urged that the nondelivery of goods should be excused where, owing to an unexpected occurrence, "the nonoccurrence of which was a basic assumption on which the contract was made," performance has been rendered commercially impracticable.

■==■

Quicknotes

IMPRACTICABILITY A doctrine relieving the parties to a contract from liability for nonperformance of their duties thereunder, if the subject matter of the contract ceases to exist.

MUTUAL MISTAKE A mistake by both parties to a contract, who are in agreement as to what the contract terms should be, but the agreement as written fails to reflect that common intent; such contracts are voidable or subject to reformation.

REPLEVIN An action to recover personal property wrongfully taken.

RESCISSION The canceling of an agreement and the return of the parties to their positions prior to the formation of the contract.

■==■

Griffith v. Brymer

Coronation viewer (P) v. Room owner (D)

King's Bench Div., 19 T.L.R. 434 (1903).

NATURE OF CASE: Action to recover sum on an agreement to rent a room.

FACT SUMMARY: Griffith (P), desirous of viewing a coronation procession, agreed to rent a room from Brymer (D) but demanded the return of his money when the procession was unexpectedly called off.

🏛 RULE OF LAW
Where both parties to a contract are under a misconception with regard to an existing state of facts about which they were contracting, and the misconception goes to the heart of the agreement, the contract is void.

FACTS: Griffith (P) rented a room overlooking the planned route for a coronation procession from Brymer (D). Brymer (D) knew that Griffith's (P) purpose in renting the room was only to view the procession. However, unbeknownst to both parties at the time the contract was entered into, the King had been taken ill, and the procession was called off. When Griffith (P) learned of the cancellation, he demanded from Brymer (D) the return of his money.

ISSUE: Will a mutual mistake which relates to the underlying and material facts of a contract void the agreement?

HOLDING AND DECISION: (Wright, J.) Yes. Where both parties to a contract are mistaken as to the existence of those facts upon which the contract is based, and the misconception goes to the heart of the agreement, the contract is void. Here, the agreement was made on the supposition that nothing had happened which made performance impossible. Since Brymer (D) knew of Griffith's (P) purpose in renting the room, which was thwarted by the cancellation of the procession, Griffith (P) is entitled to the return of his money.

▶ ANALYSIS

The First Restatement of Contracts provides for the avoidance of a contract due to mutual mistake if enforcement would be materially more onerous as a result of the mistake, except where: (1) innocent third parties will be unfairly affected; (2) the party seeking avoidance can obtain reformation or performance in accord with the parties' intentions at the time the agreement was reached; or (3) where the party injured by the mistake can be fully compensated.

Quicknotes

IMPOSSIBILITY A doctrine relieving the parties to a contract from liability for nonperformance of their duties thereunder, if the subject matter of the contract ceases to exist, a person essential to the performance of the contract is deceased, or the service or goods contracted for has become illegal.

MUTUAL MISTAKE A mistake by both parties to a contract, who are in agreement as to what the contract terms should be, but the agreement as written fails to reflect that common intent; such contracts are voidable or subject to reformation.

Lenawee County Board of Health v. Messerly

County board (P) v. Property owners (D)

Mich. Sup. Ct., 417 Mich. 17, 331 N.W.2d 203 (1982).

NATURE OF CASE: Action for injunction and related cross-actions.

FACT SUMMARY: When the Lenawee County Board of Health (P) found a defective sewage system shortly after the Pickles purchased rental property from Mr. and Mrs. Messerly (D) and sought a permanent injunction proscribing human habitation, the Pickles sought rescission of their contract on the grounds of mutual mistake.

> ## 🏛 RULE OF LAW
> A court need not grant rescission in every case in which there is a mutual mistake that relates to a basic assumption of the parties upon which the contract was made and which materially affects the agreed performances of the parties.

FACTS: When Mr. Bloom owned the property on which there was a three-unit apartment building, he installed a septic tank without a permit and in violation of the applicable health code. This was not known to the Messerlys (D) when they subsequently bought it, nor to Barnes when he purchased it on a land contract from the Messerlys (D). After Barnes defaulted on the land contract, an arrangement was made whereby the land was quit-claimed back to the Messerlys (D), and they sold it on a new land contract to the Pickles. About six days later, the Pickles discovered raw sewage seeping out of the ground. The Lenawee County Board of Health (P) condemned the property and sought an injunction against human habitation until it was brought into compliance with the sanitation code. In resulting cross-actions, the Pickles sought rescission of the contract on grounds of mutual mistake. Focusing on the "as is" clause in their land contract, the trial court denied rescission and awarded the Messerlys (D) a judgment against the Pickles on the land contract. The court of appeals reversed.

ISSUE: Is rescission always granted when there is a mutual mistake?

HOLDING AND DECISION: (Ryan, J.) No. A mutual mistake that is the prerequisite for rescission is one that relates to a basic assumption of the parties upon which the contract was made and which materially affects the agreed performance of the parties. However, rescission need not be granted in every case where there is such a mistake. It cannot be ordered to relieve a party who has assumed the risk of loss in connection with the mistake. Furthermore, where both parties are innocent, as in this case, the court exercises its equitable powers to determine which blameless party should assume the loss. Here, the "as is" clause suggests it should be the Pickles. Reversed.

▶ ANALYSIS

According to 1 Restatement Contracts, 2d, § 124, a party bears the risk of mistake if it is allocated to him by agreement of the parties, or he is aware at the time of contracting of his limited knowledge of the facts to which the mistake relates but treats his limited knowledge as sufficient, or the court allocates it to him because "it is reasonable in the circumstances to do so."

Quicknotes

INJUNCTION A court order requiring a person to do or prohibiting that person from doing a specific act.

MUTUAL MISTAKE A mistake by both parties to a contract, who are in agreement as to what the contract terms should be, but the agreement as written fails to reflect that common intent; such contracts are voidable or subject to reformation.

RESCISSION The canceling of an agreement and the return of the parties to their positions prior to the formation of the contract.

Hill v. Jones

Home purchaser (P) v. Seller (D)

Ariz. Ct. App., 151 Ariz. 81, 725 P.2d 1115 (1986).

NATURE OF CASE: Appeal from summary dismissal of action for rescission of real estate purchase contract.

FACT SUMMARY: Before buying Jones's (D) home, Hill (P) asked whether it had been infested with termites, and Jones (D) denied that there had been previous infestations, despite firsthand knowledge of them.

RULE OF LAW
Where the seller of a home knows of facts materially affecting the value of the property which are not readily observable and are not known to the buyer, the seller is under a duty to disclose them.

FACTS: During escrow for the purchase of Jones's (D) home, Hill (P) expressed concern about a "ripple" in a parquet floor. Jones (D) claimed that the problem was due to flooding from a broken water heater, when in fact it demonstrated a termite infestation. Hill (P) asked that a termite inspection report be placed in escrow. An exterminator inspected Jones's (D) home but failed to find instances of prior infestation due to strategic placement of boxes and plants. When the results of the termite report were revealed to Hill (P) by his realtor, Hill (P) closed escrow with Jones (D). After moving in, Hill (P) found termites and discovered that the previous seller of the home had paid for termite guarantees and semiannual inspections when he sold the house to Jones (D). Despite previous infestations which had been treated during Jones's (D) ownership and occupancy of the house, Jones (D) had said nothing about termites to either Hill (P) or the exterminator. Hill (P) sued to rescind the purchase contract on grounds of intentional nondisclosure of the termite damage. The trial court dismissed the action on summary judgment for failure to state a claim, and Hill (P) appealed.

ISSUE: Where the seller of a home knows of facts materially affecting the value of the property which are not readily observable and are not known to the buyer, is the seller under a duty to disclose them?

HOLDING AND DECISION: (Meyerson, J.) Yes. Where the seller of a home knows of facts materially affecting the value of the property which are not readily observable and are not known to the buyer, the seller is under a duty to disclose them to the buyer. Such a disclosure is necessary to correct mistakes of the purchaser as to a basic assumption on which he is making the contract and to protect him from misplaced trust in the vendor. The existence of termite damage in a residential dwelling is the type of material fact which gives rise to the duty to disclose

because it is a matter to which a reasonable person would attach importance in deciding whether or not to purchase such a dwelling. Here, Jones (D) failed to reveal the home's prior history of termite infestation, despite knowledge of such infestation and previous attempts to treat it. Allegations to this effect raise triable issues of material fact which must be determined by the trier of fact. Whether Hill (P) was put on reasonable notice of the termite problem despite Jones's (D) nondisclosure or whether he exercised reasonable diligence in informing himself about the termite problem should also be left to the trier of fact. Reversed and remanded.

ANALYSIS

This case is somewhat exceptional in that the court recognized a duty of disclosure between parties in an ordinary arm's-length, commercial transaction. More typically, courts will recognize a "duty to speak up" only in the presence of a confidential or fiduciary relationship. See, e.g., *Vai v. Bank of America Trust & Savings Association*, 15 Cal. Rptr. 71, 364 P.2d 247 (1961) (community property settlement set aside on grounds that husband had failed to disclose value of property involved to his wife). Beyond the existence of a confidential or fiduciary relationship, courts traditionally have imposed a duty of disclosure between businessmen only when necessary to correct a previous misstatement or mistaken impression.

Quicknotes

DUTY TO DISCLOSE The duty owed by a fiduciary to reveal those facts that have a material effect on the interests of the party that must be informed.

ESCROW A written contract held by a third party until the conditions therein are satisfied, at which time it is delivered to the obligee.

MATERIAL FACT A fact without the existence of which a contract would not have been entered.

MISREPRESENTATION A statement or conduct by one party to another that constitutes a false representation of fact.

SUMMARY JUDGMENT Judgment rendered by a court in response to a motion by one of the parties, claiming that the lack of a question of material fact in respect to an issue warrants disposition of the issue without consideration by the jury.

CHAPTER 19

The Effect of Unexpected Circumstances

Quick Reference Rules of Law

Taylor v. Caldwell

Event promoter (P) v. Facility owner (D)

Queen's Bench, 3 Best & S. 826 (1863).

NATURE OF CASE: Action for damages for breach of a contract for letting of premises.

FACT SUMMARY: Taylor (P) contracted to let Caldwell's (D) hall and gardens for four fetes and concerts, for four days, for £100 per day. Taylor (P) expended money in preparation and for advertising, but Caldwell (D) could not perform when the hall burned down without his fault.

🏛 RULE OF LAW
In contracts in which the performance depends on the continued existence of a given person or thing, a condition is implied that the impossibility of performance, arising from the perishing of the person or thing, shall excuse the performance.

FACTS: By written agreement, Caldwell (D) agreed to let the Surrey Gardens and Musical Hall, Surrey, for four days for giving four "Grand Concerts" and "Day and Night Fetes." Taylor (P) was to pay £100 for each day. Before any concerts were held, the hall was completely destroyed by fire without any fault of either of the parties. Taylor (P) alleged that the fire and destruction of the hall was a breach and that it resulted in his losing large sums in preparation and advertising for the concerts and fetes.

ISSUE: Was Caldwell (D) excused from performance by the accidental destruction of the hall and gardens which had made his performance impossible?

HOLDING AND DECISION: (Blackburn, J.) Yes. Caldwell (D) was excused from performance. First, the agreement was not a lease but a contract to "let." The entertainments that were planned could not be made without the existence of the hall. Ordinarily, where there is a positive contract to do something that is not unlawful, the contractor must perform or pay damages for not doing it even if an unforeseen accident makes performance unduly burdensome or even impossible. This is so when the contract is absolute and positive and not subject to either express or implied conditions, and if it appears that the parties must have known from the beginning that the contract could not be fulfilled unless a particular, specified thing continued to exist and there is no express or implied warranty that the thing shall exist, the contract is not positive and absolute. It is subject to the implied condition that the parties shall be excused in case, before breach, performance becomes impossible from the perishing of the thing without fault of the contractor. This appears to be within the intention of the parties when they enter into a contract. The excuse from the contract's performance is implied in law because from the nature of the contract, it is apparent it was made on the basis of the continued existence of the particular, specified thing. Rule must be absolute to enter the verdict for the defendants.

▶ ANALYSIS

It was important for J. Blackburn not to find the agreement to be a lease. Otherwise, the decision would come within direct conflict of *Paradine v. Jane*, K.B., 1647, 82 Eng. Rep. 897, which held that a lease must be performed to the letter despite unforeseen hardship or good fortune. Next, performance is excused only if the destruction of the specified thing is without fault. Had Caldwell (D) been shown to be guilty of arson in the destruction of the hall, he would not have been excused. If there is impossibility of performance due to no one's fault, the one seeking to enforce performance takes the risk. It might be said that the court was actually apportioning the loss if the contract was, in effect, a joint venture with Taylor (P) paying Caldwell (D) £100 out of each day's admission fees to the concerts (Caldwell [D] was supplying the band). The view of this case is found in U.C.C. § 2-613 where for total destruction of the specified thing, the contract is avoided, or if the specified thing is goods which had so deteriorated as to no longer conform, the contract can be avoided or the goods can be accepted with an allowance for their lesser value. Note that there is not a satisfactory distinction between a contract to let and a lease.

■■■

Quicknotes

CONDITION Requirement; potential future occurrence upon which the existence of a legal obligation is dependent.

EXPRESS WARRANTY An express promise made by one party to a contract that the other party may rely on a fact, relieving that party from the obligation of determining whether the fact is true and indemnifying the other party from liability if that fact is shown to be false.

IMPOSSIBILITY A doctrine relieving the parties to a contract from liability for nonperformance of their duties thereunder, if the subject matter of the contract ceases to exist, a person essential to the performance of the contract is deceased, or the service or goods contracted for has become illegal.

IMPLIED CONDITION A condition that is not expressly stated in the terms of an agreement, but which is inferred from the parties' conduct or the type of dealings involved.

Continued on next page.

IMPLIED WARRANTY An implied promise made by one party to a contract that the other party may rely on a fact, relieving that party from the obligation of determining whether the fact is true and indemnifying the other party from liability if that fact is shown to be false.

■━■

United States v. Wegematic Corp.

Federal government (P) v. Computer system manufacturer (D)

360 F.2d 674 (2d. Cir. 1966).

NATURE OF CASE: Action for damages for breach of a government contract to purchase computers.

FACT SUMMARY: United States (P) brought action for damages when Wegematic's (D) submitted proposal was no longer practicable and the U.S. government (P) was forced to procure equipment from another manufacturer.

🏛 RULE OF LAW
Sellers promoting technological advances accept the risk that they will be unable to develop the advances in order to perform a contract.

FACTS: In June 1956, the Federal Reserve Board of the U.S. government (P) invited five companies to submit bids on a digital computing system, stressing the importance of early delivery. The government (P) ordered an ALWAC 800 from Wegematic (D), which it touted as a "revolutionary system utilizing the latest technical advances," for delivery in June 1957. There was a liquidated damages clause providing that Wegematic (D) would pay $100 per day for delays in delivery, and if Wegematic (D) failed in any provision, the government (P) could contract elsewhere and Wegematic (D) would be liable for the extra costs. In March 1957, Wegematic (D) requested a delay in delivery for redesign and in April suggested delivery in October with a waiver of damages. After other requests for delay, Wegematic (D) stated that development of the computer was beyond technological capabilities. The government (P) obtained an IBM 650 at a rental cost of $102,000 with an option to purchase for $410,450 and filed suit for damages. The trial court awarded the government (P) damages for delay under the liquidated damages clause, reimbursement for the IBM system, and interest. Wegematic (D) appealed.

ISSUE: Do sellers who promote technological advances assume the risk of being unable to deliver the advances in order to perform the contract?

HOLDING AND DECISION: (Friendly, J.) Yes. Sellers promoting technological advances assume the risk that they will be unable to produce the advances in order to fulfill a contract. While under U.C.C. § 2-615, a delay in delivery is not a breach if performance has been made impracticable by the occurrence of a contingency, the risk of a technological breakthrough failing does not fall on the purchaser. It was reasonable to assume that Wegematic (D) had already perfected the technology when it made the agreement with the government (P). Otherwise, a purchaser would be forced to accept whatever a contractor develops while the basis for selecting the contractor may never even come to fruition. Because there was a liquidated damages clause, Wegematic (D) cannot argue that this was their understanding of the law. Affirmed.

▶ ANALYSIS

Cases involving the manufacture of new products often involve government contracts. Generally, where compliance has proved impossible under technology of the day, the contractor has been held to have assumed the risk that production was possible. However, in a limited number of cases where the government has provided specifications for manufacturing, the courts have held that the government has in effect warranted that the specifications will produce the desired result.

Quicknotes

ASSUMPTION OF RISK DOCTRINE An affirmative defense to a negligence suit by the defendant contending that the plaintiff knowingly and voluntarily subjected himself to the hazardous condition, wholly absolving the defendant of liability for injuries incurred.

IMPRACTICABILITY A doctrine relieving the parties to a contract from liability for nonperformance of their duties thereunder, if the subject matter of the contract ceases to exist.

LIQUIDATED DAMAGES An amount of money specified in a contract representing the damages owed in the event of breach.

U.C.C. § 2-615 Provides that the duty to perform be discharged where a party is subjectively unable to perform due to the occurrence of an uninsurable risk.

Transatlantic Financing Corp. v. United States

Wheat carrier (P) v. Federal government (D)

363 F.2d 312 (D.C. Cir. 1966).

NATURE OF CASE: Action for unforeseen costs in execution of a contract for carriage.

FACT SUMMARY: Transatlantic (P), under charter of the United States (D), contracted to ship a full cargo of wheat from Galveston, Texas, to Iran. Shipment was contemplated on Transatlantic's (P) SS Christos through the Suez Canal, but war broke out between Egypt and Israel, forcing the closure of the canal. The SS Christos had to steam an extra 3,000 miles around the Cape of Good Hope.

RULE OF LAW

When the issue of impossibility is raised, the court must construct a condition of performance based on changed circumstances involving the following: (1) a contingency, something unexpected, must have occurred, (2) the risk of unexpected occurrence must not have been allocated either by agreement or custom, and (3) occurrence of the contingency must have rendered performance commercially impracticable.

FACTS: Transatlantic (P), under charter to the United States (D), contracted to carry a full cargo of wheat on its SS Christos from Galveston, Texas to a safe port in Iran. On July 26, 1956, Egypt nationalized the Suez Canal. During the international crisis resulting from this, the parties contracted on October 2, 1956, for Transatlantic (P) to ship the wheat as described. The charter stated the termini of the voyage but not the route. The SS Christos sailed October 27, 1956, on a planned route through the Suez Canal. On October 29, 1956, war between Egypt and Israel broke out. On October 31, 1956, Great Britain and France invaded the Suez Canal Zone. On November 2, 1956, Egypt obstructed the canal with sunken vessels, closing it to traffic. Transatlantic (P) sought an agreement for additional compensation for a voyage around the Cape of Good Hope from a concededly unauthorized Department of Agriculture employee who advised Transatlantic (P) that it had to perform the charter according to its terms but could always file a claim. The SS Christos changed course for the Cape of Good Hope, arriving in Bandar Shapur, Iran, on December 30, 1956. The planned 10,000 mile voyage was increased by 3,000 miles. Transatlantic (P) sought the added expense of $43,972 over the $305,845 contract price. The district court dismissed the libel (an action in admiralty).

ISSUE: Was the contract legally impossible, that is, only able to be done at an excessive and unreasonable cost?

HOLDING AND DECISION: (Wright, J.) No. While it was reasonable to assume that when no route was mentioned in the charter, the usual and customary route (through the Suez Canal) would be taken. Just because this means of performance was impossible, the court must find whether the risk of the contingency (the closure of the canal) was allocated and, if not, whether performance by alternate routes was rendered impracticable. Allocation of risk of the contingency's occurrence may be expressed or implied in the agreement or found in the surrounding circumstances, including custom and usages of the trade. Nothing in the charter specified the Suez route or implied continued availability of that route for performance. Nothing in custom or trade usage, or in the surrounding circumstances, supported such a condition of performance. An implied expectation of the Suez route was hardly adequate proof of an allocation to the promisee of the risk on Transatlantic (P) as the parties knew or should have known of the crisis. Freight rates were most likely affected by the increased risk of voyage in the Suez area. While one might not have foreseen that nationalization of the canal would have brought about a subsequent closure, the circumstances did indicate Transatlantic's (P) willingness to assume abnormal risks. That legitimately causes the court to judge impracticability of performance by alternative route in stricter terms. Impracticability did not appear as the goods could be shipped in the less temperate climate. The ship and crew were fit for the longer voyage, and Transatlantic (P) was no less able than the Government (D) to purchase insurance. In fact, the ship's operator would more reasonably be expected to cover the hazards of war. To justify relief, there must be more of a variation between expected cost and the cost of performing by alternative means than was present here as the promisor can be presumed to have accepted greater than normal risk and impracticability is argued on the basis of expense alone. Affirmed.

▶ ANALYSIS

In determining impossibility, the court will look first to see which party assumed the risk of unforeseen circumstances. If that cannot be determined, then it will look to see whether performance was legally impossible. Legally impossible means impracticable, that is, at excessive and unreasonable cost. Knowledge of the crisis would tend to show assumption of the risk. The court, with respect to unreasonable cost, examined Transatlantic's (P) theory of relief. If the contract was impossible, it was a nullity from the start. Transatlantic (P) asked for quantum meruit, not

Continued on next page.

for the total performance as it should have. The court believed that Transatlantic (P) wanted to avoid losing any of what appeared to be an advantageous contract price. The court would not place a burden on one party to preserve the other's profit. Note that when the court discussed foreseeability of the risk, that foreseeability is as much a fiction as implied conditions, and the parties might honestly have not foreseen the canal's closure. Foreseeability is used as a tool in considering where the risk was to be allocated.

Quicknotes

ASSUMPTION OF RISK DOCTRINE An affirmative defense to a negligence suit by the defendant contending that the plaintiff knowingly and voluntarily subjected himself to the hazardous condition, wholly absolving the defendant of liability for injuries incurred.

CONDITION Requirement; potential future occurrence upon which the existence of a legal obligation is dependent.

CONTINGENCY Based on the uncertain happening of another event.

FORESEEABILITY A reasonable expectation that an act or omission would result in injury.

IMPOSSIBILITY A doctrine relieving the parties to a contract from liability for nonperformance of their duties thereunder, if the subject matter of the contract ceases to exist, a person essential to the performance of the contract is deceased, or the service or goods contracted for has become illegal.

IMPRACTICABILITY A doctrine relieving the parties to a contract from liability for nonperformance of their duties thereunder, if the subject matter of the contract ceases to exist.

RISK Danger of damage to or loss of property.

QUANTUM MERUIT Equitable doctrine allowing recovery for labor and materials provided by one party, even though no contract was entered into, in order to avoid unjust enrichment by the benefitted party.

TRADE USAGE A course of dealing or practice commonly used in a particular trade.

Albre Marble & Tile Co. v. John Bowen Co.

Tile subcontractor (P) v. General construction contractor (D)

Mass. Sup. Jud. Ct., 338 Mass. 394, 155 N.E.2d 437 (1959).

NATURE OF CASE: Action to recover the value of work and labor furnished.

FACT SUMMARY: Albre (P) sought to recover the value of the expenses it incurred in preparing to undertake the work that had been subcontracted out to it by John Bowen (D), the general contractor, but which never got under way because the general contract was itself declared invalid.

🏛 RULE OF LAW
The courts may permit one to recover for those expenditures made in reliance on a contract or in preparation to perform it when made pursuant to the specific request of the other party as set forth in the contract.

FACTS: As general contractor on a construction project, Bowen (D) subcontracted some of the work out to Albre (P). The subcontracts called for Albre (P) to furnish and submit all necessary or required samples, shop drawings, tests, affidavits, etc., for approval, all as ordered or specified. Albre (P) incurred expenses in preparing such samples, drawings, etc. When the general contract was held invalid in a court case, Albre (P) brought suit against Bowen (D) to recover the fair value of work and labor furnished prior to the termination of the general contract and for the aforementioned expenses incurred in preparation for performance of the subcontracted work. Bowen (D) asserted that recovery for expenses incurred in preparation for performance of contractual obligations was improper, and the court agreed. Albre (P) appealed.

ISSUE: Are there instances when recovery of expenses incurred in preparation for performance under a contract is permissible?

HOLDING AND DECISION: (Spalding, J.) Yes. There are circumstances under which recovery may be had for payments made, or obligations reasonably incurred, in preparation for performance of a contract pursuant to the specific request of the other party as set forth in the contract. The facts here are that Bowen's (D) actions directly led to its general contract being invalid and thus it had the primary involvement in creating the impossibility that rendered further performance of the subcontracts impossible. Thus, as between the two parties, Bowen (D) should suffer whatever loss was thereby sustained by Albre (P). The damages to be assessed are limited solely to the fair value of the acts Albre (P) did pursuant to the specific request of Bowen (D) as contained in the subcontracts. Plaintiff's

exceptions overruled in part and sustained in part, and the case remanded.

▶ ANALYSIS

There is case law which denies recovery even when preparatory expenses were incurred in meeting a request made by the other party to the contract. However, in those cases the supervening act rendering further performance of the contract impossible was not caused by the fault of either party, and that is a most significant difference.

Quicknotes

QUASI-CONTRACT An implied contract created by law to prevent unjust enrichment.

IMPOSSIBILITY A doctrine relieving the parties to a contract from liability for nonperformance of their duties thereunder, if the subject matter of the contract ceases to exist, a person essential to the performance of the contract is deceased, or the service or goods contracted for has become illegal.

SUPERVENING CAUSE An independent cause, which is the proximate cause of an act.

UNJUST ENRICHMENT The unlawful acquisition of money or property of another for which both law and equity require restitution to be made.

Missouri Public Service Co. v. Peabody Coal Co.

Utility company (P) v. Coal supplier (D)

Mo. Ct. App., 583 S.W.2d 721, *cert. denied*, 444 U.S. 865 (1979).

NATURE OF CASE: Appeal from decree of specific performance.

FACT SUMMARY: Peabody (D) discontinued its coal shipments to Public Service (P) after the shipments became unprofitable because of escalating costs.

🏛 RULE OF LAW
The defense of commercial impracticability may be claimed where there is a contingency, the nonoccurrence of which was a basic assumption upon which the contract was made, and by which occurrence further performance became commercially impracticable.

FACTS: Peabody (D) and Public Service (P) entered into a contract in which Peabody (D) agreed to supply Public Service (P) with coal for the production of electricity at Public Service's (P) electric plants. Faced with escalating costs, Peabody (D) unsuccessfully attempted to renegotiate the agreement by seeking a higher price for the coal. Failing in such negotiations, Peabody (D) notified Public Service (P) it was stopping its deliveries of coal. Public Service (P) treated this action as an anticipatory breach of the contract and sued Peabody (D). The court found for Public Service (P) and issued a decree for specific performance. Peabody (D) appealed, contending that its performance under the contract was a commercial impracticability.

ISSUE: May the defense of commercial impracticability be claimed only where there is a contingency, the nonoccurrence of which was a basic assumption upon which the contract was made, and by which occurrence further performance became commercially impracticable?

HOLDING AND DECISION: (Swofford, J.) Yes. The defense of commercial impracticability may be claimed only where there is a contingency, the nonoccurrence of which was a basic assumption upon which the contract was made, and by which occurrence further performance became commercially impracticable. Here, it is apparent Peabody (D) made a bad and unprofitable bargain in its contract with Public Service (P) and that Peabody (D) suffered losses as a result. But this alone does not deal with either the basic assumption on which the contract was negotiated or alter the essential nature of the performance under the contract to make performance a commercial impracticability. Affirmed.

▶ ANALYSIS

In the principal case, Peabody (D) attempted to use the defense contained in Uniform Commercial Code § 2-615 which states that: "nondelivery . . . by a seller . . . is not a breach of his duty under a contract for sale if performance as agreed upon has been made impracticable by the occurrence of a contingency the nonoccurrence of which was a basic assumption on which the contract was made." Many sellers in the 1970s and 1980s sought relief under this section based on significantly increased costs resulting from the oil crisis. In almost all cases, the sellers were unsuccessful. See, e.g., *Iowa Electric Light and Power Co. v. Atlas Corp.*, 467 F. Supp. 129 (N.D. Iowa 1978).

Quicknotes

ANTICIPATORY BREACH Breach of a contract subsequent to formation but prior to the time performance is due.

CONTINGENCY Based on the uncertain happening of another event.

IMPRACTICABILITY A doctrine relieving the parties to a contract from liability for nonperformance of their duties thereunder, if the subject matter of the contract ceases to exist.

SPECIFIC PERFORMANCE An equitable remedy whereby the court requires the parties to perform their obligations pursuant to a contract.

U.C.C. § 2-615 Provides that a delay in delivery by a seller is not a breach of his duty under a contract for sale if performance has been made impracticable by the occurrence of a contingency the nonoccurrence of which was a basic assumption on which the contract was made.

Alamance County Board of Education v. Bobby Murray Chevrolet, Inc.

Purchaser of school bus chassis (P) v. Seller of school bus chassis (D)

N.C. Ct. App., 121 N.C. App. 222, 465 S.E.2d 306 (1996).

NATURE OF CASE: Appeal from entry of summary judgment in action for breach of contract.

FACT SUMMARY: Bobby Murray (D) sought to excuse failure to deliver school bus chassis to a number of school boards (P) per contract by claiming that third party manufacturer's inability to produce the chassis was a contingency of the contract and new EPA regulations were an intervening factor.

> 🏛 **RULE OF LAW**
> A supplier's failure to deliver is not excused by third-party manufacturer's inability to perform where the supplier's contract with the purchaser is not explicitly contingent upon availability of supply.

FACTS: Bobby Murray (D) bid on and was awarded a contract to supply school bus chassis to the North Carolina Department of Administration's Division of Purchase and Contract on behalf of a number of school boards (P). Bobby Murray (D) submitted orders for the chassis to GM. During the period for performance, Bobby Murray (D) was advised by GM of potential problems with the supply of a component part of the chassis that would delay the delivery of the chassis. Bobby Murray (D) also learned of new Environmental Protection Agency (EPA) regulations that would make the chassis out of compliance by the time the chassis would become available. Bobby Murray (D) notified the school boards (P) that the chassis could not be supplied. The school boards (P) obtained chassis elsewhere and sued Bobby Murray (D) for the difference between the bid and actual price paid for the chassis. Bobby Murray (D) filed a third-party complaint against GM claiming GM breached its contract with Bobby Murray (D). Bobby Murray (D) appealed from entry of summary judgment for the school boards (P) (awarding difference damages plus interest), claiming that its failure to perform was excusable because it was contingent upon GM's ability to supply the chassis and that the new EPA regulations were an intervening factor.

ISSUE: Is a supplier's failure to deliver pursuant to a contract that does not make explicit that delivery is contingent upon supply excusable where third-party manufacturer's inability to produce the chassis causes the breach?

HOLDING AND DESCISION: (John, J.) No. Bobby Murray's (D) failure to deliver the chassis to the school boards (P) is not excused by GM's inability to perform because Bobby Murray's (D) contract with the school boards (P) was not contingent upon the available supply of chassis. Bobby Murray (D) bore the burden of making any foreseeable contingency part of the contract with the school boards (P). Bobby Murray's (D) Dealer Sales and Services Agreement with GM provides that orders placed with GM are only binding once vehicles are released to production and here, the chassis were never released to production. Bobby Murray (D) also failed to ensure delivery of the chassis with GM, relying instead on GM's history of meeting orders. The defense of the new EPA regulations is also not availing because the contract between Bobby Murray (D) and the school boards (P) specifically addressed government restrictions and Bobby Murray (D) failed to meet its obligations under the relevant contract provision. Affirmed.

▶ ANALYSIS

A middleman cannot simply rely on the past performance of a supplier and, where the ability to deliver may be influenced by the vagaries of supply, it is incumbent upon the middleman to make those contingencies part of the contract with the purchaser.

■=■

Quicknotes

BREACH OF CONTRACT Unlawful failure by a party to perform its obligations pursuant to contract.

INTERVENING CAUSE A cause, not anticipated by the initial actor, which is sufficient to break the chain of causation and relieve him of liability.

SUMMARY JUDGMENT Judgment rendered by a court in response to a motion made by one of the parties, claiming that the lack of a question of material fact in respect to an issue warrants disposition of the issue without consideration by the jury.

■=■

Krell v. Henry

Flat owner (P) v. Coronation viewer (D)

Ct. of App., 2 K.B. 740 (1903).

NATURE OF CASE: Action for damages for breach of a contract for a license for use.

FACT SUMMARY: Henry (D) paid a deposit of £25 to Krell (P) for the use of his apartment in Pall Mall, London, for the purpose of a viewing sight for King Edward VII's coronation procession. The King became ill causing a delay of the coronation upon which Henry (D) refused to pay a £50 balance for which Krell (P) sued.

> 🏛 **RULE OF LAW**
> Where the object of one of the parties is the basis upon which both parties contract, the duties of performance are constructively conditioned upon the attainment of that object.

FACTS: In two letters of June 20, 1902, Henry (D) contracted through Krell's (P) agent, Bisgood, to use Krell's (P) flat in Pall Mall, London, to view the coronation procession of King Edward VII which had been advertised to pass along Pall Mall. The contract made no mention of this purpose. The period of use of the flat was the daytime only of June 26, 27, 1902 for £75, £25 paid in deposit with the £50 remainder due on June 24, 1902. Henry (D) became aware of the availability of Krell's (P) flat as an announcement to that effect had been made which was reiterated by Krell's (P) housekeeper, who showed Henry (D) the rooms. When the king became very ill, the coronation was delayed, and Henry (D) refused to pay the £50 balance for which Krell brought suit.

ISSUE: Was the defeat of the basis upon which Henry (D) contracted a defeat of the contract?

HOLDING AND DECISION: (Williams, L.J.) Yes, it can be inferred from the surrounding circumstances that the rooms were taken for the purpose of viewing the processions and that was the foundation of the contract. It was not a lease of the rooms—they could not be used at night—this was a license for use for a particular purpose. With the defeat of the purpose of the contract, the performance is excused. Appeal dismissed.

▶ *ANALYSIS*

This case is an extension of *Taylor v. Caldwell* (3 Best & S. 826, 122 Eng. Rep. 309 [K.B. 1863]) and, as in that case, it was necessary to remove the roadblock of a lease in order to avoid a conflict with *Paradine v. Jane* (82 Eng. Rep. 897 [K.B. 1647]). The rule explained here is "frustration of purpose" or "commercial frustration." It has not been made clear whether this doctrine rests upon the failure of consideration or the allocation of the risks. While there is a

frustration, performance is not impossible. No constructive condition of performance has failed as Krell (P) made no promise that the condition would occur. Rather, a constructive condition based upon the attainment of the purpose or object has arisen. Note that the frustration should be total or nearly total, though that is a matter of degree.

■══■

Quicknotes

CONDITION Requirement; potential future occurrence upon which the existence of a legal obligation is dependent.

CONSTRUCTIVE CONDITION A condition that is not expressly stated in or implied by the terms of an agreement, but is imposed by law.

FRUSTRATION OF PURPOSE A doctrine relieving the parties to a contract from liability for nonperformance of their duties thereunder when the purpose of the agreement ceases to exist due to circumstances not subject to either party's control.

■══■

CHAPTER 20

Third-Party Beneficiaries

Quick Reference Rules of Law

Lawrence v. Fox

Lender (P) v. Third-party borrower (D)

N.Y. Ct. App., 20 N.Y. 268 (1859).

NATURE OF CASE: Action by a third party to recover damages for breach of contract.

FACT SUMMARY: Fox (D) promised Holly, for consideration, that he would pay Holly's debt to Lawrence (P).

> ## 🏛 RULE OF LAW
> A third party for whose benefit a contract is made may bring an action for its breach.

FACTS: Holly owed Lawrence (P) $300. Holly loaned $300 to Fox (D) in consideration of Fox's (D) promise to pay the same amount to Lawrence (P), thereby erasing Holly's debts to Lawrence (P). Fox (D) did not pay Lawrence (P), and now Lawrence (P) brings this action for breach of Fox's (D) promise to Holly.

ISSUE: Is a third party precluded for want of privity of contract from maintaining an action on a contract made for his benefit?

HOLDING AND DECISION: (Gray, J.) No. "[In the case of] a promise made to one for the benefit of another, he for whose benefit it is made may bring an action for its breach." This principle, which has been long applied in trust cases, is in fact a general principle of law. Affirmed.

DISSENT: (Comstock, J.) In general, there must be privity of contract. Here, Lawrence (P) had nothing to do with the promise on which he brought the action. "It was not made to him, nor did the consideration proceed from him. If [Lawrence (P)] can maintain the suit, it is because an anomaly has found its way into the law on this subject."

▶ ANALYSIS

This is the leading case which started the general doctrine of "third-party beneficiaries." In the parlance of the original Restatement of Contracts, Lawrence (P) was a "creditor" beneficiary. Restatement 2d, § 133, has eliminated the creditor/donee distinction which the original Restatement fostered and has lumped both under the label of "intended" beneficiary. Although the court in the present case went to some effort to discuss trusts and agency, ultimately the court allowed Lawrence (P) to recover because it was manifestly "just" that he should recover. Such has been the creation of many a new legal doctrine. The dissenting justices were primarily worried about freedom of contract and the continuing ability of promisor and promisee to rescind or modify their contract. As the doctrine has developed, various rules have arisen to handle these situations. Affirmed.

Quicknotes

CREDITOR BENEFICIARY A creditor who receives the benefits of a contract between a debtor and another party, pursuant to which the other party is obligated to tender payment to the creditor.

PRIVITY OF CONTRACT A relationship between the parties to a contract that is required in order to bring an action for breach.

THIRD-PARTY BENEFICIARY A party who benefits from a promise made pursuant to a contract although he is not a party to the agreement.

Seaver v. Ransom

Niece (P) v. Executor of aunt (D)

N.Y. Ct. App., 224 N.Y. 233, 120 N.E. 639 (1918).

NATURE OF CASE: Action by a third party to recover damages for breach of a contract.

FACT SUMMARY: Berman made a promise to his wife for the benefit of their niece, Seaver (P), who sued Berman's executor (D) for breach of that promise.

RULE OF LAW
A niece for whose benefit a promise was made to her aunt may successfully bring an action for breach of that promise.

FACTS: Mrs. Berman, on her death bed, wished to leave some property to her niece, Seaver (P). Her husband induced his dying wife to sign a will leaving all property to him by promising that he would leave a certain amount in his own will to Seaver (P). Mr. Berman died without making such a provision for Seaver (P). Seaver (P) brought suit against Ransom (D), as executor of Berman's estate, for Berman's breach of his promise to his dying wife.

ISSUE: Does a niece for whose benefit a promise was made to her aunt have an action for breach of that promise?

HOLDING AND DECISION: (Pound, J.) Yes. Although a general rule requires privity between a plaintiff and a defendant as necessary to the maintenance of an action on the contract, one of several exceptions to the rule is the case where a contract is made for the benefit of another member of the family. Here, Mrs. Berman was childless and Seaver (P) was a beloved niece. However, "the constraining power of conscience is not regulated by the degree of relationship alone. The dependent or faithful niece may have a stronger claim than the affluent or unworthy son. No sensible theory of moral obligation denies arbitrarily to the former what would be conceded to the latter." The reason for this "family" exception (and other exceptions) to the rule is that it is just and practical to permit the person for whose benefit a contract is made to enforce it against one whose duty it is to pay. "The doctrine of *Lawrence v. Fox* is progressive, not retrograde." Finally, in this particular case, the "equities" are with Seaver (P). Affirmed.

ANALYSIS

In this case, the court (as does the original Restatement of Contracts) uses the term "donee beneficiary" to describe Seaver (P). The Restatement 2d erases the creditor/donee distinction and labels both types of beneficiaries as "intended." Although the court here is very insistent on the close family relationship, subsequent New York cases have erased that requirement for donee beneficiaries as the doctrine governing third-party beneficiaries has expanded. These subsequent cases represent the now-prevailing view in the country.

Quicknotes

DONEE BENEFICIARY A third party, not a party to a contract, but for whose benefit the contract is entered with the intention that the benefits derived therefrom be bestowed upon the person as a gift.

INTENDED BENEFICIARY A third party who is the recipient of the benefit of a transaction undertaken by another.

PRIVITY OF CONTRACT A relationship between the parties to a contract that is required in order to bring an action for breach.

THIRD-PARTY BENEFICIARY A party who benefits from a promise made pursuant to a contract although he is not a party to the agreement.

Hale v. Groce

Beneficiary of bequest (P) v. Attorney (D)

Or. Sup. Ct., 304 Or. 281, 744 P.2d 1289 (1987).

NATURE OF CASE: Appeal from dismissal of third-party beneficiary contract claim.

FACT SUMMARY: Groce (D), an attorney, neglected to follow the directions of his client by omitting Hale (P) as a beneficiary from his client's testamentary documents.

🏛 RULE OF LAW
The intended beneficiary of an attorney's services for his client may bring a contract action as a third-party beneficiary.

FACTS: Groce (D) was directed by his client to prepare a will and related trust which bequested a specific sum to Hale (P). Groce (D) negligently failed to follow his client's directions and omitted Hale (P) as a beneficiary. After failing to obtain judicial reform of the documents, Hale (P) sued Groce (D) in tort and in contract. Groce (D) moved to dismiss Hale's (P) complaint, contending that the facts alleged did not constitute a claim under either theory and that the tort claim was barred by the statute of limitations. The circuit court dismissed both claims. On Hale's (P) appeal, the negligence claim was reinstated. Both parties appealed.

ISSUE: May the intended beneficiary of an attorney's services for his client bring a contract action as a third-party beneficiary?

HOLDING AND DECISION: (Linde, J.) Yes. The intended beneficiary of an attorney's services for his client may bring a contract action as a third-party beneficiary. Under third-party analysis the attorney/client contract creates a "duty" not only to the promisee, his client, but also to the intended beneficiary. Hale's (P) complaint alleges Groce's (D) breach of a specific promise that Groce (D) would prepare a trust document wherein his client and Hale (P) would be co-trustees and through which Hale (P) would receive the gift his client intended Hale (P) to have. Affirmed in part, reversed in part, and remanded.

▶ ANALYSIS

In *H.B. Deal & Co. v. Head*, 221 Ark. 47, 251 S.W.2d 1017 (1952), the federal government made a contract with Deal providing for Deal's construction of a plant. One provision in the contract required Deal to pay his laborers time-and-a-half for overtime. Deal's employees sued Deal under the contract. The court held that the employees could sue under the contract since they were the intended beneficiaries of the time-and-a-half contract provision.

Quicknotes

BEQUEST A transfer of property that is accomplished by means of a testamentary instrument.

INTENDED BENEFICIARY A third party who is the recipient of the benefit of a transaction undertaken by another.

THIRD-PARTY BENEFICIARY A party who benefits from a promise made pursuant to a contract although he is not a party to the agreement.

■■■

Scarpitti v. Weborg

Residential lot owners (P) v. Architect (D)

Pa. Sup. Ct., 530 Pa. 366, 609 A.2d 147 (1992).

NATURE OF CASE: Appeal from reversal of trial court's sustaining demurrer of breach of contract.

FACT SUMMARY: The Scarpittis (P), owners of real property in a subdivision, sought damages for loss of value to their property when architect Weborg (D) arbitrarily and inconsistently enforced deed restrictions, asserting that they were the intended third party beneficiaries of an implied contract between Weborg (D) and the subdivision's developer.

🏛 RULE OF LAW
Owners of lots in a residential subdivision are the intended third-party beneficiaries of an implied contract between the subdivision's developer and the architect employed to enforce the subdivision's deed restrictions.

FACTS: The Scarpittis and Hineses (Scarpitti) (P) purchased lots in a subdivision subject to deed restrictions and submitted construction plans to the architect Weborg (D), who was authorized to approve or reject proposed building plans. Weborg (D) rejected the initial plans because they violated certain deed restrictions. The Scarpittis (P) then built pursuant to plans conforming to the deed restrictions. Subsequently, Weborg (D) approved plans submitted by other lot owners that violated the same deed restrictions enforced against the Scarpittis (P). The Scarpittis (P) sued Weborg (D) claiming that they were third-party beneficiaries of the implied contract between the developer and Weborg (D) and that the arbitrary and inconsistent enforcement of the deed restrictions resulted in loss a of value to their property. The trial court sustained Weborg's (D) demurrer and dismissed the action. The appellate court reversed. Weborg (D) appealed the reversal.

ISSUE: Are purchasers of lots in a residential subdivision the intended third party beneficiaries of an implied contract between the land developer and the architect responsible for enforcing building restrictions in the subdivision?

HOLDING AND DESCISION: (Larsen, J.) Yes. Deed restrictions that control the development of lots in the subdivision are intended to benefit the purchasers of the lots such that the Scarpittis (P) were the intended beneficiaries of the implied contract between the developer of the subdivision and Weborg (D), who was tasked with enforcing the restrictions. Case law and the Restatement (Second) of Contracts, § 302, carve out an exception to the rule that both contracting parties must have expressed in the contract their intention that the third party be a

beneficiary: where the circumstances are so compelling that recognition of the beneficiaries' right is appropriate to effectuate the intentions of the parties and the performance satisfies a promise to give the beneficiary the benefit of the promised performance. Here, the Scarpittis (P) are third-party beneficiaries within the exception because the employment of Weborg (D) to review construction plans was for the benefit of homeowners in the subdivision. The judgment of the superior court is affirmed. The case is remanded to the trial court with instructions to reinstate the complaint and proceed consistently with this opinion.

▶ ANALYSIS

To fit within the exception to the third-party beneficiary rule (that the intent of the contracting parties to benefit the third party must appear in the contract), the circumstances must satisfy an obligation to pay money to the beneficiary or to give the beneficiary the benefit of the performance. Here, the court was persuaded by the notion that the only purpose of the deed restrictions and the only benefit obtained by enforcing them was to protect the financial interests of the owners of lots in the subdivision.

■═■

Quicknotes

BREACH OF CONTRACT Unlawful failure by a party to perform its obligations pursuant to contract.

DEMURRER The assertion that the opposing party's pleadings are insufficient and that the demurring party should not be made to answer.

IMPLIED CONTRACT An agreement between parties that may be inferred from their general course of conduct.

THIRD-PARTY BENEFICIARY A party who benefits from a promise made pursuant to a contract although he is not a party to the agreement.

■═■

Martinez v. Socoma Companies, Inc.

Economically depressed litigants (P) v. Private corporation (D)

Cal. Sup. Ct., 11 Cal. 3d 394, 521 P.2d 841 (1974).

NATURE OF CASE: Suit to recover damages pursuant to a contract.

FACT SUMMARY: Martinez (P) and others (P) sued for damages when Socoma (D) and other companies (D) reneged on government contracts to provide jobs and training for residents of an economically depressed area.

☷ RULE OF LAW

Persons who stand to gain from the performance of a contract between the government and a private corporation do not enjoy the status of third-party donee beneficiaries unless the government intended to make a gift to them or to confer upon them an enforceable legal right.

FACTS: In 1964, Congress enacted the Economic Opportunity Act. 1967 amendments to that Act provided for Special Impact Programs pursuant to which funds were appropriated to the Department of Labor, which was to implement a plan which called for private industry to provide jobs and training for residents of economically depressed sites. Under the program, the federal government in 1969 entered into contracts by which Socoma Companies, Inc. (D), Lady Fair Kitchens, Incorporated (D) and Monarch Electronics International, Inc. (D) agreed to hire and train a total of 1,600 residents of the East Los Angeles community. The government paid a total of more than $1 million to the companies (D), but only 276 jobs were provided and 229 of these allegedly were wrongfully terminated. Martinez (P) and others (P) eventually sued, on behalf of themselves and other disadvantaged unemployed persons, to recover more than $8 million in damages from the three companies (D) and certain of their officers (D) and directors (D). The complaint alleged that the unemployed residents (P) were third-party beneficiaries of the contracts between the government and the three companies (D) and, thus, were entitled to recover pursuant to those agreements. The trial court sustained general demurrers without leave to amend, holding that the unemployed persons (P) were only incidental beneficiaries of the contracts. An appeal followed.

ISSUE: May a person who is to secure employment as a result of a government contract sue the other party to that contract to enforce it as a third-party donee beneficiary?

HOLDING AND DECISION: (Wright, C.J.) No. Persons who stand to gain from the performance of a contract between the government and a private corporation do not enjoy the status of third-party donee beneficiaries unless the government intended to make a gift to them or

to confer upon them an enforceable legal right. Section 1559 of the Civil Code provides that, "A contract, made expressly for the benefit of a third person, may be enforced by him at any time before the parties thereto rescind it." However, these contracts were not "made expressly for the benefit of" the unemployed residents (P). These persons were clearly not creditor beneficiaries of the contract since the government owed them no duty. Nor were they donee beneficiaries, because the contract was not intended to bestow a gift upon them and did not confer any legal right. It is true that the contracts were designed to benefit society and the public at large, but they were not intended to give any specific advantage to any person or group. Section 145 of the Restatement of Contracts absolves a party who contracts with the government to provide services to "some or all of the members of the public" from liability unless the contract and the circumstances surrounding its formation manifest "an intention . . . that the promisor shall compensate members of the public." The contracts in this case manifest no intention that the companies (D) should compensate members of the public if performance does not occur. In fact, a contrary intention is indicated. Each contract, for instance, contains a liquidated damages clause which fixes the amount the companies (D) are to refund to the government in the event of noncompliance. Evidently, the liquidated damages provisions were intended to define the total extent of the companies' (D) liability. It is argued that § 145 is inapplicable because that section pertains only to contracts to perform a service to "the public" and that the unemployed residents (P) are an identifiable group distinct from the public good, and according to the legislation pursuant to which they were made, the agreements are intended to ameliorate a problem of national importance. Certain persons (P) might have been supposed to benefit more directly than others as a result of the contracts, but they were nevertheless no more than incidental beneficiaries and, therefore, lacked standing to bring the suit outlined in their complaint. Judgments of dismissal are affirmed.

DISSENT: (Burke, J.) These unemployed individuals (P) were the intended beneficiaries of the contracts. They are clearly members of that class of persons whom the contracts were supposed to benefit. The agreements were entered into to assist unemployed, poor persons in need of employment and job training. The contracts provide for the payment of a specified wage to a fixed number of persons and prescribe the duration of their initial employment. Such specific terms are obviously not intended only

Continued on next page.

to benefit society at large. These people are not merely a part of "the public" within the meaning of § 145. That section prevents "the public" from assessing third-party beneficiary status against government contractors, but the unemployed residents (P) are of a smaller and distinct class. It is inadequate to say that the companies (D) did not intend to be liable to any individuals (P). These individuals (P) were intended beneficiaries of the contracts and, therefore, should have their complaint reinstated, at least until the propriety of the class action can be ascertained by the trial court.

▶ ANALYSIS

For the most part, courts recently have been fairly liberal in allowing persons or groups to assert third-party beneficiary status. In products liability cases and in other contexts in which both tort and contract principles are involved, expansion of the third-party beneficiary doctrine seems to have particular significance. A person who can establish his status as a third-party beneficiary may thereby avoid the necessity of proving privity of contract and negligence. In fact, more widespread recognition of third-party beneficiary status may presage a greater judicial willingness to impose tort liability in cases which presently are decided on contract principles.

■■■

Quicknotes

CLASS ACTION A suit commenced by a representative on behalf of an ascertainable group that is too large to appear in court, who shares a commonality of interests and who will benefit from a successful result.

DEMURRAL The assertion that the opposing party's pleadings are insufficient and that the demurring party should not be made to answer.

DONEE BENEFICIARY A third party, not a party to a contract, but for whose benefit the contract is entered with the intention that the benefits derived therefrom be bestowed upon the person as a gift.

INCIDENTAL BENEFICIARY A person for whom a trust is not specifically created and who has no right to assert an interest in the trust, yet derives incidental benefits therefrom.

INTENDED BENEFICIARY A third party who is the recipient of the benefit of a transaction undertaken by another.

LIQUIDATED DAMAGES An amount of money specified in a contract representing the damages owed in the event of breach.

PRIVITY OF CONTRACT A relationship between the parties to a contract that is required in order to bring an action for breach.

STANDING Whether a party possesses the right to commence suit against another party by having a personal stake in the resolution of the controversy.

THIRD-PARTY BENEFICIARY A party who benefits from a promise made pursuant to a contract although he is not a party to the agreement.

■■■

Copeland v. Beard

Creditor (P) v. Property transferee (D)

Ala. Sup. Ct., 217 Ala. 216, 115 So. 389 (1928).

NATURE OF CASE: Action by third-party beneficiary to enforce a contract on an assignor.

FACT SUMMARY: As part of the consideration for the sale of real property, Beard (D) would pay the seller's debt to Copeland (P). Before Copeland (P) agreed to the contract, Beard (D) transferred the property to another who agreed to pay Copeland (P).

🏛 RULE OF LAW
In a third-party beneficiary contract, the obligation becomes fixed on the promisor when the beneficiary consents to his performance. Prior to this, either the promisor or promisee may revoke, rescind, or assign.

FACTS: Copeland's (P) debtor sold property to Beard (D), part of the consideration being that Beard (D) should pay the debtor's debt to Copeland (P). Prior to Copeland (P) accepting the contract benefits, Beard (D) transferred the property to a third party, who was to pay Copeland (P). The debtor released Beard (D) from his performance. Copeland (P) was not paid, and he sued Beard (D) on the theory that he could not be released from his obligation of performance without Copeland's (P) permission. The trial court and court of appeals found for Copeland (P).

ISSUE: May the promisee release the promisor prior to a third-party beneficiary's acceptance of the contract?

HOLDING AND DECISION: (Bouldin, J.) Yes. Prior to accepting the contract, the third-party beneficiary is not a party to it. The promisor may be released, or the contract may be rescinded. Until his acceptance, a third-party creditor beneficiary may ignore the contract and proceed against the debtor. Once he elects to accept the benefits of the contract, one of two theories applies. Either it is a novation and the debtor is released, or the promisor becomes primarily liable for the debt and the debtor acts as a surety. Since Copeland (P) did not alter his position before the assignment and had never accepted the original contract, the assignment acted as a mutual rescission between the debtor and Beard (D). Therefore, Copeland (P) may proceed against either the debtor or the assignee, but he has no action against Beard (D). Writ of certiorari granted; reversed and remanded.

▶ ANALYSIS

In *Lehman v. Stout*, 261 Minn. 384 (1961), the Stouts moved to their uncle's farm. He agreed to give their son a quarter section on his death as part of their compensation for aiding him. The parties later agreed in writing that the Stouts, rather than their son, should have a quarter section now. After the uncle died, the son sued for his quarter section on the basis that he had not released the uncle. The court held that the son had not given sufficient service to the uncle to vest the contract. The original contract was mutually rescinded with the son never having consented to it. Since the contract could not have been performed until the uncle's death, the son never assented and no one altered his or her position. There was no reason to hold the uncle's estate liable.

■■■■

Quicknotes

ASSIGNMENT OF RIGHTS The transfer of a party's interest or rights in property.

NOVATION The substitution of one party for another in a contract with the approval of the remaining party and discharging the obligations of the released party.

REVOCATION The cancellation or withdrawal of some authority conferred or an instrument drafted, such as the withdrawal of a revocable contract offer prior to the offeree's acceptance.

SURETY A party who guarantees payment of the debt of another party to a creditor.

THIRD-PARTY BENEFICIARY A party who benefits from a promise made pursuant to a contract although he is not a party to the agreement.

■■■■

Rouse v. United States

Purchaser of house (D) v. Federal government (P)

215 F.2d 872 (D.C. Cir. 1954).

NATURE OF CASE: Action by a third party to recover damages for breach of contract.

FACT SUMMARY: Rouse (D) promised to pay Bessie, Winston's creditor, but refused to do so after discovering flaws in his own contract with Bessie and in Bessie's contract with her creditor.

🏛 RULE OF LAW
A third-party beneficiary's rights against the promisor rise no higher than those of the promisee; however, its rights may rise higher against the promisor than they could against the promisee.

FACTS: The Government's (P) assignor sold a heating plant to Bessie, who gave her promissory note for $1,008.37 payable in monthly installments of $28.01. Bessie later sold her house to Rouse (D), who agreed in the contract of sale "to assume payment of $850 for the heating plant payable $28 per Mo." Bessie defaulted on her note, and the Government (P) sued Rouse (D) as a third-party beneficiary of Rouse's (D) contract with Bessie. Rouse (D) defended by alleging (1) that Bessie fraudulently misrepresented the condition of the heating plant and (2) that the Government's (P) assignor didn't install the heater properly in the first place.

ISSUE:
(1) May a promisor assert against a third-party beneficiary a defense that he would have against the promisee?
(2) May a promisor assert against a third-party beneficiary a defense which the promisee would have against the beneficiary?

HOLDING AND DECISION: (Edgerton, J.)

(1) Yes. The rights of the third-party beneficiary rise no higher than those of the promisee; or, in other words, one who promises to make a payment to the promisee's creditor can assert against the creditor any defense that the promisor could assert against the promisee. Thus, Rouse's (D) defense of fraud, which he would certainly have been entitled to show against Bessie, is equally effective against the beneficiary (or any valid assignee of the original beneficiary).

(2) No. Here, Rouse's (D) promise was to pay a specified sum of money to the beneficiary (P), and it is irrelevant whether or not the promisee (Bessie) was actually indebted in that amount. "Where the promise is to pay a specific debt . . . this interpretation will generally be the true one." (12 Williston, § 399) [The result would be different if Rouse (D) had merely promised

to discharge whatever liability the promisee was under. In that case, the promisor must certainly be allowed to show that the promisee was under no enforceable liability.] Reversed and remanded.

▶ ANALYSIS

This well-known case is a law student's dream insofar as it clearly lays out what defenses are, and are not, available to a promisor in an action by a third-party beneficiary. While the promisor usually may assert against the beneficiary any defense which he could assert against the promisee, he usually may not assert defenses which the promisee might have raised against the beneficiary. In support of its denial of Rouse's (D) second defense, the court rests on Williston's presumption as to the nature of the promisor's promise. Unless it is clearly indicated that a promisor is only undertaking to pay "the debt" of the promisee (whatever it may turn out to be), it will be presumed that the promise is to pay the specific amount, regardless of whether it is actually owed. [Whether this "presumption" necessarily effects a "just" result in all (or even most) ambiguous cases is open to some question.]

Quicknotes

ASSIGNOR A party who assigns his interest or rights to another.

CREDITOR BENEFICIARY A creditor who receives the benefits of a contract between a debtor and another party, pursuant to which the other party is obligated to tender payment to the creditor.

PROMISE The expression of an intention to act, or to forbear from acting, granting a right to the promisee to expect and enforce its performance.

PROMISOR Party who promises to render an obligation to another in the future.

THIRD-PARTY BENEFICIARY A party who benefits from a promise made pursuant to a contract although he is not a party to the agreement.

CHAPTER 21

Assignment and Negotiation

Quick Reference Rules of Law

Clapp v. Orix Credit Alliance, Inc.

Tractor purchaser (P) v. Tractor purchase financer (D)

Or. Ct. App., 192 Or. App. 320, 84 P.3d 833 (2004).

NATURE OF CASE: Appeal from denial of motion for summary judgment and grant of cross-motion for summary judgment.

FACT SUMMARY: Laser Express, Inc. (Laser) (D) purchased a tractor for Clapp (P) and assigned to her its contract with Orix Credit Alliance, Inc. (Orix) (D), the company financing the purchase of the tractor. Laser's (D) contract with Orix (D) contained a prohibition of assignment. When the tractor was destroyed in an accident, Clapp (P) sought the insurance proceeds.

RULE OF LAW

A prohibition of assignment in a contract for goods evidencing a secured transaction does not prevent the assignment of rights where the prohibition is limited to the transfer of obligations without prior written consent.

FACTS: Laser (D), a common carrier, entered into a conditional sale contract note with Orix (D), a commercial finance company, documenting an installment purchase of a highway tractor which Laser (D) was covertly buying on behalf of Clapp (P), an independent trucker. Under the contract, Laser (D) was not permitted to assign the contract without first obtaining the written consent of Orix (D). Without obtaining such consent, Laser (D) assigned the contract to Clapp (P). Clapp (P) paid the down payment and made all payments received by Orix (D). The tractor was totaled in an accident and Clapp (P) advised Orix (D) of her assignment interest and claimed any net insurance proceeds in excess of the balance owing on the tractor. Orix (D) received the insurance proceeds, paid off the balance owing on the tractor and paid the insurance proceeds to Laser (D). Clapp sued Laser (D) and Orix (D) for the proceeds. Clapp's (P) motion for summary judgment was denied and Orix's (D) cross-motion for summary judgment was granted. Clapp (P) appealed.

ISSUE: Does the prohibition of assignment without Orix's (D) consent restrict Clapp's (P) rights in the contract to purchase the tractor?

HOLDING AND DESCISION: (Brewer, J.) No. The prohibition of assignment did not prevent the transfer to Clapp (P) of Laser's (D) rights under the contract. The issue is governed by U.C.C. Articles 2 (goods) and 9 (secured transactions). Orix (D) was the "holder" of the note on the tractor and by the terms of the prohibition on assignment, the prohibition was concerned only with Laser's (D) obligations to the holder of the note. Nothing in the contract suggests that the prohibition concerned the potential assignment of Laser's (D) rights and the assignment of rights did not materially alter Orix's (D) duties, burden of risk or chance of obtaining return performance on the contract. Therefore, under U.C.C. § 2-210 relating to sale of goods, the transfer of rights was valid. U.C.C. § 9-401 (2) governs the alienability of Orix's (D) rights in collateral and provides that the agreement between Laser (D) and Orix (D) that precludes an assignment of Laser's (D) rights does not prevent the transfer from taking effect. The dispute here concerns the assignment of the right to receive the proceeds of collateral on the debt owed to Orix (D). Accordingly, since Laser (D) assigned to Clapp (P) the right to receive the proceeds of collateral for the debt owed to Orix (D), the prohibition against assignment did not prevent the transfer to Clapp (P) of the right to the insurance proceeds. Because Orix (D) had notice of the assignment, the trial court erred in denying Clapp's (P) motion for summary judgment. Reversed and remanded.

ANALYSIS

The decision hinges on the distinction between rights and obligations under the contract. The case concerned only the disposition of the insurance proceeds and whether Clapp (P) had acquired the right to those proceeds by virtue of the assignment. Within that very narrow focus, U.C.C. Articles 2 and 9 permitted the assignment. The effect of the assignment to Clapp (P) of Laser's (D) obligations to Orix (D) was not before the court.

Quicknotes

ASSIGNMENT A transaction in which a party conveys his or her entire interest in property to another.

SUMMARY JUDGMENT Judgment rendered by a court in response to a motion made by one of the parties, claiming that the lack of a question of material fact in respect to an issue warrants disposition of the issue without consideration by the jury.

Evening News Ass'n v. Peterson

News association (P) v. Anchorman (D)

477 F. Supp. 77 (D.D.C. 1979).

NATURE OF CASE: Action for a declaration of rights and injunctive relief.

FACT SUMMARY: A year after Evening News (P) acquired the District of Columbia station at which Peterson (D) had worked as a newscaster-anchorman for Post-Newsweek, Peterson (D) began insisting that his contract of employment with Post-Newsweek was non-assignable.

🏛 RULE OF LAW
Contract rights, which are assignable as a general rule, are not assignable if the contract calls for the rendition of personal services based on a relationship of confidence between the parties or if the assignment would vary materially the duty of the obligor, increase materially the burden of risk imposed by the contract, or impair materially the obligor's chance of obtaining return performance.

FACTS: Peterson (D) had a long-term contract under which he worked for Post-Newsweek at a District of Columbia television station as a newscaster-anchorman. Evening News (P) purchased the station and Peterson (D) continued to work as a newscaster-anchorman for a year. After a year, he began insisting that his contract with Post-Newsweek had been non-assignable because it required him to perform unique and unusual services and because of the personal relationship he had with Post-Newsweek and the parties who ran the news department under Post-Newsweek. It just so happened that Peterson (D) had negotiated an employment contract with a competing station. So, Evening News (P) sought a declaration of the rights and legal relations of the parties under the contract and permanent injunctive relief against Peterson (D).

ISSUE: Is a contract non-assignable if it calls for the rendition of personal services based on a relationship of confidence between the parties or if the assignment would vary materially the duty of the obligor, increase materially the burden of risk imposed by the contract, or impair materially the obligor's chance of obtaining return performance?

HOLDING AND DECISION: (Parker, J.) Yes. There are exceptions to the general rule that contract rights are assignable. One arises when the contract calls for the rendition of personal services based on a relationship of confidence between the parties. Another arises if the assignment would vary materially the duty of the obligor, increase materially the burden of risk imposed by the contract, or impair materially the obligor's chance of obtaining

return performance. Neither of those situations exists in this case. Thus, the contract was assignable. Order consistent with the Memorandum Opinion will be entered.

▶ ANALYSIS

As Corbin explains: "In almost all cases where a 'contract' is said to be non-assignable because it is personal, what is meant is not that the contractor's right is not assignable, but that the performance required by his duty is a personal performance and that an attempt to perform by a substituted person would not discharge the contractor's duty." Contracts, Corbin, § 865.

■━■

Quicknotes

ASSIGNMENT A transaction in which a party conveys his or her entire interest in property to another.

INJUNCTIVE RELIEF A remedy imposed by the court ordering a party to cease the conduct of a specific activity.

■━■

Macke Co. v. Pizza of Gaithersburg, Inc.

Coffee company purchaser (P) v. Pizza company (D)

Md. Ct. App., 259 Md. 479, 270 A.2d 645 (1970).

NATURE OF CASE: Appeal in an action for damages for breach of contract.

FACT SUMMARY: The Pizza Corporations (D), claiming that their contracts with Virginia Coffee Services were for personal services, refused to honor the contracts' assignment to the Macke Co. (P).

🏛 RULE OF LAW
Unless otherwise agreed, contractual duties can be delegated unless they require such unique personal service that this would materially change the nature of performance.

FACTS: Pizza Corporations (D) contracted to have Virginia Coffee Service install and service its vending machines. The contract contained no clause excluding an assignment. Accordingly, when the Macke Co. (P) purchased Virginia Coffee, Macke (P) received an assignment of the Pizza (D) contract. When Pizza (D) attempted to terminate the contract, Macke (P) sought damages for breach. Pizza (D) argued that the contractual duties were not delegable because these were personal service contracts, entered into only because Pizza (D) relied on Virginia's skill, judgment, and reputation. Macke (P) replied that servicing vending machines required no special skill such that a delegation would materially change the performance due under the contracts. Macke (P) appealed the trial court's ruling for Pizza (D).

ISSUE: Are contractual duties delegable when they do not require such unique personal service that a delegation would materially change the nature of performance?

HOLDING AND DECISION: (Singley, J.) Yes. Unless otherwise agreed, contractual duties can be delegated when they do not require such unique personal services that a delegation would materially change the nature of performance. But we do not regard these agreements as personal service contracts. They were either a license or a concession entitling Virginia to lease of portion of Pizza's (D) premises and pay Pizza (D) a percentage of the vending machine sales. This did not require rare genius or extraordinary skill. Our holding accords with the Restatement, Contracts § 160(3) allowing delegation unless "performance by the person delegated varies ... materially from the performance by the person named in the contract as the one to perform, and there has been no ... assent to the delegation." Reversed as to liability.

ANALYSIS

Assignment questions should be analyzed separately in terms of assignment of rights, delegation of duties, or both. It is necessary to keep in mind the distinction between assignment of rights and delegation of duties. An assignment is a transfer of rights. A delegation is a transfer of duties of performance. Often, an assignment would also involve a delegation without the contract explicitly stating that fact.

Quicknotes

ASSIGNMENT A transaction in which a party conveys his or her entire interest in property to another.

DELEGATION The authorization of one person to act on another's behalf.

LICENSE A right that is granted to a person allowing him or her to conduct an activity that without such permission he or she could not lawfully do, and which is unassignable and revocable at the will of the licensor.

PERSONAL SERVICES CONTRACT A contract whose bargained-for performance includes specific conduct or activity that must be performed by one party.

CHAPTER 22

The Obligation to Perform in Good Faith

Quick Reference Rules of Law

Patterson v. Meyerhofer

Landowner (P) v. Purchasers (D)

N.Y. Ct. App., 204 N.Y. 96, 97 N.E. 472 (1912).

NATURE OF CASE: Appeal from judgment denying damages in breach of contract action.

FACT SUMMARY: After Meyerhofer (D) agreed to buy four parcels of property from Patterson (P) that Patterson (P) was to purchase at a foreclosure sale, Meyerhofer (D) outbid Patterson (P) for the properties.

RULE OF LAW
Every contract contains an implied promise that each party will not intentionally and purposely do anything to prevent the other party from performing.

FACTS: Benjamin Patterson (P) and Anna Meyerhofer (D) entered into a contract in which Patterson (P) agreed to sell Meyerhofer (D) four parcels of land. When the contract was executed, Patterson (P) was not the owner of the properties. However, Patterson (P) expected to purchase the properties at a foreclosure sale. Meyerhofer (D) attended the foreclosure sale and outbid Patterson (P) for each of the four properties. The result was that Meyerhofer (D) acquired the parcels for $620 less than she was obligated to pay Patterson (P) under the contract. Patterson (P) sued Meyerhofer (D) for damages in the amount of $620. The court found for Meyerhofer (D) holding that Meyerhofer (D) had no duty to refrain from buying the parcels at the sale. Patterson (P) appealed.

ISSUE: Does every contract contain an implied promise that each party will not intentionally and purposely do anything to prevent the other party from performing?

HOLDING AND DECISION: (Bartlett, J.) Yes. Every contract contains an implied promise that each party will not intentionally and purposely do anything to prevent the other party from performing. Here, by entering into the contract to buy the parcels from Patterson (P), Meyerhofer (D) impliedly promised that she would do nothing to prevent him from acquiring the property at the foreclosure sale. If Meyerhofer (D) didn't outbid Patterson (P), Patterson (P) would probably have been able to purchase the parcels for the same prices at which Meyerhofer (D) purchased them. Patterson (P) could have then sold the parcels to Meyerhofer (D), realizing the $620 profit. That sum, therefore, accurately represents Patterson's (P) damages. Reversed.

ANALYSIS

In *Kirke LA Shelle Co. v. Paul Armstrong Co.*, 263 N.Y. 79, 188 N.E. 163 (1933), the court described the implied covenant of good faith and fair dealing: "In every contract there is an implied covenant that neither party shall do anything which will have the effect of destroying or injuring the rights of the other party to receive the fruits of the contract, which means that in every contract there exists an implied covenant of good faith and fair dealing."

Quicknotes

FORECLOSURE SALE Termination of an interest in property, usually initiated by a lienholder upon failure to tender mortgage payments, resulting in the sale of the property in order to satisfy the debt.

IMPLIED COVENANT OF GOOD FAITH AND FAIR DEALING An implied warranty that the parties will deal honestly in the satisfaction of their obligations and without an intent to defraud.

IMPLIED PROMISE A promise inferred by law from a document as a whole and the circumstances surrounding its implementation.

Iron Trade Products Co. v. Wilkoff Co.

Rail purchaser (P) v. Supplier (D)

Pa. Sup. Ct., 272 Pa. 172, 116 A. 150 (1922).

NATURE OF CASE: Action to recover damages for breach of contract.

FACT SUMMARY: Wilkoff (D) contracted to deliver rails to Iron Trade (P) but refused to do so after Iron Trade (P) reduced the available supply and made Wilkoff's (D) performance more difficult.

🏛 RULE OF LAW
Mere difficulty of performance will not excuse a breach of contract even though that difficulty was created by the other contracting party.

FACTS: Iron Trade (P) contracted to purchase 2,600 tons of rails from Wilkoff (D) at the rate of $41 per ton. Iron Trade (P) thereafter purchased additional rails from one of the very few rail suppliers, thereby reducing the overall rail supply and driving up the market price. Because of the reduced supply and increased price of rails, it became difficult and unprofitable for Wilkoff (D) to procure rails for Iron Trade (P). Wilkoff (D) failed to deliver. Iron Trade (P) subsequently covered at a higher price and sued for damages.

ISSUE: Does one party's conduct, which renders performance by the second party more difficult, excuse that second party's refusal to perform?

HOLDING AND DECISION: (Walling, J.) No. "If a party seeking to secure all the merchandise which he could, entered into a contract for a quantity of the required goods, and subsequently made performance of the contract by the seller more difficult by making other purchases which increased the scarcity of the available supply, his conduct would furnish no excuse for refusal to perform the prior contract" (Williston). Here, Iron Trade's (P) conduct did not render performance by Wilkoff (D) impossible, only more difficult. Mere difficulty of performance will not excuse a breach of contract. (The case of *U.S. v. Peck*, 102 U.S. 64, in which one party cut off the other party's only available source of supply, thus rendering performance impossible, is not parallel.) Finally, there was no restriction in the contract on subsequent purchases by Iron Trade (P). Assignments of error overruled and judgment affirmed.

▶ ANALYSIS

Although there is no straightforward rule which explains the result in all the cases similar to the present one, perhaps the connecting thread is an assumption-of-risk notion. The court here undoubtedly felt that a deflated supply (and the resulting inflated market price) was a foreseeable commercial risk which Wilkoff (D) undertook when he entered the contract. However, if Iron Trade (P) had interfered with what it knew to be Wilkoff's (D) only source of supply, Wilkoff's (D) duty might have been discharged since Wilkoff (D) would not be held to have assumed the risk of Iron Trade's (P) knowing interference. [See *Patterson v. Meyerhofer*, 204 N.Y. 96 (1912).] A court will use its instinct for "justice" in each case.

■■■

Quicknotes

ASSUMPTION OF RISK DOCTRINE An affirmative defense to a negligence suit by the defendant contending that the plaintiff knowingly and voluntarily subjected himself to the hazardous condition, wholly absolving the defendant of liability for injuries incurred.

IMPOSSIBILITY A doctrine relieving the parties to a contract from liability for nonperformance of their duties thereunder, if the subject matter of the contract ceases to exist, a person essential to the performance of the contract is deceased, or the service or goods contracted for has become illegal.

RISK Danger of damage to or loss of property.

■■■

Best v. United States National Bank

Depositors at bank (P) v. Bank (D)

Or. Sup. Ct., 303 Or. 557, 739 P.2d 554 (1987).

NATURE OF CASE: Appeal of a class action suit against a bank alleging bad faith.

FACT SUMMARY: When United States National Bank (D) raised its fee for processing checks written on insufficient funds, Lonnie and Teresa Best (P) brought a class action suit alleging that Bank (D) breached its obligation to set fees in good faith.

🏛 RULE OF LAW
Whether a specified price violates the obligation of good faith is determined by the reasonable contractual expectations of the parties.

FACTS: The United States National Bank (D) charges its checking account depositors a fee for processing non-sufficient funds checks written on their accounts. Between 1973 and 1979, Bank (D) increased its fees for returned checks from $3 to $5 per check. The Bests (P) were among depositors whose accounts were assessed such fees, and they brought a class action suit to recover the charges. They alleged: (1) that Bank (D) breached its obligation to set fees in good faith; (2) that the fees were unconscionable; and (3) that the fees were an unlawful penalty for breach of contract. The circuit court granted Bank's (D) motion for summary dismissal of all of the claims, but the court of appeals reversed and remanded on the issue of breach of good faith. Both Bank (D) and Best (P) petitioned for review.

ISSUE: Is the determination of whether a specified price violates the obligation of good faith measured by the reasonable contractual expectations of the parties?

HOLDING AND DECISION: (Lent, J.) Yes. Whether a specified price violates the obligation of good faith is determined by the reasonable contractual expectations of the parties. Although, in some cases, the term specified may be so high or low that the party will be deemed to have acted in bad faith regardless of the reasonable expectations of the other party, this is not the case with Bank's (D) fees. There is a genuine issue of material fact whether Bank (D) set its fees for insufficient funds checks within the reasonable expectations of account holders. The sole reference to the fees was in the account agreement signed by depositors when the account was opened, and it stated only that depositors would be liable for service charges in effect at the time the service was to be performed. Assuming that Bank's (D) obligation of good faith required it to set the fees in accordance with its costs and ordinary profit margin, there is some evidence that Bank (D) breached the obligation. The court of appeals

properly reversed and remanded the decision of the circuit court on the issue of breach of good faith. Affirmed.

▶ ANALYSIS

It would seem only fair that a bank should be required to send notices to its customers when fees for services are raised. However, banks make a distinction between fees for ordinary account services, such as regular checking fees, and other service charges. With increasing competition among banks, elimination of certain ordinary fees has become a way to lure business; however, they make up the difference with higher service charges for other types of transactions.

■▬■

Quicknotes

CLASS ACTION A suit commenced by a representative on behalf of an ascertainable group that is too large to appear in court, who shares a commonality of interests and who will benefit from a successful result.

OBLIGATION A debt; a duty that a person is legally or morally bound to perform; an action or forbearance that a party promises to do or refrain from doing.

UNCONSCIONABLE A situation in which a contract, or a particular contract term, is unenforceable if the court determines that such term(s) are unduly oppressive or unfair to one party to the contract.

■▬■

Bloor v. Falstaff Brewing Corp.

Trustee (P) v. Brewery business (D)

601 F.2d 609 (2d Cir. 1979).

NATURE OF CASE: Action to recover for breach of contract.

FACT SUMMARY: Bloor (P), as Reorganization Trustee of a brewery business, brought suit claiming that Falstaff (D) had breached its contract with the brewery by failing to live up to a clause promising to use its "best efforts" to promote and maintain a high volume of sales of Ballantine brands.

🏛 RULE OF LAW
One breaches a contractual clause obligating him to use his "best efforts" to promote and maintain a high volume of sales of a particular product by following policies which stress profit at the expense of sales volume.

FACTS: The contract by which Falstaff (D) purchased the Ballantine brewing labels, trademarks, accounts receivable, distribution systems, and other property (excluding the brewery) contained a clause which obligated Falstaff (D) to "use its best efforts to promote and maintain a high volume of sales" of Ballantine products. By another clause, Falstaff (D) was to pay a $.50 per barrel royalty for a period of six years. If it substantially discontinued distribution of beer under the brand name "Ballantine" during the royalty period, Falstaff (D) was to pay liquidated damages as specified. Bloor (P), as Reorganization Trustee of the brewery, brought suit claiming that Falstaff (D) had breached the "best efforts" clause by following policies which stressed overall profit to Falstaff (D) at the expense of sales of Ballantine products. He also claimed that these policies resulted in what effectively was a discontinuance of distribution of Ballantine beer and that the liquidated damages provision was thus triggered. The trial court found the best efforts clause had been breached and awarded damages but held that the liquidated damages provision was not triggered.

ISSUE: Does one breach a clause promising to use best efforts to promote sales of a product if he follows policies based on considerations of profit at the expense of sales volume?

HOLDING AND DECISION: (Friendly, J.) Yes. One who has contracted to use his best efforts to promote and maintain a high volume of sales of a particular product breaches the contract where, as in this case, he follows policies based on considerations of profit at the expense of sales volume. Failure to give due consideration to the effect of such policies on sales volume rendered Falstaff (D) liable for damages measured by the reasonable estimate of royalties which would have been paid had such a breach not occurred. Affirmed.

▶ *ANALYSIS*

In a footnote, the court noted several New York cases in which the courts had attempted to define precisely what a "best efforts" clause requires of one. A number of the cases suggest that such a clause imposes an obligation to act with good faith in light of one's own capabilities.

■═■

Quicknotes

BEST EFFORTS In order to enforce an agreement, pursuant to which only one party appears to be furnishing consideration, the court will imply a promise on the part of the other party to use its best efforts.

LIQUIDATED DAMAGES An amount of money specified in a contract representing the damages owed in the event of breach.

■═■

Market Street Associates v. Frey

Commercial property lessee (P) v. Lessor (D)

941 F.2d 588 (7th Cir. 1991).

NATURE OF CASE: Appeal from summary judgment dismissing action seeking specific performance.

FACT SUMMARY: A principal of Market Street Associates (P) allegedly deliberately failed to notify General Electric Pension Trust (D) of an obscure clause that could result in forfeiture of General Electric's (D) property.

> 🏛 **RULE OF LAW**
> A party to a contract may not intentionally exploit the other party's oversight of an important fact.

FACTS: J.C. Penney entered into a sale-leaseback arrangement with General Electric Pension Trust (D) on a property. A clause in the lease provided that if General Electric (D) failed to negotiate with the lessee regarding future financing, the property could be purchased at less than market value. Years later, Market Street Associates (P), J.C. Penney's assignee, attempted to negotiate financing with General Electric (D). General Electric (D), no longer being aware of the clause, refused to negotiate. Market Street (P) then sought to exercise its option and sued for specific performance. At his deposition, the principal of Market Street (P) primarily responsible for the property testified that his counterpart at General Electric (D) might not be aware of the clause and that he had realized it during negotiations. Based on this, the district court entered summary judgment dismissing the action, holding Market Street (P) to have acted in bad faith. Market Street (P) appealed.

ISSUE: May a party to a contract intentionally exploit the other party's oversight of an important fact?

HOLDING AND DECISION: (Posner, J.) No. A party to a contract may not intentionally exploit the other party's oversight of an important fact. That parties to a contract must act in good faith does not mean, as some courts seem to believe, that the parties must act in an altruistic or fiduciary manner toward each other; they need not do so. Furthermore, it is quite legitimate for a party to use his superior knowledge to drive an advantageous bargain. However, it is one thing to have superior knowledge, but it is quite another to know that the other party is unaware of a crucial fact and take advantage of this ignorance. This constitutes sharp practice, which departs from good faith. Here, the district court held that Market Street's (P) principal had engaged in such conduct. This may be true, but it is a factual issue, addressable only at trial, not at the summary judgment level. Reversed and remanded.

▌ **ANALYSIS**

A mutual mistake is grounds for nullifying a contract or a term thereof. Unilateral mistake may or may not be. As the court stated here, unilateral mistake combined with an opponent's overreaching may be grounds for rescission.

Quicknotes

GOOD FAITH An honest intention to abstain from any unconscientious advantage of another.

MUTUAL MISTAKE A mistake by both parties to a contract, who are in agreement as to what the contract terms should be, but the agreement as written fails to reflect that common intent; such contracts are voidable or subject to reformation.

SPECIFIC PERFORMANCE An equitable remedy whereby the court requires the parties to perform their obligations pursuant to a contract.

SUMMARY JUDGMENT Judgment rendered by a court in response to a motion by one of the parties, claiming that the lack of a question of material fact in respect to an issue warrants disposition of the issue without consideration by the jury.

UNILATERAL MISTAKE Occurs when only one party to an agreement makes a mistake and is generally not a basis for relief by rescission or reformation.

The Doctrine of Substantial Performance

Quick Reference Rules of Law

Jacob & Youngs v. Kent

Homebuilder (P) v. Buyer (D)

N.Y. Ct. App., 230 N.Y. 239, 129 N.E. 889 (1921).

NATURE OF CASE: Action for damages for breach of a construction contract.

FACT SUMMARY: Jacobs (P) was hired to build a $77,000 country home for Kent (D). When the dwelling was completed, it was discovered that, through an oversight, pipe not of Reading manufacture (though of comparable quality and price), which had been specified in the contract, was used. Kent (D) refused to make final payment of $3,483.46 upon learning of this.

🏛 RULE OF LAW
An omission, both trivial and innocent, will sometimes be atoned for by allowance of the resulting damage and will not always be the breach of a condition to be followed by forfeiture. For damages in construction contracts, the owner is entitled merely to the difference between the value of the structure if built to specifications and the value it has as constructed.

FACTS: Jacobs (P) built a country home for $77,000 for Kent (D) and sues for $3,483.46 which remains unpaid. Almost a year after completion, Kent (D) discovered that not all pipe in the home was of Reading manufacture as specified in the contract. Kent (D) ordered the plumbing replaced, but as it was encased in the walls, except in those spots where it must necessarily remain exposed, Jacobs (P) refused to replace the pipe, stating that the pipe used was of comparable price and quality. It appears that the omission was neither fraudulent nor willful and was due to oversight. Kent (D) refused to pay the balance of the construction cost still due.

ISSUE: Was the omission by Jacobs (P) so trivial and innocent so as not to be a breach of the condition?

HOLDING AND DECISION: (Cardozo, J.) Yes. Where the significance of the default or omission is grievously out of proportion to the oppression of the forfeiture, the breach is considered to be trivial and innocent. A change will not be tolerated if it is so dominant and pervasive as to frustrate the purpose of the contract. The contractor cannot install anything he believes to be just as good. It is a matter of degree judged by the purpose to be served, the desire to be gratified, the excuse for deviation from the letter, and the cruelty of enforced adherence. Under the circumstances, the measure of damages should not be the cost of replacing the pipe, which would be great. Instead, the difference in value between the dwelling as specified and the dwelling as constructed should be the measure even though it may be nominal or nothing. Usually, the owner is entitled to the cost of completion, but not where it is grossly unfair and out of proportion to the good to be obtained. This simply is a rule to promote justice when there is substantial performance with trivial deviation. Order should be affirmed, and judgment absolute directed for the plaintiff.

▶ ANALYSIS

Substantial performance cannot occur where the breach is intentional, as it is the antithesis of material breach. The part unperformed must not destroy the purpose or value of the contract. Because here there is a dissatisfied landowner who stands to retain the defective structure built on his land there arises the problem of unjust enrichment. Usually, it would appear that the owner would pocket the damages he collected rather than remedying the defect by tearing out the wrong pipe and replacing it with the specified pipe. The owner would have a home substantially in compliance and a sum of money greatly in excess of the harm suffered by him. Note that under the doctrine of de minimis non curat lex, that is, the law is not concerned with trifles, trivial defects, even if willful, will be ignored. The party who claims substantial performance has still breached the contract and is liable for damages, but in a lesser amount than for a willful breach.

■■■

Quicknotes

DE MINIMUS NON CURAT LEX Not of sufficient significance to invoke legal action.

FORFEITURE The loss of a right or interest as a penalty for failing to fulfill an obligation.

FRUSTRATION OF PURPOSE A doctrine relieving the parties to a contract from liability for nonperformance of their duties thereunder when the purpose of the agreement ceases to exist due to circumstances not subject to either party's control.

MATERIAL BREACH Breach of a contract's terms by one party that is so substantial as to relieve the other party from its obligations pursuant thereto.

SUBSTANTIAL PERFORMANCE Performance of all the essential obligations pursuant to an agreement.

UNJUST ENRICHMENT The unlawful acquisition of money or property of another for which both law and equity require restitution to be made.

■■■

Kreyer v. Driscoll

Home builder (P) v. Buyer (D)

Wis. Sup. Ct., 39 Wis.2d 540, 159 N.W.2d 680 (1968).

NATURE OF CASE: Suit to recover contract price.

FACT SUMMARY: Kreyer (P) and Mr. and Mrs. Driscoll (D) entered into an oral contract to build the Driscolls (D) a house for $47,046.62. Kreyer (P) failed to complete the house and the Driscolls (D) alleged a breach and refused to finish payments on the contracts.

RULE OF LAW

Where substantial performance has not occurred on a building contract and the non-breaching party accepted the benefit of the rendition of part performance with knowledge of the breach, the contractor may recover in quantum meruit for services rendered.

FACTS: Kreyer (P) and Mr. and Mrs. Driscoll (D) entered into an oral contract to build the Driscolls (D) a house for $47,046.62. Kreyer (P) failed to complete the house, leaving one-half of the plumbing to be done at a cost of $800; one-half of the electrical work to be done at a cost of $800; one-half of the heating work to be done at a cost of $800; one-half of the tile work to be done at a cost of $1,500, and all of the linoleum work to be done at a cost of $560, and about one-fourth of the decorating to be done. The Driscolls (D) refused to pay the remaining amount of the contract and Kreyer (D) sued. The trial court found in Kreyer's (P) favor, holding that he had substantially performed the contract, but deducted from the contract price the following: $740 for imperfect workmanship; $1,233.32 damages for unreasonable delay in completion; $23,460 for payments made to Kreyer (P); and $13,433.32 for payments the Driscolls (D) made to subcontractors to satisfy liens or to pay off their accounts; $4,650 for work performed after difficulties arose between the parties. Judgment was entered in favor of Kreyer (P) for the balance of $10,967.81. The Driscolls (D) appealed.

ISSUE: Where substantial performance has not occurred on a building contract but there was a good-faith effort on the part of the contractor, and the non-breaching party accepted the benefit of the rendition of part performance with knowledge of the breach, may the contractor recover in quantum meruit for services rendered?

HOLDING AND DECISION: (Hallows, C.J.) Yes. Where substantial performance has not occurred on a building contract but there was a good-faith effort on the part of the contractor, and the non-breaching party accepted the benefit of the rendition of part performance with knowledge of the breach, the contractor may recover in quantum meruit for services rendered. On the facts of this case, it is clear that Kreyer (P) did not render substantial performance. The court made no finding on the good faith of Kreyer (P), and if one presumes an affirmative finding on that question was impliedly made, it is not a saving grace because the house was not constructed to the point of completeness which could be called substantial performance. The trial court was in error to permit recovery on the theory of substantial performance. However, recovery can be granted on the theory of quantum meruit. When a plaintiff has rendered part performance which is of no benefit to the defendant and he accepts performance with knowledge of the breach, the contractor can get judgment, with some exceptions, for the amount of such benefit in excess of harm he has caused by his breach, but in no case exceeding a ratable proportion of the agreed compensation. Thus, the cost of completion plus the cost of any additional harm is subtracted from the contract price as the measure of quasi-contractual recovery, except that it must never exceed the benefit actually received by the owner. The Driscolls (D) have a house which now meets the contract with adjustments made for delay and for faulty and incomplete work. It would be unjust to allow them to retain $10,967.81, since they should not receive a windfall. The trial court found that the dwelling was reasonably worth the purchase price and thus the amount found due Kreyer (P) by the court does not exceed the benefit actually received. Judgment is affirmed since the total recovery remains the same—not based on the theory of substantial performance, but rather on the theory of quantum meruit.

ANALYSIS

The doctrine of substantial performance is applied when the unperformed portion does not destroy the purpose or value of the contract. Of course, this is like saying that the breach must not be material. Here, when the Jacobs (D) occupied the house, they showed that it served its purpose and thereby assumed the burden to show that performance was not substantial to the terms of the contract. The primary application of the doctrine of substantial performance is with building contracts where fairly large defaults have been treated as immaterial, while a small default is often sufficient to breach a sales contract due to practical considerations. The unhappy buyer can return the goods or refuse delivery. The unhappy landowner keeps the incomplete structure; hence, greater are the possibilities for unjust enrichment.

Continued on next page.

Quicknotes

MATERIAL BREACH Breach of a contract's terms by one party that is so substantial as to relieve the other party from its obligations pursuant thereto.

QUANTUM MERUIT Equitable doctrine allowing recovery for labor and materials provided by one party, even though no contract was entered into, in order to avoid unjust enrichment by the benefited party.

SUBSTANTIAL PERFORMANCE Performance of all the essential obligations pursuant to an agreement.

T.W. Oil, Inc. v. Consolidated Edison Co.

Fuel oil company (P) v. Utility company (D)

N.Y. Ct. App., 57 N.Y.2d 574, 443 N.E.2d 932 (1982).

NATURE OF CASE: Appeal from award of damages in breach of contract action.

FACT SUMMARY: T.W. (P) delivered fuel oil to ConEd (D) that ConEd (D) rejected for having an unacceptable sulfur content.

RULE OF LAW
If a buyer rejects nonconforming tender which the seller had reasonable grounds to believe would be accepted, the seller has a reasonable time to substitute a conforming tender if he seasonably notifies the buyer of such substitution.

FACTS: ConEd (D), a public utility, purchased a cargo of fuel oil from T.W. (P) which, at delivery, had a sulfur content that was .92%. ConEd (D) rejected the shipment, even though T.W. (P) offered a fair price reduction and ConEd (D) regularly burned oil with a sulfur content of up to 1%. The next day, T.W. (P) offered to cure the defect by substituting conforming oil that would arrive a week later. ConEd (D) summarily rejected this offer also since it knew the price of fuel oil was dropping and it could buy cheaper substitute fuel oil elsewhere. T.W. (P) sued ConEd (D) for breach of contract on the grounds that ConEd (D) unreasonably rejected T.W.'s (P) offer to substitute conforming goods. T.W. (P) was awarded damages. ConEd (D) appealed on the basis that T.W. (P) knowingly made a nonconforming tender and the cure provisions of the Uniform Commercial Code § 2-508 applied only to unknowing tenders.

ISSUE: If a buyer rejects nonconforming tender which the seller had reasonable grounds to believe would be accepted, does the seller have a reasonable time to substitute a conforming tender if he seasonably notifies the buyer of such substitution?

HOLDING AND DECISION: (Fuchsberg, J.) Yes. If a buyer rejects nonconforming tender which the seller had reasonable grounds to believe would be accepted, the seller has a reasonable time to substitute a conforming tender if he seasonably notifies the buyer of such substitution. Here, ConEd (D) rejected the oil; T.W. (P) reasonably believed ConEd (D) would accept oil with .92% sulfur content since it regularly accepted oil with up to 1% sulfur content; and T.W. (P) seasonably notified ConEd (D) that it was ready to substitute conforming oil that was to arrive a week later. Therefore, T.W. (P) satisfies the requirements of the Uniform Commercial Code § 2-508 cure provision. Affirmed.

ANALYSIS

In *Zabriskie Chevrolet, Inc. v. Smith*, 99 N.J. Super. 441, 240 A.2d 195 (1968), Zabriskie, a car dealer, sold a new car to Smith that had transmission problems. After Zabriskie repaired the transmission, Smith refused to accept the repaired car. The court held for Smith, stating that: "For a majority of people, the purchase of a new car is a major investment, rationalized by the peace of mind that flows from its dependability. Once their faith is shaken, the vehicle loses not only its real value in their eyes, but becomes an instrument whose integrity is substantially impaired and whose operation is fraught with apprehension. The attempted cure in the present case was ineffective."

Quicknotes

CURE In a commercial transaction, the seller has a right to correct a delivery of defective goods within the time originally provided for performance as specified in the contract.

NONCONFORMING GOODS Goods tendered pursuant to a contract for sale that do not conform with the contract's requirements or which are otherwise defective in some way.

RIGHT OF REJECTION The right of a buyer of goods to reject a delivery that does not conform to the contract requirements.

Express Conditions

Quick Reference Rules of Law

Oppenheimer & Co. v. Oppenheim, Appel, Dixon & Co.

Sublessor (P) v. Subtenant (D)

N.Y. Ct. App., 86 N.Y.2d 685, 660 N.E.2d 415 (1995).

NATURE OF CASE: Appeal from reinstatement of jury verdict for plaintiff in a breach of contract action.

FACT SUMMARY: When an express condition precedent was not satisfied, Oppenheim, Appel (D) declared a sublease agreement void, and Oppenheimer (P) sued for breach of contract, claiming substantial performance.

🏛 RULE OF LAW
Substantial performance is not applicable to excuse the nonoccurrence of an express condition precedent.

FACTS: Oppenheimer (P) moved to the World Financial Center in Manhattan and entered into a conditional letter agreement with Oppenheim, Appel (D) to sublease Oppenheimer's former office space on the 33rd floor at One New York Plaza, since Oppenheim, Appel (D) already leased space on the 29th floor there. The letter agreement provided that the proposed sublease would be executed only upon the satisfaction of certain conditions. Oppenheimer (P) was to submit its plans and obtain the prime landlord's written consent to the proposed "tenant work," involving construction of a telephone communication linkage system between the 29th and 33rd floors. If the prime landlord's written consent was not received by the agreed date, both the agreement and the sublease were to be deemed null and void. Oppenheimer (P) timely satisfied the first condition, but never delivered the written consent on or before the modified deadline date. The written consent was eventually received by Oppenheim, Appel (D) 23 days after the deadline. The day after the deadline, Oppenheim, Appel (D) declared the agreement and sublease were invalid for failure to timely deliver the written consent. Oppenheimer (P) then commenced this action for breach of contract, asserting that Oppenheim, Appel (D) was estopped by virtue of its conduct from insisting on physical delivery of the written consent by the deadline, and that Oppenheimer (P) had substantially performed the conditions set forth in the letter agreement. The jury awarded Oppenheimer (P) damages, after finding that he had substantially performed the conditions set forth in the letter agreement. Oppenheim, Appel's (D) motion for judgment notwithstanding the verdict was granted by the court, which ruled as a matter of law that the doctrine of substantial performance had no application to this dispute, since the letter was free of any ambiguity. The Appellate Division reversed the judgment on law and facts, and reinstated the jury verdict because it found that the failure to deliver the prime landlord's written consent was inconsequential. Oppenheim, Appel (D) appealed.

ISSUE: Is substantial performance applicable to excuse the nonoccurrence of an express condition precedent?

HOLDING AND DECISION: (Ciparick, J.) No. Substantial performance is not applicable to excuse the nonoccurrence of an express condition precedent. Inasmuch we are not dealing here with a situation where Oppenheimer (P) stands to suffer some forfeiture or undue hardship, we perceive no justification for engaging in a "materiality-of-the-nonoccurrence" analysis. To do so would frustrate the clearly expressed intention of the parties. Also, the issue of substantial performance is not one for the jury to resolve, but rather one for judges to determine. Reversed.

▶ ANALYSIS

The letter agreement in this case contained a further provision stating that the sublease would be invalid "unless and until" all conditions had been satisfied. The agreement further stated that failure of the conditioning event would cause the agreement to be of "no further force and effect." In such event, neither party would have any rights against or obligations to the other.

■═■

Quicknotes

AMBIGUITY Language that is capable of more than one interpretation.

BREACH OF CONTRACT Unlawful failure by a party to perform its obligations pursuant to contract.

CONDITION PRECEDENT The happening of an uncertain occurrence, which is necessary before a particular right or interest may be obtained or an action performed.

JUDGMENT N.O.V. A judgment entered by the trial judge reversing a jury verdict if the jury's determination has no basis in law or fact.

SUBLEASE A transaction in which a tenant or lessee conveys an interest in the leased premises that is less than his own or retains a reversionary interest.

SUBSTANTIAL PERFORMANCE Performance of all the essential obligations pursuant to an agreement.

■═■

Merritt Hill Vineyards, Inc. v. Windy Heights Vineyard, Inc.

Vineyard buying stock (P) v. Vineyard selling stock (D)

N.Y. Ct. App., 61 N.Y.2d 106, 472 N.Y.S.2d 592, 460 N.E.2d 1077 (1984).

NATURE OF CASE: Appeal from summary judgment in an action for breach of contract in real estate sale.

FACT SUMMARY: Merritt Hill (P) brought suit against Windy Heights (D) for the return of a deposit and consequential damages when a deal to purchase a vineyard fell through.

RULE OF LAW

While a contracting party's failure to fulfill a condition excuses performance by the other party whose performance is so conditioned, it is not, without an independent promise to perform the condition, a breach of contract subjecting the nonfulfilling party to liability for damages.

FACTS: Merritt Hill (P) and Windy Heights (D) entered into an agreement under which Merritt Hill (P) would purchase a majority stock interest in Windy Heights's (D) vineyard. Merritt Hill (P) tendered a $15,000 deposit, and the agreement provided that if the sale did not close, Windy Heights (D) would retain the deposit as liquidated damages unless Windy Heights (D) failed to satisfy specified precedent conditions. These conditions included that a requirement that Windy Heights (D) obtain a title insurance policy and give confirmation that certain mortgages on the vineyard were in effect. At closing, Merritt Hill (P) discovered that neither of the conditions had been met, so they refused to close and requested the return of their deposit. When Windy Heights (D) would not return the deposit, Merritt Hill (P) filed suit seeking return of the deposit and consequential damages. The trial court denied Merritt Hill's (P) motion for summary judgment, but the appellate division reversed and granted summary judgment for Merritt Hill (P) for the return of the deposit, and for Windy Heights (D) on the consequential damages action. Both parties appealed.

ISSUE: Does a contracting party's failure to fulfill a condition constitute a breach of contract subjecting the nonfulfilling party to liability for damages?

HOLDING AND DECISION: (Kaye, J.) No. While a contracting party's failure to fulfill a condition excuses performance by the other party whose performance is so conditioned, it is not, without an independent promise to perform the condition, a breach of contract subjecting the nonfulfilling party to liability for damages. The contract requirements were conditions, not promises. The wording in the contract stating that closing was subject to fulfillment of requirements is not the language of a promise. Windy Heights's (D) promise was agreeing to

sell the vineyard, and Merritt Hill's (P) promise was to pay the agreed upon price. The proper remedy is the return of the deposit to Merritt Hill (P), as the parties had expressly agreed upon. Order affirmed without costs.

ANALYSIS

The court was careful to distinguish what is a promise and what is merely a condition upon which the promise hinges. Promises are what must be performed in order to discharge contract duties. Conditions are used to determine when and if the duties defined in the agreement are subject to breach. Therefore, failure to satisfy a condition does not constitute a breach.

Quicknotes

CONDITION Requirement; potential future occurrence upon which the existence of a legal obligation is dependent.

CONDITION PRECEDENT The happening of an uncertain occurrence, which is necessary before a particular right or interest may be obtained or an action performed.

CONSEQUENTIAL DAMAGES Monetary compensation that may be recovered in order to compensate for injuries or losses sustained as a result of damages that are not the direct or foreseeable result of the act of a party, but that nevertheless are the consequence of such act and which must be specifically pled and demonstrated.

LIQUIDATED DAMAGES An amount of money specified in a contract representing the damages owed in the event of breach.

PROMISE The expression of an intention to act, or to forbear from acting, granting a right to the promisee to expect and enforce its performance.

SUMMARY JUDGMENT Judgment rendered by a court in response to a motion by one of the parties, claiming that the lack of a question of material fact in respect to an issue warrants disposition of the issue without consideration by the jury.

Howard v. Federal Crop Insurance Corp.

Tobacco grower (P) v. Insurance company (D)

540 F.2d 695 (4th Cir. 1976).

NATURE OF CASE: Appeal from denial of proceeds of an insurance policy.

FACT SUMMARY: Federal Crop Insurance Corp. (FCIC) (D) claimed that Howard's (P) violation of a condition precedent negated its obligation to pay.

🏛 RULE OF LAW
Where it is doubtful whether words create a promise or an express condition, they are usually interpreted as creating a promise, thereby avoiding a forfeiture.

FACTS: Howard (P) suffered losses to his tobacco crop due to alleged rain damage. He notified FCIC (D), with whom he had an insurance policy, of the loss. However, before an FCIC (D) agent was able to come out and inspect the land, Howard (P) plowed under the tobacco field, including the damaged stalks, in order to plant a cover crop of rye, which he claimed was necessary for preservation of the soil. The plowing under of the damaged crop was in violation of a provision in the FCIC (D) insurance policy. Claiming that the provision constituted a condition precedent to its obligation to pay, FCIC (D) refused to settle the claim. Howard (P) brought suit to recover on the policy, but the trial court found for FCIC (D). Howard (P) appealed, arguing that the subject provision constituted a promise, rather than a condition precedent.

ISSUE: Where it is doubtful whether words constitute a promise or express condition, should they be interpreted as constituting a promise?

HOLDING AND DECISION: (Widener, J.) Yes. It is a well established maxim that the law abhors a forfeiture. Therefore, a provision which does not clearly constitute a condition precedent should be interpreted as creating a mere promise. In such a manner, the imposition of a forfeiture is avoided. In the instant case, the offending clause did not specify that Howard's (D) agreement not to destroy evidence of an asserted claim constituted a condition precedent to FCIC's (D) obligation to pay. Thus, a condition precedent will generally not be found. Accordingly, summary judgment in FCIC's (D) favor was improperly granted. Vacated and remanded.

▶ ANALYSIS

The distinction between a condition and a mere promise, on which the *Howard* decision primarily rests, was described by one court as follows: "A condition is distinguished from a promise in that it creates no right or duty in and of itself but is merely a limiting or modifying factor. . . . If the condition is not fulfilled, the right to enforce the contract does not come into existence." See *Lach v. Cahill*, 138 Conn. 418, 85 A.2d 481 (1951).

Quicknotes

CONDITION PRECEDENT The happening of an uncertain occurrence, which is necessary before a particular right or interest may be obtained or an action performed.

EXPRESS CONDITION A condition that is expressly stated in the terms of a written instrument.

FORFEITURE The loss of a right or interest as a penalty for failing to fulfill an obligation.

PROMISE The expression of an intention to act, or to forbear from acting, granting a right to the promisee to expect and enforce its performance.

Vanadium Corp. v. Fidelity & Deposit Co.

Assignee of lease (P) v. Bond issuer (D)

159 F.2d 105 (2d Cir. 1947).

NATURE OF CASE: Action to collect on a surety bond.

FACT SUMMARY: Vanadium Corp. (P) wanted to be repaid for the advance payment it made on mining leases because the Department of the Interior would not approve the leases.

🏛 RULE OF LAW
Whenever the cooperation of one of the contracting parties is necessary for the performance of the contract, there is a condition implied that the cooperation will be given.

FACTS: Wade, Curran, and Redington (D) obtained mining leases to mine vanadium on the Navajo Indian Reservation in Arizona. In return for the payment of $13,000, Redington (D) assigned his interests in the leases to Vanadium Corp. (P). Because the mines were on Indian lands, the transfer of the lease had to be approved by the Secretary of the Interior. The contract of sale provided that in the event the assignments were not approved, Redington (D) would repay the purchase price and the agreement would be deemed canceled. To insure payment in case the assignments were not approved, Redington (D) executed a bond with Fidelity & Deposit Co. (D). Vanadium Corp. (P) had difficulty in reaching agreement with Curran and Wade for the mining of the leases. The Secretary of the Interior refused to approve the assignment of the lease unless an operating agreement could be reached with Curran and Wade. Vanadium Corp. (P) decided that it was not possible to get the assignments approved and, therefore, it brought this action against Fidelity & Deposit Co. (D) to collect on the bond. Redington (D) intervened as party defendant. He claimed that Vanadium Corp. (P) had not made an adequate attempt to get the leases approved and, therefore, did not have a right to the return of its money. The district court found for Fidelity & Deposit Co. (D).

ISSUE: Whenever the cooperation of one of the contracting parties is necessary for the performance of the contract, is there a condition implied that the cooperation will be given?

HOLDING AND DECISION: (Clark, J.) Yes. There was an obligation on both parties to this contract to attempt in good faith to secure the prerequisite approval of the leases. In fact, Vanadium Corp. (P) probably had a greater burden because only Vanadium Corp. (P) could file the assignment for approval. Whenever the cooperation of the contracting parties is necessary for the performance of the contract, as it was in this case, there is a condition implied in the contract that the cooperation will be given. Vanadium Corp. (P) was, therefore, obligated to make a good-faith effort to get the assignment of the lease approved. The facts show that once Vanadium Corp. (P) saw that it was going to be difficult to get the assignment approved on the terms it wanted, it did not make any further effort to secure approval and, in fact, notified the Secretary of the Interior not to reconsider the assignment. Because Vanadium Corp. (P) failed to perform the implied condition of cooperation in gaining approval of the assignment, it did not have a right to the return of its $13,000. Judgment of the district court was affirmed.

▶ ANALYSIS

This case represents the majority view in the United States. It is also the view set forth in the Second Restatement of Contracts. Other cases have held that a suit may be brought to force specific performance of the implied condition where such enforcement is deemed to be feasible.

■══■

Quicknotes

ASSIGNMENT A transaction in which a party conveys his or her entire interest in property to another.

IMPLIED CONDITION A condition that is not expressly stated in the terms of an agreement, but which is inferred from the parties' conduct or the type of dealings involved.

■══■

Morin Building Products Co. v. Baystone Construction, Inc.

Aluminum siding supplier (P) v. Construction company (D)

717 F.2d 413 (7th Cir. 1983).

NATURE OF CASE: Appeal of award of damages for breach of contract.

FACT SUMMARY: General Motors Corp. refused, for aesthetic reasons, to approve aluminum siding installed by Morin Building Products (P), which was subsequently not paid.

🏛 RULE OF LAW
Acceptance of performance in a contract whose purpose is primarily functional will be based on an objective standard.

FACTS: As part of a construction project for General Motors Corp., Baystone Construction, Inc. (D) subcontracted with Morin Building Products (P) to install aluminum siding. General Motors retained final approval rights. A General Motors agent rejected the siding due to a minor aesthetic flaw. The purpose of the siding was strictly functional. Baystone (D) had another subcontractor redo the job and refused to pay Morin (P), which sued for breach. The trial court held that the standard of acceptability of Morin's (P) performance was objective, and the jury held it objectively adequate. Baystone (D) appealed.

ISSUE: Will acceptance of performance in a contract whose purpose is primarily functional be based on an objective standard?

HOLDING AND DECISION: (Posner, J.) Yes. Acceptance of performance in a contract whose purpose is primarily functional will be based on an objective standard. The majority rule is that where the contract in question involves performance of commercial quality, an objective, reasonable man standard will be used in determining whether performance was adequate. It is unreasonable to expect a party to such a contract to permit his financial outcome to depend on whim. Therefore, in the absence of explicit language to the contrary, only if performance is inadequate objectively will performance be considered inadequate. Affirmed.

▶ ANALYSIS

Generally speaking, a party will not be held to an objective standard when assessing the adequacy of performance when the nature of the contract is aesthetic. Even then, the law usually does not grant unfettered discretion. A good faith requirement will generally be read into the contract.

Quicknotes

GOOD FAITH REQUIREMENT An implied warranty that the parties will deal honestly in the satisfaction of their obligations and without an intent to defraud.

REASONABLE MAN STANDARD A hypothetical person whose judgment represents the standard to which society requires its members to act in their private affairs and in their dealings with others.

■=■

Koch v. Construction Technology, Inc.

Painting subcontractor (P) v. General contractor (D)

Tenn. Sup. Ct., 924 S.W.2d 68 (1996).

NATURE OF CASE: Appeal from ruling denying motion to modify damages award in action for breach of contract.

FACT SUMMARY: Painter Koch (P) entered into a subcontract with general contractor CTI (D) that provided that Koch would be paid "when and as" CTI (D) was paid.

🏛 RULE OF LAW
A "pay when paid" clause in a contract is not a condition precedent to a promise to pay for work performed.

FACTS: Construction Technology, Inc. (CTI) (D) was the general contractor on a Memphis Housing Authority (MHA) construction project. CTI (D) subcontracted the painting portion of the contract to Koch (P) pursuant to a contract that provided that payments to Koch (P) would be made "when and as" payments were received by CTI (D). After completion of the painting, Koch (P) determined that the amounts paid did not cover the work performed under the subcontract and brought suit against CTI (D) for breach of contract. The trial court considered the work performed and payments made and awarded Koch (P) the amount it calculated MHA had paid to CTI (D) for work performed by Koch (P). Koch's (P) motion to increase judgment to cover the amount owing on work performed by Koch (P) for which CTI (D) had not been paid by MHA was denied and Koch (P) appealed. The appellate court affirmed, holding that the clause providing that Koch (P) would be paid when and as CTI (D) was a condition precedent to CTI's (D) promise to pay. Koch (P) appealed. Reversed and remanded.

ISSUE: Is a "pay when paid" clause in a contract a condition precedent to a promise to pay for work performed?

HOLDING AND DECISION: (Drowota, J.) No. The clause in the subcontract providing that Koch (P) would be paid when and as CTI (D) was paid by MHA is not a condition precedent to CTI's (D) obligation to fulfill its promise to pay Koch (P) for the work performed. Conditions precedent are not favored in a contract. Most jurisdictions construe such clauses as affecting the timing of payment and not the underlying obligation to pay the subcontractor. Because there is no evidence that the parties intended to shift the risk of MHA's nonpayment from the general contractor, CTI (D), to the subcontractor, Koch (P), the payment by MHA is not a condition precedent to CTI's (D) obligations to Koch (P). Moreover, the clear and specific language used elsewhere in the contract to create a condition precedent regarding the presentation of documentation precludes construing the ambiguous language of the "pay when paid" clause as a condition precedent. Reversed and remanded.

▶ ANALYSIS

The record established both that Koch (P) had performed more work than he had been paid for and that all payments made to CTI (D) by MHA had been passed on to Koch (P) by virtue of the trial court's judgment. Thus, the court here was presented with the perfect opportunity to join the overwhelming majority of jurisdictions in negating the unintended confiscatory impact of "pay when paid" clauses.

■==■

Quicknotes

BREACH OF CONTRACT Unlawful failure by a party to perform its obligations pursuant to contract.

CONTRACT DAMAGES Monetary compensation awarded by the court to a party as the result of a breach of contract by another party.

SUBCONTRACTOR A contractor who enters into an agreement with a principal contractor, or other subcontractor, to perform all or a part of a contract.

■==■

Aetna Casualty and Surety Co. v. Murphy

Insurance company (P) v. Lessor of insurer (D)

Conn. Sup. Ct., 206 Conn. 409, 538 A.2d 219 (1988)

NATURE OF CASE: Appeal from summary judgment denying payment of insurance proceeds.

FACT SUMMARY: Murphy (D) delayed over two years in notifying his insurance company of a claim against him.

🏛 RULE OF LAW
An insured who belatedly gives notice of an insurance claim may nonetheless recover on the insurance contract by rebutting the presumption that the delay prejudiced the insurer.

FACTS: When Murphy (D) terminated a lease with Aetna's (P) insured, he damaged the premises, which gave rise to a claim for those damages. Although Murphy (D) was served with the complaint on November 21, 1983, he did not notify his insurance company of the claim until January 10, 1986. Murphy's (D) insurer, Chubb, became a third-party defendant by Murphy's (D) impleading. Murphy's (D) insurance contract provided: "In the event of an occurrence, written notice . . . shall be given by or for the insured to the company . . . as soon as practicable." Murphy (D) delayed over two years in notifying Chubb of the claim against him. Chubb claimed that Murphy (D) had inexcusably and unreasonably delayed in complying with the notice provision in the insurance contract and obtained summary judgment. This appeal followed.

ISSUE: Can an insured who belatedly gives notice of an insurance claim nonetheless recover on the insurance contract by rebutting the presumption that the delay prejudiced the insurer?

HOLDING AND DECISION: (Peters, C.J.) Yes. An insured who belatedly gives notice of an insurance claim may nonetheless recover on the insurance contract by rebutting the presumption that the delay prejudiced the insurer. Three considerations are key to deciding this case. First is that the contract is one of adhesion. Because the contract is drawn up by the insurer, the insured, who merely "adheres" to it, has little choice as to its terms. Clearly, Murphy (D), like any other insured, had no opportunity to bargain as to the consequences of delayed notice of a claim. Second is that the insured's noncompliance with the notice provision will cause a forfeiture. Because he will lose his insurance coverage despite dutiful payment of insurance premiums, Murphy's (D) failure to comply with the notice provision operates as a forfeiture. Third, the insurer's legitimate purpose of assuring itself a fair opportunity to investigate accidents and claims can be protected by demanding strict compliance with regard to

the notice requirement in the contract. A proper balance between the interests of the insurer and the insured requires a factual inquiry into whether, in the circumstances of a case, the insurer has been prejudiced by its insured's delay in providing notice of a claim. Here, Chubb (D) was not automatically discharged of its contract duties because of Murphy's (D) delay; however, summary judgment was warranted because Murphy's (D) affidavit opposing summary judgment contained no factual basis for a claim that Chubb (D) had not been materially prejudiced by the delay. Affirmed.

▶ ANALYSIS

There exists a split of authority on the issue of whether an insured can attempt to rebut the presumption of prejudice to the insurer. Some states allow the insured to prove lack of prejudice, while other jurisdictions continue to enforce delayed notice provisions literally. This all translates into a question of materiality. Generally, express conditions in a contract must be strictly performed, while constructive or implied-in-fact conditions can be satisfied by substantial performance. Either type of condition must meet the requirement that it is material to allow a party relief from the other party's noncompliance.

■━■

Quicknotes

ADHESION CONTRACT A contract, usually in standardized form, that is prepared by one party and offered to another, whose terms are so disproportionately in favor of the drafting party that courts tend to question the equality of bargaining power in reaching the agreement.

EXPRESS CONDITION A condition that is expressly stated in the terms of a written instrument.

FORFEITURE The loss of a right or interest as a penalty for failing to fulfill an obligation.

IMPLIED-IN-FACT CONTRACT Refers to conditions which arise by physical or moral inference: (a) prerequisites or circumstances which a reasonable person would assume necessary to render or receive performance; and (b) the good-faith cooperation of the promisee in receiving the performance of the promisor.

REBUTTABLE PRESUMPTION A rule of law, inferred from the existence of a particular set of facts, that is conclusive in the absence of contrary evidence.

SUBSTANTIAL PERFORMANCE Performance of all the essential obligations pursuant to an agreement.

Continued on next page.

SUMMARY JUDGMENT Judgment rendered by a court in response to a motion by one of the parties, claiming that the lack of a question of material fact in respect to an issue warrants disposition of the issue without consideration by the jury.

■══■

CHAPTER 25

Breach and Response

Quick Reference Rules of Law

Kanavos v. Hancock Bank & Trust Co.

Stock purchaser (P) v. Bank (D)

Mass. Sup. Jud. Ct., 395 Mass. 199, 479 N.E.2d 168 (1985).

NATURE OF CASE: Appeal from award of damages in breach of contract action.

FACT SUMMARY: After the Bank (D) gave a right of first refusal to Kanavos (P) to purchase stock, the Bank (D) sold the stock to a third party without first notifying Kanavos (P).

RULE OF LAW
When performance under a contract is concurrent, one party cannot put the other in default unless he is ready, willing and able to perform and has manifested this by some offer of performance.

FACTS: Bank (D) gave Kanavos (P) the right of first refusal to acquire all the stock in a corporation whose only asset was an apartment building. The Bank (D) offered to pay Kanavos (P) $40,000 if he would surrender his option to purchase and gave Kanavos (P) the option to match the price of sale of the property to a third party for a sixty-day period from the time the offer was received. Kanavos (P) did not respond to the Bank's (D) offer. The Bank (D) then sold the stock to a third party purchaser for $760,000 without giving Kanavos (P) notice and the opportunity to purchase the stock. Kanavos (P) sued the Bank (D). The jury awarded Kanavos (P) $780,000 in damages. The Bank (D) appealed on the basis that the judge failed to instruct the jury that Kanavos (P) had to be ready, willing, and able to pay the bank $760,000 within 60 days of the offer from the third-party purchaser of the stock.

ISSUE: When performance under a contract is concurrent, may one party put the other in default if he is not ready, willing, and able to perform and has manifested this by some offer of performance?

HOLDING AND DECISION: (Wilkins, J.) No. When performance under a contract is concurrent, one party cannot put the other in default unless he is ready, willing, and able to perform and has manifested this by some offer of performance. The financial ability of a prospective buyer is a material issue in his action for damages against a repudiating defendant for breach of an agreement to sell that property for an established price. Here, the Bank's (D) obligation to sell the shares and Kanavos' (P) obligation to pay for them were concurrent obligations. Kanavos (P) has the burden of proof to show his ability to match the offer of the third-party purchaser. Remanded for retrial on the question: If Kanavos (P) had proper notice of his right to purchase the stock, would Kanavos (P) have been ready, willing, and able to do so during the option period?

ANALYSIS

In *Ilemar Corp. v. Krochmal*, 44 N.Y.2d 702, 405 N.Y.S.2d 444 (1978), the court stated: "In order to place the vendor of realty under a contract of sale in default for a claimed failure to provide clear title, the purchaser normally must first tender performance himself and demand good title.... Tender of performance by the purchaser is excused only if the title defect is not curable, for in such case it would serve no purpose to require the purchaser to go through the fruitless motions of tendering performance."

Quicknotes

CONCURRENT CONDITIONS Dependent conditions that are to be performed at the same time.

RIGHT OF FIRST REFUSAL Allows one to meet the terms of a proposed contract before it is executed.

TENDER OF PERFORMANCE The seller's delivery of conforming goods to the buyer pursuant to the requirements of a sales contract.

K & G Constr. Co. v. Harris

Construction company (P) v. Subcontractor (D)

Md. Ct. App., 223 Md. 305, 164 A.2d 451 (1960).

NATURE OF CASE: Action for breach of contract.

FACT SUMMARY: After Harris (D) allegedly negligently injured K & G Construction's (P) property, K & G (P) refused to make progress payments due to Harris (D).

🏛 RULE OF LAW
Where there is a breach of a mutually dependent clause, the non-breaching party may suspend his performance, and the breaching party remains under a duty to continue to perform.

FACTS: K & G Construction (P) hired Harris and Brooks (D) to perform subcontract work. Progress payments were to be made for work performed by Harris (D). All work was to be performed in a workmanlike manner, in accordance with best practices. Harris (D) was required to obtain liability insurance to cover any damage caused by them. One of Harris's (D) employees allegedly was negligent in operating a bulldozer, which caused the collapse of a wall. The claim was submitted to Harris's (D) insurer, but Harris (D) disclaimed all liability. The damage was estimated at $3,400. K & G (P) refused to make the progress payment due Harris (D) of $1,484.50. Harris (D) continued to work for one more month, and then stopped performing for nonpayment. K & G (P) sued for damages for breach of contract and for damages done to the house (the insurer had denied the claim). Harris (D) cross-complained for the money due for services rendered. The court granted judgment for Harris (D), finding that while his employee was negligent, this did not excuse K & G's (P) duty to make the progress payments. K & G (P) appealed, alleging that this constituted a substantial breach of the contract and this excused its duty to make the progress payments since they were dependent on Harris's (D) duty to perform in a workmanlike manner.

ISSUE: Where performance is found to be mutually dependent, does a breach by one party excuse performance by the other party while still leaving the breaching party obligated to perform?

HOLDING AND DECISION: (Prescott, J.) Yes. Today, covenants are almost universally construed as creating dependent duties. If one party breaches his duty, the other party is relieved of his obligation to perform. The breaching party remains obligated to continue his performance, even though the nonbreaching party has ceased to perform. Here, Harris's (D) duty was to perform in a workmanlike manner. This was one of the central parts of the agreement. The damage caused by the negligence of

Harris's (D) employee was substantial. This excused K & G's (P) duty to make the progress payments and Harris (D) remained obligated to perform. When Harris (D) ceased performance, this constituted a second breach. Merely submitting the claim to the insurer while disclaiming liability was not an attempt to cure the breach. Reversed.

▶ ANALYSIS

If the breach is not material, the nonbreaching party may not suspend his performance and may seek only damages. If the work/performance is divisible, breach during one part of the contract will normally not excuse suspension of performance during other segments of the contract. A material breach prevents a finding of substantial performance by the breaching party.

■=■

Quicknotes

COVENANT A written promise to do, or to refrain from doing, a particular activity.

MATERIAL BREACH Breach of a contract's terms by one party that is so substantial as to relieve the other party from its obligations pursuant thereto.

SUBSTANTIAL PERFORMANCE Performance of all the essential obligations pursuant to an agreement.

■=■

Walker & Co. v. Harrison

Neon sign company (P) v. Sign renter (D)

Mich. Sup. Ct., 347 Mich. 630, 81 N.W.2d 352 (1957).

NATURE OF CASE: Action to recover damages for breach of contract.

FACT SUMMARY: Harrison (D) rented a neon sign and sought to repudiate the rental agreement when Walker (P) delayed in repairing the sign.

🏛 **RULE OF LAW**
A party attempting to repudiate a contract must convince the court that the other party has materially breached the contract.

FACTS: Walker (P) contracted to rent a neon sign to Harrison (D). The rental agreement included repair service "as deemed necessary by Walker (P) to keep sign in first class advertising condition." Shortly after the sign was installed, someone hit it with a tomato. Rust was allegedly visible on the chrome and cobwebs had collected in the corners. Harrison (D) made several calls to Walker (P) complaining of the sign's condition, but maintenance was not forthcoming. Harrison (D) repudiated the contract and Walker (P) sued for the rent. [Walker (P) subsequently repaired the sign.]

ISSUE: May one party to a contract repudiate that contract under circumstances which do not amount to a "material breach" by the other party?

HOLDING AND DECISION: (Smith, J.) No. It is essential to one party's repudiation of a contract that he demonstrate a "material breach" by the other party. As to the criterion for "materiality," there is no single touchstone. Here, although Walker's (P) delay in rendering service was certainly irritating, it cannot be said as a matter of law that the delay was a material breach. The trial court, on this phase of the case, held as follows: "The tomato . . . was up on the clock; that would be outside [Harrison's (D)] reach, without a stepladder or something. The cobwebs are within easy reach of Mr. Harrison and so would the rust be. I think that [the] argument that these were not materially a breach would clearly be true as to the cobwebs and I really can't believe in the face of all the testimony that there was a great deal of rust seven days after the installation of this sign. And that really brings it down to the tomato . . . I really can't find that was such a material breach of the contract as to justify rescission. I really don't think so." (It is not clear whether the court defers to these findings of the trial court or whether the court draws its own independent conclusion in agreement with the trial court's judgment.) Affirmed.

The primary advantage in alleging "material breach" is that the alleging party, if successful, may rescind the whole contract. If a breach is not material, the breachee may recover damages flowing therefrom but may not cancel the contract. In the present case, for example, it would not be surprising to find that Harrison (D) wanted out of his contract for reasons other than the breach and alleged "materiality" as a means to that end. As the court indicates, there is no simple test for materiality (which is unfortunate since so much can hinge on the characterization). Among the factors often considered are: (1) to what extent has the contract been performed prior to the breach; (2) was the breach willful; (3) was the breach "quantitatively serious;" and (4) what will be the consequences of the determination (e.g., will it work extreme hardship on one of the parties). Some of the above factors should undoubtedly be given more weight than others and, arguably, some of them overlap. Perhaps the most important factor is the last one which openly acknowledges "materiality" as a conclusory label to be applied insofar as a sense of "justice" requires it.

Quicknotes

MATERIAL BREACH Breach of a contract's terms by one party that is so substantial as to relieve the other party from its obligations pursuant thereto.

RESCISSION The canceling of an agreement and the return of the parties to their positions prior to the formation of the contract.

REPUDIATION The actions or statements of a party to a contract that evidence his intent not to perform, or to continue performance, of his duties or obligations thereunder.

Anticipatory Breach, Prospective Inability to Perform, and Adequate Assurance of Performance

Quick Reference Rules of Law

Hochster v. De La Tour

Employee (P) v. Employer (D)

Queen's Bench, 2 Ellis. & Bl. 678 (1853).

NATURE OF CASE: Action to recover damages for breach of contract.

FACT SUMMARY: Before Hochster (P) was due to perform his contract of employment for De La Tour (D), De La Tour (D) announced his intention to repudiate the contract whereupon Hochster (P) immediately commenced an action for breach of contract.

🏛 RULE OF LAW
A party to a contract who renounces his intention to perform may not complain if the other party, instead of waiting until performance is due, elects to sue immediately for breach of contract.

FACTS: In April, Hochster (P) contracted to serve as De La Tour's (D) employee beginning on June 1. On May 11, De La Tour (D) wrote to Hochster (P) that it had changed its mind and declined Hochster's (P) services. On May 22, Hochster (P) brought this action for breach of contract.

ISSUE: When the time for performance has not arrived, but one party nevertheless indicates his intention not to perform, must the other party wait until the performance should have occurred before bringing action for breach of contract?

HOLDING AND DECISION: (Campbell, C. J.) No. "The man who wrongfully renounces a contract into which he has deliberately entered cannot justly complain if he is immediately sued for a compensation in damages by the man whom he has injured; and it seems reasonable to allow an option to the injured party, either to sue immediately, or to wait until the time when the act was to be done." If Hochster (P) had to wait until June 1 to sue, he would not be able to enter any employment which would interfere with his promise to begin work at that time. But it is surely more rational that after renunciation by De La Tour (D), Hochster (P) should be at liberty to consider himself absolved from any future performance. Thus, he would be free to seek other employment in mitigation of damages. De La Tour's (D) renunciation may be treated as a breach of contract. Judgment for plaintiff.

▶ ANALYSIS

This is the leading case on the so-called doctrine of "anticipatory breach." The court's reasoning is erroneous insofar as it felt that Hochster (P) would otherwise be caught in a dilemma: to remain idle and hope for a favorable future judgment or to obtain other employment and thereby forfeit his rights against De La Tour (D). The court overlooked the rule that where a party manifests prospective unwillingness to perform, the other party may suspend his performance and change his position without surrendering his right to sue after the breach occurs. In other words, the court could have considered the repudiation as (1) a defense to an action brought by De La Tour (D) and (2) an excuse of the constructive condition that Hochster (P) be ready, willing, and able to perform on June 1.

■═■

Quicknotes

ANTICIPATORY REPUDIATION Breach of a contract subsequent to formation but prior to the time performance is due.

CONSTRUCTIVE CONDITION A condition that is not expressly stated in or implied by the terms of an agreement, but is imposed by law.

MITIGATION OF DAMAGES A plaintiff's implied obligation to reduce the damages incurred by taking reasonable steps to prevent additional injury.

■═■

Wholesale Sand & Gravel, Inc. v. Decker

Property owner (P) v. Driveway builder (D)

Me. Sup. Jud. Ct., 630 A.2d 710 (1993).

NATURE OF CASE: Appeal from judgment in a breach of contract claim.

FACT SUMMARY: Decker (D) hired another contractor to complete work begun by Wholesale (P) when Wholesale (P) refused to finish the job.

🏛 **RULE OF LAW**
An anticipatory repudiation of a contract is a definite and unequivocal manifestation of an intention on the part of the repudiator that he will not render the promised performance when the time fixed for it in the contract arrives.

FACTS: On June 13, 1989, Decker (D) and Wholesale Sand & Gravel (P) entered into a contract whereby Wholesale (P) agreed to perform earth work, including the installation of a gravel driveway, on Decker's (D) property. The contract contained no provision specifying a completion date for the project, and the only reference to time was that payment was to be made within ninety days. Goodenow, the president of Wholesale (P), told Decker (D) that the driveway portion of the work would be completed within one week. Wholesale (P) began work the following weekend but experienced immediate difficulties when their bulldozers became stuck in the mud. Because the ground was too wet to allow Wholesale (P) to perform the work without substantially exceeding the contract price, Goodenow decided that they should wait for the ground to dry out. On July 12, 1989, Decker (D) contacted Goodenow concerning the lack of work on the driveway and Goodenow responded that he would "get right on it." Decker (D) called again to inquire on July 19, 1989, and informed Goodenow that they had one week to complete the driveway. Weeks later, Wholesale (P) still had not started work again, so Decker (D) hired another contractor to complete the work. Wholesale (P) commenced an action for breach of contract; however, the trial court entered a judgment in favor of Decker (D) finding that Wholesale's (P) conduct constituted an anticipatory repudiation of the contract. Wholesale (P) appealed.

ISSUE: Is an anticipatory repudiation a definite and unequivocal manifestation of an intention on the part of the repudiator that he will not render the promised performance when the time fixed for it in the contract arrives?

HOLDING AND DECISION: (Roberts, J.) Yes. An anticipatory repudiation of a contract is a definite and unequivocal manifestation of an intention on the part of the repudiator that he will not render the promised performance when the time fixed for it in the contract arrives.

Wholesale (P) removed its equipment from the work site and never returned, despite repeated promises. It was reasonable for Decker (D) to conclude that Wholesale (P) would never complete the work under the contract. The trial court properly found that Wholesale's (P) conduct reflected an unequivocal and definite unwillingness or inability to perform within a reasonable time. Affirmed.

DISSENT: (Wathen, C. J.) This court and the trial court misapplied the doctrine of anticipatory repudiation. The record does not contain any explicit words or conduct that show that Wholesale (P) did not intend to perform, but merely that they were waiting for circumstances to permit performance.

▶ **ANALYSIS**

The common law doctrine of anticipatory repudiation, or voluntary disablement, was devised to allow one party to be excused from performance because of the actions or inactions of the other party. Without this doctrine, the party with less leverage or bargaining power can be held at the mercy of the other party and without alternatives. However, the standard for enforcing application of the rule is stringent, and the actions of the repudiating party must show a definite, unequivocal, and unyielding renunciation of intent to perform.

━━■

Quicknotes

ANTICIPATORY REPUDIATION Breach of a contract subsequent to formation but prior to the time performance is due.

━━■

Oloffson v. Coomer

Corn buyer (P) v. Farmer (D)

Ill. Ct. App., 11 Ill. App. 3d 918, 296 N.E.2d 871 (1973).

NATURE OF CASE: Action for breach of a sales contract.

FACT SUMMARY: Coomer (D) contracted to sell to Oloffson (P) 40,000 bushels of corn. Later, Coomer (D) repudiated but Oloffson (P) insisted upon delivery. When the tender date expired without delivery, Oloffson (P) brought suit.

RULE OF LAW
When a buyer receives an anticipatory repudiation by the seller, the buyer may wait a commercially reasonable time before accepting the repudiation and pursuing the appropriate contractual remedies.

FACTS: Coomer (D), a farmer, contracted to sell to Oloffson (D) 40,000 bushels of corn. Delivery was to be made in the following year. During the summer, at planting time, Coomer (D) told Oloffson (D) that because the season had been too wet, he was not going to plant corn and to arrange to acquire corn elsewhere. Oloffson (P) refused to accept the repudiation and insisted upon delivery per the contract. Such insistence continued until the tender date, at which time Oloffson (P) brought suit for damages. The trial court found that Coomer (D) was in breach, that he had made an anticipatory repudiation, but that it was unreasonable for Oloffson (P) not to accept the repudiation. Therefore, damages would be measured from the date of the repudiation as opposed to the date of delivery. Oloffson (P) appeals on the issue of damages.

ISSUE: May a buyer refuse to accept an anticipatory repudiation by the seller and instead wait before accepting the repudiation?

HOLDING AND DECISION: (Alloy, J.) Yes. A buyer may refuse to accept an anticipatory repudiation by the seller and may wait a commercially reasonable time before accepting the repudiation and pursuing the appropriate contractual remedies. Damages would then be, if no cover was effectuated, the difference between the contract price and the market price at the end of the commercially reasonable period. In this case, however, as the date of the anticipatory repudiation by Coomer (D) occurred at approximately the same time in which he was required to plant his corn, it would appear that there was no commercially reasonable waiting period. We believe then that Oloffson's (P) refusal to accept the repudiation was made in bad faith. We conclude that as there was no commercially reasonable period to wait as permitted by U.C.C. § 2-610, the damages must be measured from the date

of the repudiation as opposed to the date of delivery. Affirmed.

ANALYSIS

Under the traditional rule before the U.C.C., damages were measured from the date of the anticipatory repudiation. The Code via § 2-610 modified this rule to permit a buyer to await a commercially reasonable period of time before being required to accept the repudiation. What is a commercially reasonable period of time is a question of fact which is governed by the general rule of good faith. The principal case is an example of this application. Note that the result in the principal case would have been the same had the U.C.C. not been in existence.

Quicknotes

ANTICIPATORY REPUDIATION Breach of a contract subsequent to formation but prior to the time performance is due.

COVER The purchase of an alternate supply of goods by a buyer, after a seller has breached a contract for sale, for which the buyer may recover the difference between the cost of the substituted goods and the price of the original goods pursuant to the contract, so long as the buyer purchases the alternate goods in good faith and without unreasonable delay.

Pittsburgh-Des Moines Steel Co. v. Brookhaven Manor Water Co.

Water tank builder (P) v. Water company (D)

532 F.2d 572 (7th Cir. 1976).

NATURE OF CASE: Action alleging repudiation of contract.

FACT SUMMARY: PDM (P) asserted that it was entitled to demand that the purchase price of the tank it was manufacturing for Brookhaven (D) be placed in escrow or that the president of Brookhaven (D) personally guarantee the purchase price and suspend manufacture until such was forthcoming.

🏛 RULE OF LAW
If either party under a sales contract has reasonable grounds for insecurity with respect to the performance of the other, U.C.C. § 2-609(1) gives him the right to demand in writing adequate assurance of due performance and, if commercially reasonable, to suspend any performance for which he has not already received the agreed return until such assurance is received.

FACTS: PDM (P) contracted to build a one-million-gallon water tank for Brookhaven (D), with the purchase price due and payable within 30 days after the tank had been tested and accepted. Just one month later, PDM (P) wrote a letter requesting assurances that the $175,000 contract price would be held in escrow until completion of the tank and stating that the order would be held in abeyance until receipt of such assurance. No action was taken on the request. Thereafter, PDM (P) learned that Brookhaven (D) was still in the process of negotiating its purchase money loan. It thus sent a letter to the president of Brookhaven (D) demanding that he mail his personal guarantee of payment of the contract price. Such was not forthcoming. PDM (P) stopped work on the tank. Within a couple of weeks, a meeting was held. There, PDM (P) said it could complete and deliver the tank in a few weeks, to which the president of Brookhaven (D) replied that he had no need for the tank until the following year. PDM (P) sued, alleging repudiation of the contract. Brookhaven (D) recovered on its counterclaim for breach of contract, the court finding that PDM (P) had requested assurances to which it was not entitled.

ISSUE: Must a party have reasonable grounds for insecurity before he can request assurance of performance under U.C.C. § 2-609(1)?

HOLDING AND DECISION: (Pell, J.) Yes. According to U.C.C. § 2-609(1), if either party to a sales contract has reasonable grounds for insecurity with respect to the performance of the other, he can demand in writing

adequate assurance of due performance and, if commercially reasonable, suspend any performance for which he has not already received the agreed return until such assurance is received. Here, the performance to which PDM (P) was entitled was the full payment of the purchase price within a specified time after the completion of the tank. However, the letters which PDM (P) sent conveying what it wanted done before it would pursue its obligations under the contract demanded more than that to which PDM (P) was entitled. Furthermore, the demand was not founded upon what was an actuating basis for the applicability of U.C.C. § 2-609(1). PDM's (P) actions in demanding either the escrowing of the purchase price or a personal guarantee lacked the necessary predicate of reasonable grounds for insecurity having arisen. The contract negates the existence of any basis for insecurity at the time of contracting, when PDM (P) was willing to wait 30 days beyond completion for payment. The fact that Brookhaven (D) had not completed its loan negotiations does not constitute reasonable grounds for insecurity when the money in question was not to be needed for some months. Thus, PDM's (P) action in stopping performance and in making its demands constituted a repudiation of the contract. That means that Brookhaven's (D) request to put off the contract for one year came after the contract had already been repudiated and was indicative of nothing more than that Brookhaven (D) was willing to undertake a new arrangement with PDM (P) a year hence. Therefore, Brookhaven (D) was entitled to suspend its own performance, by virtue of PDM's (P) anticipatory repudiation, and bring suit to recover damages. Affirmed.

CONCURRENCE: (Cummings, J.) Reasonable men could certainly conclude that PDM (P) had legitimate grounds to question Brookhaven's ability to pay for the water tank. When the contract was signed, the parties understood that Brookhaven would obtain a loan to help pay for the project. When the loan failed to materialize, a prudent businessman would have "reasonable grounds for insecurity." U.C.C. § 2-609(1) was, I believe, designed to cover instances where an underlying condition of the contract, even if not expressly incorporated into the written document, fails to occur. Whether, in a specific case, the breach of the condition gives rise to "reasonable grounds for insecurity" is a question of fact for the jury. It is to be recognized, however, that U.C.C. § 2-609(1) does not give the alarmed party a right to redraft the contract. Here, the district court could properly conclude that PDM (P) had

Continued on next page.

demanded assurances that would work significant changes in the contract so that its requests demanded more than a commercially "adequate assurance of due performance."

▶ *ANALYSIS*

If a party is entitled to the assurance requested, U.C.C. § 2-609(4) provides a time frame for receipt of the requested assurance. It provides that "failure to provide within a reasonable time not exceeding 30 days such assurance of due performance as is adequate under the circumstances of the particular case is a repudiation of the contract."

■═■

Quicknotes

REPUDIATION The actions or statements of a party to a contract that evidence his intent not to perform, or to continue performance, of his duties or obligations thereunder.

U.C.C. § 2-609 Provides that a contract imposes an obligation on each party that the other's expectation of receiving due performance will not be impaired.

■═■

Norcon Power Partners v. Niagara Mohawk Power Corp.

Seller (P) v. Buyer (D)

N.Y. Ct. App., 92 N.Y.2d 458, 705 N.E.2d 656 (1998).

NATURE OF CASE: Certified question following summary judgment for defendant in counter claim for declaratory judgment.

FACT SUMMARY: When Niagara (D) sought adequate assurance of future repayment under a contract it had signed with Norcon (P), Norcon (P) sought a declaratory judgment that N.Y. law precluded such a demand.

RULE OF LAW

A party has the right to demand adequate assurance of future performance when reasonable grounds arise to believe that the other party will commit a breach by non-performance of a contract governed by New York law, where the other party is solvent and the contract is not governed by the U.C.C.

FACTS: Niagara Mohawk Power Corp. (D), a public utility provider, agreed to purchase electricity from Norcon (P) under terms of a contract signed in 1989 for twenty-five years. The contract provided for three pricing periods. In 1994, Niagara (D) sent a letter to Norcon (P) stating its belief that, based on revised avoided costs estimates, Norcon (P) would not be able to satisfy the daily escalating credits in the third period, and demanding adequate assurance of Norcon's timely future performance under the repayment obligations of the original contract. Norcon (P) then sued Niagara (D) in federal court, seeking a declaratory judgment that Niagara (D) had no contractual right under N.Y. law to demand adequate assurance, and also sought a permanent injunction to prevent Niagara (D) from anticipatorily terminating the contract. Niagara (D) counter claimed, seeking a counter declaration that it properly invoked a right to demand future assurance. The district court granted Norcon's (P) motion for summary judgment, reasoning that N.Y. common law recognized a right to demand future assurance only when a promisor became insolvent or when the statutory sale of goods U.C.C. section applied, and that neither of these exceptions applied, in fact or by analogy, to this case. The Second Circuit Court of Appeals preliminarily agreed with the district court but, because of the uncertainty concerning non-U.C.C. commercial law disputes, certified the question to the N.Y. Court of Appeals as an aid to its correct application of N.Y. law.

ISSUE: Does a party have the right to demand adequate assurance of future performance when reasonable grounds arise to believe that the other party will commit a breach by non-performance of a contract governed by New York law, where the other party is solvent and the contract is not governed by the U.C.C.?

HOLDING AND DECISION: (Bellacosa, J.) Yes. A party has the right to demand adequate assurance of future performance when reasonable grounds arise to believe that the other party will commit a breach by non-performance of a contract governed by New York law, where the other party is solvent and the contract is not governed by the U.C.C. Up to now, New York has refrained from extending the right to demand adequate assurance of performance beyond the U.C.C. The policies underlying the U.C.C. 2-609 counterpart apply with similar cogency for the resolution of this kind of controversy. The extension of the doctrine of demand for adequate assurance, as a common law analogue, is recognized for cases involving long-term commercial contracts between corporate entities, which are complex and not reasonably susceptible of all security features being anticipated, bargained for, and incorporated into the original contract. The certified question is answered in the affirmative.

ANALYSIS

The court declined to agree to Niagara's (D) request for a comprehensive adaptation of the exceptional demand tool. It chose rather to proceed to limit the application of its decision to the facts of this case. This was consistent with the proven benefits of the maturation process of common law, including the area of anticipatory repudiation, which spawned this relatively newer demand for assurance corollary.

Quicknotes

ANTICIPATORY REPUDIATION Breach of a contract subsequent to formation but prior to the time performance is due.

BREACH OF CONTRACT Unlawful failure by a party to perform its obligations pursuant to contract.

CERTIFIED QUESTION A question that is taken from federal court to the state supreme court so that the court may rule on the issue, or that is taken from a federal court of appeals to the United States Supreme Court.

COMMON LAW A body of law developed through the judicial decisions of the courts as opposed to the legislative process.

Continued on next page.

COUNTERCLAIM An independent cause of action brought by a defendant to a lawsuit in order to oppose or deduct from the plaintiff's claim.

SUMMARY JUDGMENT Judgment rendered by a court in response to a motion by one of the parties, claiming that the lack of a question of material fact in respect to an issue warrants disposition of the issue without consideration by the jury.

Glossary

Common Latin Words and Phrases Encountered in the Law

A FORTIORI: Because one fact exists or has been proven, therefore a second fact that is related to the first fact must also exist.

A PRIORI: From the cause to the effect. A term of logic used to denote that when one generally accepted truth is shown to be a cause, another particular effect must necessarily follow.

AB INITIO: From the beginning; a condition which has existed throughout, as in a marriage which was void ab initio.

ACTUS REUS: The wrongful act; in criminal law, such action sufficient to trigger criminal liability.

AD VALOREM: According to value; an ad valorem tax is imposed upon an item located within the taxing jurisdiction calculated by the value of such item.

AMICUS CURIAE: Friend of the court. Its most common usage takes the form of an amicus curiae brief, filed by a person who is not a party to an action but is nonetheless allowed to offer an argument supporting his legal interests.

ARGUENDO: In arguing. A statement, possibly hypothetical, made for the purpose of argument, is one made arguendo.

BILL QUIA TIMET: A bill to quiet title (establish ownership) to real property.

BONA FIDE: True, honest, or genuine. May refer to a person's legal position based on good faith or lacking notice of fraud (such as a bona fide purchaser for value) or to the authenticity of a particular document (such as a bona fide last will and testament).

CAUSA MORTIS: With approaching death in mind. A gift causa mortis is a gift given by a party who feels certain that death is imminent.

CAVEAT EMPTOR: Let the buyer beware. This maxim is reflected in the rule of law that a buyer purchases at his own risk because it is his responsibility to examine, judge, test, and otherwise inspect what he is buying.

CERTIORARI: A writ of review. Petitions for review of a case by the United States Supreme Court are most often done by means of a writ of certiorari.

CONTRA: On the other hand. Opposite. Contrary to.

CORAM NOBIS: Before us; writs of error directed to the court that originally rendered the judgment.

CORAM VOBIS: Before you; writs of error directed by an appellate court to a lower court to correct a factual error.

CORPUS DELICTI: The body of the crime; the requisite elements of a crime amounting to objective proof that a crime has been committed.

CUM TESTAMENTO ANNEXO, ADMINISTRATOR (ADMINISTRATOR C.T.A.): With will annexed; an administrator c.t.a. settles an estate pursuant to a will in which he is not appointed.

DE BONIS NON, ADMINISTRATOR (ADMINISTRATOR D.B.N.): Of goods not administered; an administrator d.b.n. settles a partially settled estate.

DE FACTO: In fact; in reality; actually. Existing in fact but not officially approved or engendered.

DE JURE: By right; lawful. Describes a condition that is legitimate "as a matter of law," in contrast to the term "de facto," which connotes something existing in fact but not legally sanctioned or authorized. For example, de facto segregation refers to segregation brought about by housing patterns, etc., whereas de jure segregation refers to segregation created by law.

DE MINIMIS: Of minimal importance; insignificant; a trifle; not worth bothering about.

DE NOVO: Anew; a second time; afresh. A trial de novo is a new trial held at the appellate level as if the case originated there and the trial at a lower level had not taken place.

DICTA: Generally used as an abbreviated form of obiter dicta, a term describing those portions of a judicial opinion incidental or not necessary to resolution of the specific question before the court. Such nonessential statements and remarks are not considered to be binding precedent.

DUCES TECUM: Refers to a particular type of writ or subpoena requesting a party or organization to produce certain documents in their possession.

EN BANC: Full bench. Where a court sits with all justices present rather than the usual quorum.

EX PARTE: For one side or one party only. An ex parte proceeding is one undertaken for the benefit of only one party, without notice to, or an appearance by, an adverse party.

EX POST FACTO: After the fact. An ex post facto law is a law that retroactively changes the consequences of a prior act.

EX REL.: Abbreviated form of the term ex relatione, meaning upon relation or information. When the state brings an action in which it has no interest against an individual at the instigation of one who has a private interest in the matter.

FORUM NON CONVENIENS: Inconvenient forum. Although a court may have jurisdiction over the case, the action should be tried in a more conveniently located court, one to which parties and witnesses may more easily travel, for example.

GUARDIAN AD LITEM: A guardian of an infant as to litigation, appointed to represent the infant and pursue his/her rights.

HABEAS CORPUS: You have the body. The modern writ of habeas corpus is a writ directing that a person (body) being detained (such as a prisoner) be brought before the court so that the legality of his detention can be judicially ascertained.

IN CAMERA: In private, in chambers. When a hearing is held before a judge in his chambers or when all spectators are excluded from the courtroom.

IN FORMA PAUPERIS: In the manner of a pauper. A party who proceeds in forma pauperis because of his poverty is one who is allowed to bring suit without liability for costs.

INFRA: Below, under. A word referring the reader to a later part of a book. (The opposite of supra.)

IN LOCO PARENTIS: In the place of a parent.

IN PARI DELICTO: Equally wrong; a court of equity will not grant requested relief to an applicant who is in pari delicto, or as much at fault in the transactions giving rise to the controversy as is the opponent of the applicant.

IN PARI MATERIA: On like subject matter or upon the same matter. Statutes relating to the same person or things are said to be in pari materia. It is a general rule of statutory construction that such statutes should be construed together, i.e., looked at as if they together constituted one law.

IN PERSONAM: Against the person. Jurisdiction over the person of an individual.

IN RE: In the matter of. Used to designate a proceeding involving an estate or other property.

IN REM: A term that signifies an action against the res, or thing. An action in rem is basically one that is taken directly against property, as distinguished from an action in personam, i.e., against the person.

INTER ALIA: Among other things. Used to show that the whole of a statement, pleading, list, statute, etc., has not been set forth in its entirety.

INTER PARTES: Between the parties. May refer to contracts, conveyances or other transactions having legal significance.

INTER VIVOS: Between the living. An inter vivos gift is a gift made by a living grantor, as distinguished from bequests contained in a will, which pass upon the death of the testator.

IPSO FACTO: By the mere fact itself.

JUS: Law or the entire body of law.

LEX LOCI: The law of the place; the notion that the rights of parties to a legal proceeding are governed by the law of the place where those rights arose.

MALUM IN SE: Evil or wrong in and of itself; inherently wrong. This term describes an act that is wrong by its very nature, as opposed to one which would not be wrong but for the fact that there is a specific legal prohibition against it (malum prohibitum).

MALUM PROHIBITUM: Wrong because prohibited, but not inherently evil. Used to describe something that is wrong because it is expressly forbidden by law but that is not in and of itself evil, e.g., speeding.

MANDAMUS: We command. A writ directing an official to take a certain action.

MENS REA: A guilty mind; a criminal intent. A term used to signify the mental state that accompanies a crime or other prohibited act. Some crimes require only a general mens rea (general intent to do the prohibited act), but others, like assault with intent to murder, require the existence of a specific mens rea.

MODUS OPERANDI: Method of operating; generally refers to the manner or style of a criminal in committing crimes, admissible in appropriate cases as evidence of the identity of a defendant.

NEXUS: A connection to.

NISI PRIUS: A court of first impression. A nisi prius court is one where issues of fact are tried before a judge or jury.

N.O.V. (NON OBSTANTE VEREDICTO): Notwithstanding the verdict. A judgment n.o.v. is a judgment given in favor of one party despite the fact that a verdict was returned in favor of the other party, the justification being that the verdict either had no reasonable support in fact or was contrary to law.

NUNC PRO TUNC: Now for then. This phrase refers to actions that may be taken and will then have full retroactive effect.

PENDENTE LITE: Pending the suit; pending litigation underway.

PER CAPITA: By head; beneficiaries of an estate, if they take in equal shares, take per capita.

PER CURIAM: By the court; signifies an opinion ostensibly written "by the whole court" and with no identified author.

PER SE: By itself, in itself; inherently.

PER STIRPES: By representation. Used primarily in the law of wills to describe the method of distribution where a person, generally because of death, is unable to take that which is left to him by the will of another, and therefore his heirs divide such property between them rather than take under the will individually.

PRIMA FACIE: On its face, at first sight. A prima facie case is one that is sufficient on its face, meaning that the evidence supporting it is adequate to establish the case until contradicted or overcome by other evidence.

PRO TANTO: For so much; as far as it goes. Often used in eminent domain cases when a property owner receives partial payment for his land without prejudice to his right to bring suit for the full amount he claims his land to be worth.

QUANTUM MERUIT: As much as he deserves. Refers to recovery based on the doctrine of unjust enrichment in those cases in which a party has rendered valuable services or furnished materials that were accepted and enjoyed by another under circumstances that would reasonably notify the recipient that the rendering party expected to be paid. In essence, the law implies a contract to pay the reasonable value of the services or materials furnished.

QUASI: Almost like; as if; nearly. This term is essentially used to signify that one subject or thing is almost analogous to another but that material differences between them do exist. For example, a quasi-criminal proceeding is one that is not strictly criminal but shares enough of the same characteristics to require some of the same safeguards (e.g., procedural due process must be followed in a parole hearing).

QUID PRO QUO: Something for something. In contract law, the consideration, something of value, passed between the parties to render the contract binding.

RES GESTAE: Things done; in evidence law, this principle justifies the admission of a statement that would otherwise be hearsay when it is made so closely to the event in question as to be said to be a part of it, or with such spontaneity as not to have the possibility of falsehood.

RES IPSA LOQUITUR: The thing speaks for itself. This doctrine gives rise to a rebuttable presumption of negligence when the instrumentality causing the injury was within the exclusive control of the defendant, and the injury was one that does not normally occur unless a person has been negligent.

RES JUDICATA: A matter adjudged. Doctrine which provides that once a court of competent jurisdiction has rendered a final judgment or decree on the merits, that judgment or decree is conclusive upon the parties to the case and prevents them from engaging in any other litigation on the points and issues determined therein.

RESPONDEAT SUPERIOR: Let the master reply. This doctrine holds the master liable for the wrongful acts of his servant (or the principal for his agent) in those cases in which the servant (or agent) was acting within the scope of his authority at the time of the injury.

STARE DECISIS: To stand by or adhere to that which has been decided. The common law doctrine of stare decisis attempts to give security and certainty to the law by following the policy that once a principle of law as applicable to a certain set of facts has been set forth in a decision, it forms a precedent which will subsequently be followed, even though a different decision might be made were it the first time the question had arisen. Of course, stare decisis is not an inviolable principle and is departed from in instances where there is good cause (e.g., considerations of public policy led the Supreme Court to disregard prior decisions sanctioning segregation).

SUPRA: Above. A word referring a reader to an earlier part of a book.

ULTRA VIRES: Beyond the power. This phrase is most commonly used to refer to actions taken by a corporation that are beyond the power or legal authority of the corporation.

Addendum of French Derivatives

IN PAIS: Not pursuant to legal proceedings.

CHATTEL: Tangible personal property.

CY PRES: Doctrine permitting courts to apply trust funds to purposes not expressed in the trust but necessary to carry out the settlor's intent.

PER AUTRE VIE: For another's life; during another's life. In property law, an estate may be granted that will terminate upon the death of someone other than the grantee.

PROFIT A PRENDRE: A license to remove minerals or other produce from land.

VOIR DIRE: Process of questioning jurors as to their predispositions about the case or parties to a proceeding in order to identify those jurors displaying bias or prejudice.

Casenote Legal Briefs